# GLOBAL MEMBER CARE

"The strength of *Pearls and Perils* is its emphasis on growth and reflection as well as its supportive resources for member care practitioners. It will be another major reference for the member care movement here in the Philippines and in other countries."

—Grace Margaret Alag, MA
programs operations director, Asian Center for Missions, The Philippines

"*Pearls and Perils* is superb. It will be widely welcomed by an increasingly diverse range of workers, trainers, caregivers, and senders at this exciting time, when faith-based organizations are becoming increasingly prominent and strategic."

—Ted Lankester
director of health services, InterHealth, United Kingdom

"Dr. O'Donnell's engaging writing style will touch your heart and definitely hold your interest. *Pearls and Perils* is not just for academicians but for all those who care deeply about promoting health within/through the mission/aid sector."

—Ann Yeh, M.A., Ph.D.
student, Fuller Theological Seminary, School of Psychology, United States

"*Pearl and Perils* brings together a wealth of wisdom and resources to address many key issues for us in the Middle East. I really appreciate the materials from different disciplines, international settings, and Scriptures. Thank you for this creative and valuable contribution for us in the mission/aid community."

—Fayez Ishak, LLB
Kasr El Dobarah Evangelical Church, Egypt

"As an Africa-based practitioner, I have watched the member care field shift its focus from caring for mission/aid workers from the North who serve the rest of the world to embracing a global call to care for the diversity of workers around the world. Dr. O'Donnell's book not only reflects this shift but also helps steer it both emphatically and practically in this global direction."

—Gladys K. Mwiti, Ph.D.
consulting clinical psychologist, founder and CEO, Oasis Africa, Kenya

"*Pearls and Perils* will help us weave member care further in the practical fabric of how we do mission and how we support staff. I greatly appreciate Dr. O'Donnell's emphases on new/crucial directions for member care, good governance and management, and human rights and responsibilities. Many thanks."

—JJ Ratnakumar, MBA
general coordinator, Mission Upholders Trust (MUT), India

"Dr. O'Donnell is a well-known psychologist in the mission and church community. He has contributed significantly to our understanding of the holistic needs of mission/aid workers and humans. In COMIBAM, and throughout the Spanish and Portuguese speaking world, we have benefited greatly from his knowledge and experience. Those serving cross-culturally are able to stay longer, be more productive, and impact more lives. This book takes us deeper and more specifically into the core issues related to member care."

—Decio de Carvalho
executive director, COMIBAM International

"Dr. O'Donnell once again competently launches us further into the practical realities of doing member care well. He provides an up to date and comprehensive review of organizational and interpersonal support in mission/aid. He also boldly discusses the need to upgrade our approaches to ethics, corruption, management, and leadership plus provides many tools and examples to do so."

—John Fawcett, MSW
international human resources consultant, editor,
*Stress and Trauma Handbook*, New Zealand

"Dr. O'Donnell offers a clarion call for good practice in the burgeoning field of global member care. With Christians sent out from nearly all countries to all countries, member care is now a truly global undertaking. The depth of insight Dr. O'Donnell provides in his analysis of the past, present, and future of member care shows that he understands this reality."

—Todd M. Johnson, Ph.D.
director, Center for the Study of Global Christianity,
Gordon-Conwell Theological Seminary, United States

"*Pearls and Perils* expands our thinking about member care and provides many resources to address some of the complex and difficult issues in organizational settings. How do we make decisions, how is power handled in organizations, and how do we respond to violations of ethics or codes of conduct? These challenges may "shake things up," but they also point a road to follow!"

—Cynthia B. Eriksson, Ph.D.
assistant professor, Fuller Theological Seminary,
School of Psychology, United States

# KELLY O'DONNELL

# GLOBAL MEMBER CARE

## VOLUME ONE:

## THE PEARLS AND PERILS OF GOOD PRACTICE

**WILLIAM CAREY**
LIBRARY

Unless otherwise noted, all scripture is taken from the
NEW AMERICAN STANDARD BIBLE®,
Copyright © 1960,1962,1963,1968,1971,1972,1973,1975,1977,1995
by The Lockman Foundation. Used by permission.

Naomi Bradley-McSwain, copyeditor
Hugh Pindur, graphic design
Felicia Hartono, graphic design intern
Rose Lee-Norman, indexer

Published by
William Carey Library
1605 E. Elizabeth Street
Pasadena, CA 91104 | www.missionbooks.org

William Carey Library is a ministry of the
U.S. Center for World Mission
Pasadena, CA | www.uscwm.org

Printed in the United States of America

15 14 13 12 11    5 4 3 2 1    BP1000

For updates on the Global Member Care series, including new links and resources, visit www.membercareassociates.org.

---

Library of Congress Cataloging-in-Publication Data

O'Donnell, Kelly S.
  Global member care : the pearls and perils of good practice / [Kelly O'Donnell].
    p. cm.
  Includes bibliographical references and index.
  ISBN 978-0-87808-113-4
  1. Missionaries--Supervision of. 2. Personnel management. 3. Missions. 4. Humanitarian assistance. I. Title.
  BV2091.O36 2010
  266.0068'3--dc22
                          2010017126

For my special pearls:

*Michèle, Erin, Ashling*

and the global member care community

# Contents

# Application

## Part Two: Promoting Health in Mission/Aid

### Chapter 5: Unmasking Dysfunction

### Chapter 6: Upgrading Relational Resiliency

### Chapter 7: Supporting Good Governance and Good Management

### Chapter 8: Resources for Good Practice

**Part Three: Developing Guidelines in Mission/Aid**

# Preface

"THE WORLD IS INDEED FULL OF PERIL, AND IN IT THERE ARE MANY DARK PLACES;
BUT STILL THERE IS MUCH THAT IS FAIR, AND THOUGH IN ALL LANDS LOVE IS NOW
MINGLED WITH GRIEF, IT GROWS PERHAPS THE GREATER."
J.R.R. TOLKIEN, THE FELLOWSHIP OF THE RING

---

If you are interested in growing as a person, developing your member care skills, and bringing love to dark places, then you have come to the right place. This book and the upcoming books in the *Global Member Care* series are for you. Welcome!

Member care is an interdisciplinary field that focuses on supporting the diversity of mission/aid personnel and sending groups. This field has clear roots that can be traced back to the 1960s and 1970s although its phenomenal growth has occurred during the last two decades. Just about everyone is aware of member care. It has become increasingly international and contextualized. The wealth of concepts, resources, practices, and practitioners (the pearls!) have contributed greatly to the people and purposes of the mission/aid community. These contributions will only increase in the coming years as the member care field further expands and develops.

This *Global Member Care* series is dedicated to the diversity of people around the world in mission/aid who have member care responsibility. This includes people who are probably very much like you: field and team leaders, mission/aid workers themselves, personnel department staff, professionally trained caregivers, and many others in recognized member care roles. The three books in the series build especially upon the 2002 edited book, *Doing Member Care Well: Perspectives and Practices from Around the World*. Together they represent the ongoing efforts to help all of us in the mission/aid community get a better sense of the vast domain of member care. They are designed to further equip us all with the knowledge and skills necessary for good practice.

Book one reviews member care milestones, future directions, and the crucial issues of health/dysfunction and ethics/human rights. Book two encourages us to cross into sectors such as humanitarian assistance, human resources, and health care for mutual learning and good practice. Book three advocates for member care to go to and from all people groups and gives many examples from around the world. We have endeavored to make the *Global Member Care* series as practical, cutting edge, and interesting as possible. For updates on the *Global Member Care* series, including new links and resources, visit www.membercareassociates.org.

We emphasize the importance of personal and professional growth in this series. Character and competence, permeated with compassion, are needed in order to provide good practice. This focus on growth is seen in the many exercises and resources that are included throughout the books. Be sure to use them for personal reflection and when possible group discussions. Member care goes broadly around the world and we grow deeply in our inner person. It's a powerful combination!

Permeating the *Global Member Care* series is the compelling biblical vision to creatively provide and develop member care on behalf of all people groups. In other words people from all the *ethnê* (the thousands of sociocultural groupings of people) are to be included in the practice of member care. Member care is embedded in the gospel and so it travels with the gospel from *ethnê* to *ethnê*. All people groups can thus both receive and provide member care. Member care, like the gospel, is an *ethnê* to *ethnê* strategy.

We are grateful for our many colleagues and friends over the years who have supported our work and helped to shape our practice in international member care. We also sincerely appreciate the colleagues from around the world who have given us such helpful feedback on the materials that we have included in book one of *Global Member Care*. Special thanks to Laura Adams, John Fawcett, Rand Guebert, James Morehead, Jean Morehead, Michèle O'Donnell, Charles Schaefer, Vance Shepperson, and William Watson.

## THE PEARLS AND PERILS OF GOOD PRACTICE

As you can probably imagine, there is a good reason why we have also titled this book, *The Pearls and Perils of Good Practice*. The title is a direct reflection of the refining process that we all go through both in life and in member care practice. Our character and competence, like *pearls* in an oyster shell, continue to be developed through the various challenges—and at times *perils*—that we encounter. The cover art of this first book reflects our ongoing development. The thorn-crowned pearl bears solemn witness to the inseparable reality of suffering/pain and growth/life.

For the last twenty-five years we have lived in five countries, and consulted with workers/agencies (faith-based and secular) in some forty countries. Overall the challenges have been well-worth it and we have a sense of deep satisfaction in being able to work in this field. At times though we have had to carefully navigate tricky, overlapping issues. These issues have involved relationship struggles, personality disorders, personal weaknesses, organizational politics, misunderstandings, major international fraud, discrediting, dismissals, and what can only be described as egregious "demonic" opposition. It has frankly been *perilous* at times.

We were not always adequately prepared to deal with such difficult and potentially debilitating issues. And we have made mistakes at times as we sought to protect others and promote group health. We have had to consult and read widely to better understand "dysfunction, deviance, and devils" as well as our own weaknesses. Much of this learning is summarized in book one in the four chapters that deal with *Promoting Health in Mission/Aid.* We have also had to hone our "contextual" skills for managing the multi-faceted settings (contexts) in which we provide our services. Different settings have different preferences and capacities for being transparent and accountable, for negotiating different agendas and differences in hierarchical power, for dealing with relational friction, and for being open to receive constructive suggestions from staff. "Develop your contextual skills" and "know your settings" have become both watchwords and safeguards for us.

Like our fellow mission/aid workers, some of our greatest challenges then have been to maintain hope and perspective in spite of experiencing helplessness, injustice, and relational malaise. We have been sustained by the gentle, affirming voice of God inside of us. We have also appreciated the many wise words of family, friends and scripture, especially the Psalms. Many thanks again and again to our dear friends and family members for helping us to stay the course.

Trust in the LORD and do good; dwell in the land and cultivate faithfulness. Delight yourself in the LORD, and He will give you the desires of your heart. Commit your way to the LORD, trust also in Him, and He will do it. He will bring forth your righteousness as the light, and your judgment as the noonday. (Ps 37: 3-6)

## MEMBER CARE AND TRUE LOVE

Member care is founded upon the biblical command to love one another (John 13:34-35) and on the ethical sense of duty to help vulnerable people (Prov. 24:11-12). This commitment to love one another and duty to others is tested in many ways for all of us, individually and collectively. The testing is often in the "furnace of health, relational, and organizational struggles." So in other words the *pearls* of our character and our competencies will get refined by the many challenges and at times *perils* that we all face. We also believe that our relationship with God (the *Pearl of Great Price*) is what ultimately upholds us throughout our life and as we confront the works of the Evil One (the *peril of great vice*).

My child, if you aspire to serve the Lord, prepare yourself for an ordeal. Be sincere of heart, be steadfast, and do not be alarmed when disaster comes. Cling to him and do not leave him, so that you may be honoured at the end of your days. Whatever happens to you, accept it, and in the uncertainties of your humble state, be patient, since gold is tested in the fire, and the chosen in the furnace of humiliation. Trust him and he will uphold you, follow a straight path and hope in him. (Sirach 2:1-6, *NJB*)

Member care above all involves the trans-cultural practice of fervently loving one another. Such love, as affirmed in 1 Cor. 13:8, never fails. It is both sacrificial and celebratory. We grow together in the mission/aid community, we celebrate life together, and by God's grace, as human vessels full of strengths and weaknesses, we do our utmost to stay close together. Resilient love is the ultimate measure of the effectiveness of our member care.

Kelly and Michèle O'Donnell
Geneva, Switzerland
September 2010

사랑은 언제까지든지 떨어지지

Axebbeṛ n wayen i d-yeṭṭasen

Kasih tidak berkesudahan

Anbu orukallum ozliyathu

Хайр хэзээ ч дуусдаггүй

Ljubav nikad ne prestaje

الْمَحَبَّةُ فَتَدُومُ وَ لَا تَنْتَهِي

Armastus ei hävi ilmaski

ความรักไม่มีวันสูญสิ้น

לעולם תבל לא האהבה

Ime eque carpis

爱 是 永 不 止 息

Սէրը քաш'ւ չhյնшр

Mbëggeel amul àpp

Uthando aluze lutshitshe

ፍቅር ለዘወትር አይወድቅም

Dashuria nuk ligshtohet kurrë

Kærleikurinn fellur aldrei úr gildi

Die liefde vergaan  nimmermeer

Quintlasohtla nochipa in oc sequin

愛はいつまでも絶えることがない

Любовь никогда не перестает

Upendo hauna kikomo kamwe

A szeretet soha el  nem fogy

E kore rawa te aroha e taka

Die Liebe höret nimmer auf

La charité ne périt jamais

Caritas numquam excidit

Miłość nigdy nie ustaje

O amor jamais acaba

Renmen pa janm fini

Kärleken förgår aldrig

Sevgi asla son bulmaz

Láska nikdy nevypadá

Meilė niekada nesibaigia

Kasih tidak berkesudahan

El amor nunca deja de ser

Charitatea nehoiz-ere ezta erorten

Tình yêu thương chẳng hề hư mất bao giờ

Ang pagibig ay hindi nagkukulang kailan man

# ἡ ἀγάπη οὐδέποτε πίπτει

*Love never fails.*

*1 Cor 13:8*

# Growing Together in Mission/Aid

This book is written to help us continue to move forward together in the member care field. We want to grow in our understanding of member care by *stepping back to reflect* on where we have come from in the past forty years and by *stepping forward to reflect on* where we need to go in the upcoming years. We want to continue to provide and develop good practice and to grow together, in light of the serious issues and opportunities that we face in the world.

*Pearls and Perils* offers a great deal of new material and new thinking that is organized in three broad areas:

Part One. Exploring Member Care in Mission/Aid
Historical notes on member care, adjustment and research issues for workers, and future directions.

Part Two. Promoting Health in Mission/Aid
Suggestions and safeguards for developing healthy staff/senders and for managing dysfunction.

Part Three. Developing Guidelines in Mission/Aid
Ethical principles and human rights commitments to further establish and upgrade member care.

Interwoven throughout *Pearls and Perils* you will find many exercises for reflection and discussion. Many chapters also have a summary chart at the beginning that lists ten of the main points or "take aways." I have listed these points in terms of *five pearls* and *five perils*. In total there are forty-five pearls and forty-five perils that summarize good practice principles. In addition, the final chapter in each of the three parts includes several materials designed for your personal and professional growth.

This book can serve as a contemporary text for training purposes in universities, seminaries, and mission/aid settings. It also provides many principles and resources that make it a handbook for member care workers, sending groups, and those with member care responsibility. The intended audience is primarily the faith-based community in the mission/aid sectors although people in other sectors will find the material to be very relevant as well.

I was privileged to present the core parts of Pearls and Perils in February 2009 as the guest lecturer for the annual Integration Symposium at Fuller Seminary in the USA. The lectures are available online for free in written, audio, and video formats at http://www.fuller.edu/academics/school-of-psychology/integration-symposium-2009.aspx. I am grateful for the encouragement that I received from several faculty and staff at Fuller School of Psychology, in particular Dr. Al Dueck and Dr. Cynthia Eriksson.

I use the term "mission/aid" throughout the book. This is a broad, inclusive term that represents the increasing focus and contributions of faith-based, Christian work around the world. By "mission" I am referring to the efforts of both Christian workers serving in cross-cultural settings and national Christian workers located in their home/passport countries. The former group is estimated to be about 400,000 and the latter group about 12 million people. This term also includes the efforts of Christians who relocate for economic, sociopolitical, and other reasons (e.g., tentmakers, international workers, refugees) and in the process bring their faith and good works with them. By "aid" I am referring to the extensive area of humanitarian assistance. This area, or sector, encompasses relief and development operations by civil society, NGOs, the United Nations, faith-based groups, etc. Mission and aid overlap with each other and using the term mission/aid reflects this practical reality.

*Pearls and Perils* focuses on providing and developing member care for both mission/aid workers and sending groups. It also emphatically points us to the *raison de être* for our mission/aid efforts: improving the lives of fellow-humans, many who are impoverished, devoid of basic human rights, and living in places beset with protracted calamities and intractable conflicts. This book will help you to help others; to think deeply about member care practice; and link you to supportive resources for yourself and those with whom you work. I trust it will be both a "guide and goad" as you go more broadly in your work and as you grow more deeply in your life.

# PART ONE

## Resilient People in Difficult Places: Exploring Member Care in Mission/Aid

*"The providence of God has led us all into a new world of opportunity, danger, and duty"*

WORLD MISSIONARY CONFERENCE, EDINBURGH, 1910

A Somali woman at the gate of the UNHCR compound prior to registration and admission to a refugee camp in Dadaab, Kenya. © 2008 Manoocher Deghati/IRIN. www.irinnews.org

OPPORTUNITY, DANGER, DUTY, HELL. Life can be as difficult as it can be wonderful. And helping those whose life is even more difficult than our own can be very difficult indeed! There is so much misery that requires the interventions of the faith-based, government, and civil society sectors (e.g., natural and human made disasters, poverty, HIV-AIDS, malaria/diarrheic disease, and internecine war, to name a few). For the mission/aid community, helping can often involve staying sane—and alive—in unstable, insane places. It is not that mission/aid work always deals with life-threatening experiences, of course. Rather it is just that helping to relieve the "maims and moans" of creation takes its toll. Mission/aid workers, like the people they are helping, have some special challenges and needs for resiliency.

## "Better a big heart than a big house."
### FAMILY PROVERBS

The purpose of Part One is to provide a panoramic view of both the member care field and the common struggles of Christian workers in mission/aid. How has member care developed as a viable means to help mission/aid workers stay safe, sane, and effective in their work? Where are we now and where have we come from (historical milestones) and where are we going in the member care field (future directions)?

I begin this first part in *Pearls and Perils* with some reflections on developments that have shaped this field (Chapter 1). I also share some of the future directions for us to consider in light of global realities and new ways of doing mission/aid (Chapter 3).

In between chapters one and three and at the core of Part One are many examples of the adjustment challenges for Christian workers via short stories and research summaries (Chapter 2). I include personal accounts and research, with an emphasis on workers from the African, Asian, Latin American, and Arabic-Turkic world (referred to as the *A4 Regions*).

Interspersed throughout Part One are a number of "Health Promoter" exercises to help you apply the material. It concludes with helpful materials to stimulate your personal and professional growth in member care including a core listing of books and Web sites related to member care (Chapter 4). In addition, my wife and I have a narrated PowerPoint related to Part One called *God in the Global Office*. We share about our work in member care and ways to connect/contribute to this remarkable field. See www.slideshare.net/MCAresources/god-in-the-global-office.

*"If you are going through hell, keep going."*
WINSTON CHURCHILL

We thus want to consider how best to practice member care in light of our historical foundations and in light of both current and future realities. We must especially consider the diversity of member care workers and sending groups, including those workers who may have no sending group per se! This international and interdisciplinary field continues to flourish with the hard work of so many resilient people over the years who have labored together on behalf of mission/aid workers and the many needy people in our troubled world.

# PEARLS
## ENHANCING AND ENRICHING GOOD PRACTICE

*Member care is an ongoing movement of committed, diverse people.*

*Member care continues to grow as an international and interdisciplinary field.*

*Love is the foundation for the member care services that we provide.*

*Social relationships are key protective factors for longevity and effectiveness.*

*Embracing both the intrinsic worth and strategic worth of mission/aid workers.*


# PERILS
## ENCUMBERING AND ENDANGERING GOOD PRACTICE

*Belief that personal struggles and needs are a sign of weakness.*

*Belief that sacrifice and faith alone are needed for success in mission/aid.*

*Waiting for crises to happen in order to develop member care more.*

*National/local staff often get overlooked or have access to fewer supportive resources.*

*Dysfunctional practices in personnel and organizational management wreak havoc.*

CHAPTER 1

# Highlighting Member Care History

MEMBER CARE HAS A FASCINATING HISTORY THAT IS WELL-WORTH REVIEWING. OUR HISTORY AS A FIELD INFLUENCES OUR CURRENT WORK AND SHAPES OUR FUTURE PRACTICE. LET'S EXPLORE IT!

———————

Over the last twenty years, a special ministry within the Christian mission/aid sector, really a movement, has developed around the world that is called *member care*. At the core of member care is a commitment to provide ongoing, supportive resources to further *develop* mission/aid personnel. Currently there are an estimated 400,000 full-time "foreign missionaries" and over 11.8 million national Christian workers from all denominations (Johnson, Barrett, and Crossing, 2010). Our member care parish (or catchment area), so to speak, is huge! But these figures do not reflect the number of Christians involved in the overlapping area of humanitarian aid, nor do they reflect the unknown number of "tentmakers" or Christians who intentionally work in different countries while also sharing their good works and faith. Sending organizations and churches, colleagues and friends, specialist providers, and also locals who are befriended are key sources of such care.

The development of member care is reflected in the many conferences and special training symposia that have taken place. Such events have been occurring in the USA for thirty-plus years, gaining major momentum in the 1990s and beyond. Similar events have also occurred over the last fifteen years in countries like India, Singapore, Malaysia, Indonesia, Hong Kong, The Philippines, Korea, Ivory Coast, Cameroon, Nigeria, Cyprus, Germany, The Netherlands, Brazil, El Salvador, Canada, New Zealand, and Australia. Member care has truly become international, is increasingly mainstreamed into the ethos of sending groups, and is considered to be a central part of mission/aid strategy.

The member care ministry and movement did not develop easily. It was often through crises, mistakes, and failure that we began to realize that Christian workers needed quality support in order to help them in their challenging tasks. One of the first books written to help with this need was written by Marjorie Collins in 1974, providing many ideas for how churches and friends could better support mission personnel (*Who Cares About the Missionary?*). Previously in 1970 Joseph Stringham, a psychiatrist and missionary working in South Asia published two landmark articles in *Evangelical Missions Quarterly* on the mental health of missionaries. Stringham identified a number of external and internal challenges including culture shock, being disillusioned with others, children, medical care, etc. (external) and resentment, sexual issues, marital struggles, dishonesty, guilt, spirituality, trauma/deprivation in earlier life, motivation etc. (internal).

The third international consultation, Global Member Care Resources (MemCa), Vancouver, 2003

Mental health practitioners in particular who ventured into mission/aid were frequently faced with a belief that the desire for special/additional support might mean that Christian workers were being unspiritual or weak, and not trusting the Lord enough. As Tucker and Andrews point out in their article "Historical Notes on Missionary Care" (1992): "Mission societies held high the ideal of sacrifice. Strong faith in God, it was reasoned, was the prescription for a healthy mind and spirit...Self-reliance was the mark of a missionary—tempered only by dependence on God through prayer" (p. 24). But in retrospect, and at the expense of over generalizing a bit, we (speaking inclusively) were overlooking our own *humanness*, sometimes trying to be something that we were not created or called to be. We in the mission/aid community began to better appreciate our biblical need for one another—as seen in the dozens of "one another" verses in the New Testament. We began to understand that the issue was not so much our having a lack of faith, but rather our need to clearly see God's plan and His provision of care.

I remember how much I needed better training and support during my first cross-cultural ministry trip (thirty-five years ago!). I was a young, enthusiastic believer of nineteen. What delight I felt when I heard that I could join a short-term agricultural team to work with a Nahuatl indigenous group in the mountains of southern Mexico.

However it ended up being a mixed experience for me, as can sometimes happen with mission experiences. Not surprisingly I got sick with stomach problems (unclean water), confused by the language (a different dialect of Spanish was used), and was often cold (did not bring the right jacket), tired (from the high altitude and reduced oxygen), and hungry (little food was available in this poor area). I had received no pre-field training and had never met my teammates before. By the time I returned to my home country, I was not very excited about doing mission work again. I probably did make a small contribution to the team and its work, but some of my struggles could have been easily prevented. I returned to this same area/indigenous group a few years later, as part of a team that was better prepared.

Nahautl community in mountain villages in the state of Puebla, Mexico, 1983

Member care, I have learned over and over again, is not about creating a comfortable lifestyle. Nor is it about trusting people instead of trusting God. Rather, it is about further developing the resiliency to do our work well which includes our character, competencies, and social support. It is also about developing relational resiliency, which includes working through the inevitable differences and impasses with international and local fellow-workers.

Member care helps to balance the realistic demands of suffering and sacrifice with the realistic needs for support and nurture in our lives. We can pray for greater strength to endure, yet at times we must also find additional ways to lighten the load on ourselves and our colleagues. Biblically, the call to take up our cross daily is also understood in light of the fact that we are to support each other as we bear our crosses together. As my brother the dentist says: "The only teeth you really need to floss are the ones you want to keep." In member care parlance, this equates to "The only people to whom we really need to provide member care are the ones we want to keep!"

### *Health Promoter 1. Reflection and Discussion*
## MANAGING VIRTUE AND VICE

What I have gone through in my experience as a psychologist in mission/aid seems so minor compared to what so many others have had to endure throughout history. Perhaps you feel the same way too at times about your own struggles? As an example, let's look at some of the experiences of WWII Prisoners of War (POWs) in Asia and how some of their struggles can relate to those of mission/aid workers. Specifically how do the field experiences of pain, poverty, trauma, lack of safety, etc. affect our inner world—our souls? And what does one need to do in order to "survive" and remain effective? Here is a telling quote from one former POW, John Stewart. The quote is from his 1988 memoirs, *To the River Kwai (pp. 164-165)*, and quoted in *Surviving the Sword* (2005, p. 169), a book about POWs in Asia by Brian MacArthur.

"When starved and worked to death in jungle camps, thoughts of home and freedom only served to widen the gap between the reality and the hope. Only the present counted, not the past or the future. Everything and every circumstance around it was utterly new and unexpected. We had been prepared for none of it. Not for our extraordinary habitat, the rain forest; not for our closeness to another people and its culture...; and certainly not for the breakdown of our own group structure. With its societal skin flayed, human nature became visible as never before. Greed, cowardice and vanity, perseverance, altruism and generosity, in brief the wide panoply of virtue and vice, were there to be observed in the open, without pretence, with no place to hide"

**Applications:**
1.  How have you experienced both human virtue and vice in difficult circumstances? (in your own life and in those around you).
2.  How could such experiences "bring out the best in you and not the worst" (see Luke 6:27-30, *The Message*)

# REMEMBERING OUR ROOTS

The development of member care really has its origins in the biblical admonitions to "love one another" (John 13:34), "bear one another's burdens" (Gal. 6:2), "be kind to one another" (Eph. 4:32), "teach and admonish one another" (Col. 3: 16), "encourage one another day after day" (Heb. 3:13) and scores of similar "one another" verses that fill the New Testament. Member care, in this sense, is nothing new.

Christians and Christian workers, for better or for worse, have been trying to practice these relationship principles down through the centuries. Yet what is new are the more organized attempts all over the world to develop comprehensive, sustainable member care approaches to support cross-cultural Christian workers. These attempts have drawn on the contributions of practitioners from such diverse health care fields as travel and tropical medicine, psychology and psychiatry, intercultural and transition studies, pastoral care and coaching, personnel and human resource development, and recovery and trauma care.

Another way of looking at member care is to see it as a *discipline* for sending groups and workers to cultivate and work into their organizational ethos and personal lives, respectively. The same discipline that Paul said is needed to "run to win" (1 Cor. 9:24-27) is also needed so that Christian workers can "rest to win" (Matt. 11:25-30). I think of member care as a type of discipline. It is a personal, community, and biblical practice. It is an *intentional* practice to help renew workers, to help them remain resilient, and to help them remain effective. The foundations of member care—loving one another— are embedded in the gospel, and hence are to accompany Christian workers wherever they go. See also "A Theological Perspective on Missionary Care" by Glenn Taylor in *Enhancing Missionary Vitality* (2002).

Member care was originally a secular term used in the business world. I first became aware of the term in 1988 at a workshop organized by Missionary Internship in the United States (shortly after my wife and I published *Helping Missionaries Grow; Readings in Mental Health and Missions* in 1988). The workshop was "Member Care and the Development of Missionaries" facilitated by Sam Rowen and Ken Harder. One of the purposes of this workshop was to emphasize an approach to missionary care that harmonized personal development and growth with the prevalent model of clinical/therapeutic care. This approach fit well with my background in both clinical and community psychology, the latter of which emphasized the roles of non-professionals, developing resources, human strengths, and community participation. Lights went on for me philosophically and practically. Subsequently my wife and I chose to use this term widely within the evangelical mission community, and along with others we helped to popularize it internationally.

The term *member care* was especially useful since it also connoted the mutual responsibility that people (members) in a group had to each other. So member care from the start was conceived as a "two-way street," as both senders and goers had responsibilities to each other. It also implied *belonging*: the sense of a community between members who are part of a group. Finally, member care was a neutral term, which could be more readily used in settings where surveillance and security were an issue. The term has continued to take root over the last two decades internationally, primarily within the Christian mission/aid sector. Similar terms that have been used include: personnel development, human resource management, psychosocial support, staff care and development, and people care.

As Christians who practiced psychology in member care, we were committed to value staff as *humans with intrinsic worth*, and not just *resources with strategic worth*. We believed healthy people and healthy organizations were key for successful projects involving Christian witness. We were thus also committed to both the integrity of the sending organization and its purposes and the well-being of staff/leaders. Member care was to be holistic and broadly speaking was involve everyone in mission work.

\*\*\*\*

*Member care seeks to implement an adequate flow of care from recruitment through retirement.*

\*\*\*\*

Member care began to be defined more formally in the early 1990s. It was and continues to be seen as the ongoing *investment of resources* by sending groups, service organizations, and workers themselves, for the *nurture and development* of personnel. It focuses on *every member* of the organization, including children and home office staff. It includes preventative, developmental, supportive, and restorative care. A core part of member care is the *mutual care* that workers provide each other. Workers receive it and they give it. Connecting with resources and people in *the local/host community* is also key. Member care seeks to implement an adequate *flow of care* from *recruitment through retirement*. The goal is to develop resilience, skills, and virtue, which are key to helping personnel stay *healthy and effective* in their work. Member care thus involves both developing *inner resources* (e.g., perseverance, stress tolerance) and providing *external resources* (e.g., team building, logistical support, skill training).

The above understanding of member care has been very influential and has circulated broadly. A similar description was first published in 1990 in an article by my wife and me "The Increasing Scope of Member Care" (*Evangelical Missions Quarterly*, p. 418). I am grateful to Dick Hawthorne and Tim Lewis with Frontiers and Sam Rowen and Ken Harder with Missionary Internship for their ideas on member care in the late 1980s and early 1990s.

## MORE REFLECTIONS ON DEVELOPING MEMBER CARE

Another interesting historical note that not too many may recall related specifically to supporting mission personnel who were working with unreached people groups. In 1981 and 1983 there were two special conferences held in California. These conferences were called "Psychological Resources for Frontier Missions." I was delighted to attend the first one, which was held at the US Center for World Missions. The second one was held at Biola University. Here are some paraphrased notes that I took from the presentations by Ralph and Roberta Winter. You will notice their emphasis on how self-discipline and spiritual disciplines can influence mental health.

> *Ralph*: Psychological fitness involves appropriate behavioral patterns and habits. We want to rebuild a daily devotional discipline that will reach to the ends of the earth. Something must occur daily in our life in order to dominate our life.

> *Roberta*: Spiritual disciplines are very important for spiritual health. Belief and obedience are important. The will is involved in believing, the will can influence spiritual health. Both emotional and encouraging support are important. Physical heath is also important. Balanced meals are an example—sometimes there can be simple solutions for our struggles—don't over-spiritualize. Culture shock can influence everything—spiritual, physical, and psychological health. Finally be aware of spiritual warfare, including psychological attacks. Claim God's promises and use your authority over Satan.

Keep in mind that the blending of psychology and missions was still pretty much in its early stages in the early 1980s. It was still a tenuous integrative leap for many in missions. There were however some mental health practitioners providing services like assessment, counseling, and seminars to North American mission agencies in the 1960s and 1970s. Two examples are the Wycliffe Counseling Department set up in 1968 by Phil and Barbara Grossman as well as the work of Marjory Foyle in South Asia in the 1970s and 1980s (see her autobiography, *Can It Be Me?* 2006). It was not until the year 1980 that "a strong desire was voiced to interact with others doing similar work" in mental health and missions (Powell and Wickstrom, 2002, p. 4). This strong desire led to the first meeting in 1980 of what later became the annual Mental Health and Missions Conference in the USA.

Member care was recognized as a *field* in the early 1990s. It owes much to the pioneering work and positive influence of mental health professionals, largely but not entirely from North America, as well as concerned mission leaders. I believe it would be accurate to say that the status of member care as a field was significantly clarified and confirmed via the comments in the 1992 book *Missionary Care: Counting the Cost for World Evangelization.*

> It is encouraging to note the growing contributions to missionary care by agencies, consultants, and missionaries themselves. So much so in fact, that a field has now emerged devoted entirely to the care of mission personnel. *Member care*, a term which is frequently used to describe this field, refers to the commitment of resources for the development of missionary personnel by mission agencies, sending churches, and other mission-related groups. It is basically synonymous with *missionary care*, and I use both terms interchangeably throughout this volume (pp. 1, 2) . . . member care is an interdisciplinary field, drawing on the concepts and contributions from the behavioral and mental health sciences. It has a growing recognized body of literature, specific types of practitioners/helpers, and various techniques for effecting staff development. (p. 11).

In the early 1990s I began to explore the viability of developing more coordinated member care efforts at both the international and interagency levels. I became convinced that the time had come to deliberately pursue a consensually-derived "macro model" of member care in order to further support the church's mission efforts, especially among unreached people groups. My initial ideas were published in an article "An Agenda for Member Care in Frontier Missions," I concluded with these words: "I am convinced that the time has come to actively pull together the various pockets of member care workers around the world. It is also time to systematically train and mobilize many others for this strategic ministry. And the time is here for anointed leaders to step forward and help steer this field in response to the Lord's direction" (O'Donnell, 1992, pp. 111-112).

These aspirations for a more global and coordinated member care approach were neither unrealistic nor without precedent. Cooperative endeavors were being seen in the rise of national and international missionary associations, and in the formation of partnerships of ministries/organizations focusing on specific unreached people groups (e.g., see the books on mission partnerships by Eddie Addicott, *Body Matters* 2005 and Phill Butler, *Well Connected* 2005). Likewise in the area of missionary care, there had been some encouraging cooperative developments via the three previous International Conferences on Missionary Kids (ICMK, in 1984, 1987, 1989). These historic gatherings, in retrospect served as the main interagency, international forums for member care workers to come together in the 1980s, albeit in the context of MK care and educational issues. ICMK eventually evolved into three regional groups for the Americas, Asia, and Europe/Africa, and also several local chapters (Wilcox, 1998).

The member care field has also greatly benefited from three outstanding conferences that have brought people together in the USA over the years: Pastors to Missionaries Conference beginning in 1988 (www.barnabas.org); Mental Health and Missions Conference which began in 1980 (www.mti.org); and the Personnel Conference which goes back to at least the early 1970s (www.crossgloballink.org). One additional USA-based conference is Families in Global Transition (www.figt.org), now in its twelfth year, which brings together people working in several international sectors for foreign service, business, education, mission, military, and non-profit. The conference is a tangible expression of the growing interest in the emerging field of expatriate adjustment and transitions (e.g., see Melissa Hess and Patricia Linderman's *The Expat Expert: Your Guide to Successful Relocation Abroad*, 2007; Robin Pascoe's *Raising Global Nomads: Parenting Abroad in an On-Demand World*, 2006; and Tina Quick's *The Global Nomad's Guide to University Transition* (2010).

Member care, like missions, was rapidly growing in the 1980s. By the early 1990s, as described above, it had developed into its own specialized field (O'Donnell, 1997). A next step was to see various professional streams come together (e.g., psychologists, residential care centers, crisis care specialists, mission pastors) not just for mutual support and additional training, but to more systematically provide/develop additional resources for the mission community (e.g., counseling, training, crisis care, screening, reentry, retreats).

Several joint member care projects were launched in the 1990s. Examples include the MK-CART/CORE group's research on missionary kids and school personnel (see the results/analyses in *The Family in Mission: Understanding and Caring for Those Who Serve*, 2004); the 1992 book *Missionary Care* which was the collaborative effort of six consulting editors and twenty-three authors; the 1997 WEA book on missionary attrition called *Too Valuable To Lose,* a landmark book in that it included authors from all over the world; special gatherings that have brought together member care workers, like the First European Member Care Consultation held near Geneva (June 1997), and smaller, informal day consultations in Singapore to address member care topics via case studies; the formation of separate interagency member care groups for the regions of the Middle East (1993), North Africa (1994), Europe (1997), Asia (1998), Central Asia (1998), and Latin America (1999); and launching the global member care group (MemCa) by Dave Pollock and myself as part of the World Evangelical Alliance's Mission Commission.

Mission and member care were not developing in a social vacuum. Similar developments were making and continue to make their mark on the health science sector, where the increased emphasis on international, interdisciplinary cooperation has been called upon to tackle human problems. For instance, within the field of professional psychology in 1998, there are over sixty international psychological associations and related organizations (APA Office of International Affairs, 1998). International psychology, seen as both a vast network and a social movement, was increasingly active as a health care partner around the globe. Pawlik and d'Ydewale (1996) comment:

> The role of international cooperation and exchange (of persons, knowledge, and experience) may seem all too obvious in the interest of developing cross-national understanding and good will among people of different nationality, ethnic, or other background. Psychology has been opening up to and has become a partner in many such initiatives, too numerous to be cited in detail... A more recent example is the initiative (through the International Union of Psychological Science Committee for the Psychological Study of Peace) to help mitigate postwar stress disorders in war stricken Rwanda and Burundi. Other examples are psychology's contributions to international educational programs (Gelman & Lee, 1995) or to world-wide health education initiatives under the aegis of the World Health Organization (WHO) (p. 489).

Another example of coordinated efforts is seen in the early 1990s with the establishment of psychosocial support programs for both victims of disasters as well as the relief personnel who work in such stressful settings. The intentional inclusion of this support for both victims/survivors and helpers was spearheaded by the International Federation of the Red Cross and Red Crescent Societies. This was followed by the efforts of many other groups such as the Antares Foundation in The Netherlands, (www.antaresfoundation.org), Mental Health Workers Without Borders (www.mhwwb.org), People In Aid (www.peopleinaid.org), and the stress and trauma programs developed by World Vision International.

****
*Another example of coordinated efforts is seen in the early 1990s with the establishment of psychosocial support programs for both victims of disasters as well as the relief personnel who work in such stressful settings.*
****

In the aftermath of a number of disasters in the early 1990s, the necessity and importance of addressing the psychological needs of victims were amply demonstrated. This led to the establishment of the psychological support programme (PSP) of the International Federation in May 1991. However, a series of conflict situations brought to light another category of people psychologically affected by disasters: relief workers. Many Red Cross and Red Crescent delegates who had worked in relief operations (Rwanda and Somalia, for example) came back feeling lost, isolated, depressed and completely exhausted and suffering from nightmares and flashbacks. They often found it difficult to talk about their feelings of helplessness and horror to family, friends and colleagues who could not fully understand what they had been through or were not interested. It became increasingly apparent, therefore, that delegates needed specialized psychological debriefings (Psychological Support Programme for Delegates, *Psychological Support: Best Practices from Red Cross and Red Crescent Programmes*, 2001, p. 18).

These developments in the humanitarian aid world concerning psychosocial support for staff parallel what was also happening in the Evangelical mission world. An additional and crucial development has been to focus on the needs of local/national staff in addition to the needs of international/expatriate staff. Yael Daneli, one of the foremost voices on the need for psychosocial support for "international protectors and providers" (e.g., military peacekeepers, aid workers, humanitarian journalists), concludes her edited work *Sharing the Front Line and the Back Hills* (2002):

> National staff do not receive the security and support afforded their international colleagues, including remuneration and insurance, nor are they respected for their credentials, experience, and knowledge of local culture…Most of all when missions leave or evacuate they stay, often in danger to themselves and their families. Indeed, international protectors and providers report feeling outrage, incompleteness, and guilt when locally-recruited colleagues and their families are left to this fate (p. 386).

People In Aid's *Code of Good Practice* (1997 and revised 2003) is another timely example of the cooperation and advances that have benefited the mission/aid sector. This document, formulated by several humanitarian aid organizations from the United Kingdom and Ireland, discusses seven core principles for the management and support of aid personnel. Recognizing the draining realities of this labor-intensive profession, guidelines were drawn up to help ensure the security and well-being of staff. Organizations, both religious and non-religious, have been encouraged to discuss these principles, weave them into their ethos, and hold themselves accountable for their implementation. Funding for projects will likely increasingly include a budget for aid and mission organizations to provide resources for staff support and hence to put this or similar codes into practice.

In 2000 at the Mental Health and Missions Conference, some twenty-five member care leaders/workers attended from all over the world. The conference was followed up by a special retreat for them organized by Global Member Care Resources (MemCa) and the Narramore Christian Foundation. The main emphasis of the retreat was simply meeting one another, exchanging personal/member care stories, and praying together.

This group of international colleagues connected well with each other and their North American colleagues. They also heard first hand how member care was being practiced in/from North America. They brought back to their respective countries many new ideas for developing member care along with a sense that they were part of a growing field and network.

2000 International Member Care Retreat, after the Mental Health and Missions Conference, USA

As for the first decade of the 2000s, the list of developments fans out across the globe and across specialty areas. Books such as *Worth Keeping* (2007), *The Family in Mission* (2004), *Stress and Trauma Handbook* (2003), *Doing Member Care Well* (2002), *Enhancing Missionary Vitality* (2002), the revision of *Honourably Wounded* (2001), and also going back to the 1999 book with its 2009 revision, *The TCK Experience*, reflect the maturation of member care practice. Also of great importance are the many fine human resource materials from the humanitarian assistance sector, ranging from the research, stories, and practices that fill the pages of *Sharing the Frontlines and the Back Hills* (2001) to the research-based suggestions in *Approaches to Staff Care in International NGOs* (2009). Add to these the many organizations, articles, conferences, workshops, projects, and Web sites, and it becomes readily apparent how member care has been established all around the world.

The year 2000 marked the launch of an international *macro model* for member care that included five spheres of care (a model for which I was yearning some ten years earlier). This model has been widely used to "guide and goad" the provision and development of member care. It is described in "Going Global: A Member Care Model for Best Practice," in *Doing Member Care Well* (2002).

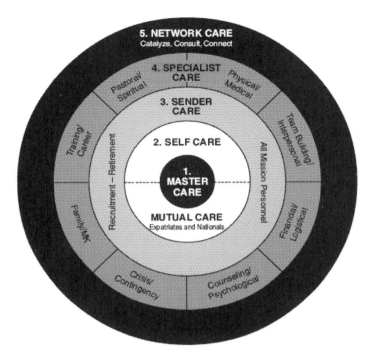

Fig. 1

Four noteworthy adjustments to the model that I have made are: a) referring to "Specialist Care" also as "Special Care" (sphere four) in order to emphasize the skills needed to support workers by both specialists (Parks, 2010) *and* others with member care responsibilities such as field and team leaders; b) the need for supportive input for sending groups, member care workers, and member care networks themselves; c) the reality that many Christian workers are not necessarily sent out by a sending group like a church/agency and they too need member care resources including support teams to back them up (sphere three, "Sender Care"); and d) "Network Care" (sphere five) and Specialist/Special Care" (sphere four) overlap with many related sectors which can inform and contribute to our member care practice (e.g., international business, human resources, human rights, health sciences). The model continues to emphasize "growth and development" (Fawcett, 2003, p.10) and holistic care—"comprehensive multidimensional wellness" (Keckler *et al*, 2008, p. 206)—in the context of sacrifice/demanding work.

## Ongoing Flows

I like to think of the historical development of member care in terms of Ps. 46:4 which says: "There is a river whose streams make glad the city of God, the dwelling place of the Most High." The member care field is like a growing stream of encouragement that flows into and from the lives of mission/aid personnel to support them in their difficult settings. Here is a list of four such streams—which I will call *flows*—that continue to shape the member care field (Box 1). These flows are part of a Divine and human movement that is refreshing the diversity of mission/aid personnel around the world.

## Box 1. Member Care Flows

1. **Flow of *Culture.*** This flow is the organizational/group ethos which embraces member care. The practice of member care is understood to be thoroughly biblical (e.g., Ps. 78:72; Prov. 27:23,24; Heb. 3:13 and many "one-another" verses). It is also increasingly acceptable and "safe" to talk about personal struggles and give/receive help. Self-care and mutual care are seen as being normative. They are OK and a sign of strength not weakness!

2. **Flow of *Concepts.*** This flow refers to ideas, values, principles, and tools that guide/shape the member care field. Member care has a growing body of literature, models, and good practices. The consolidated learning continues to develop. Member care practice is informed by many sectors/disciplines and overlapping areas such as human resource management, travel medicine, and trauma response.

3. **Flow of *Caregivers.*** This flow represents the member care workers who provide and develop member care. There are many service organizations and health professionals around the world who devote all or part of their time for mission/aid personnel. The diversity of caregivers, including staff with member care responsibilities, increases both the relevance and the internationalization of the member care field.

4. **Flow of *Connections.*** This flow includes the new technologies and special gatherings to build relationships, train, and exchange updates. There are national and regional-level member care events, plus workshops at mission, aid, health, and human resource conferences. Email forums/updates, global briefings, Web sites, radio, and internet telephony build upon and complement face to face interactions.

I would be remiss to simply talk in terms of the positive flows of member care, as encouraging and influential as these are. I need to also acknowledge that there are some important areas that we as a field must address more. From my perspective there are three areas in particular that need attention (see Box 2). These can be seen as something like "detrimental flaws" and in sharp contrast to the refreshing flows mentioned above. I am an optimist by nature. Give me and give us a challenge and we can overcome it for sure! Hence I am quite optimistic that we in the member care field, as we continue to internationalize and grow, will be able to develop the relational resiliency and skill capacity needed to deal with these areas.

> ### Box 2. Changing Flaws into Flows
>
> 1.  **Flaw of *Disparities*.** Let us grow and work together and improve the allocation of member care resources to both mission/aid workers and member care workers. Many local/national workers from the A4 Regions in particular have limited access to needed resources such as medical attention, education for children, and finances. How can we share and exchange much more as we continue onward as an international field?
> 2.  **Flaw of *Deficits*.** Let us grow and work together as we attend to the world's most vulnerable people. We can devote more of our time (services, training) to supporting mission/aid workers and sending groups who are prioritizing the needs of the world's poorest people, victims of protracted calamities and conflicts, people in poverty, and the less-reached people groups. How can we get the practical training, adjust our emphases, and seek out the opportunities to help such vulnerable people?
> 3.  **Flaw of *Dysfunction*.** Let us grow and work together to significantly upgrade our personnel practices and organizational governance. Organizational cultures and leaders must foster genuine transparency and accountability. Guidelines for managing conflicts, grievances, and whistle blowing for organizational misconduct must be developed and practiced. Abusive leadership, inept management, harassment, low morale, excessive staff turnover, and political maneuvering are definitely and sadly part of the mission/aid sector. How can we learn from organizations that are modeling healthy personnel/organizational practices? Will we have the courage to bring our struggles into the light and change as needed?

## FINAL THOUGHTS

We have explored several member care highlights in this chapter. What a fascinating history we have! However, so much more could be said in this brief overview and especially for the most recent decade (2000-2010) in which member care has gone so far and wide. Many names, events, materials, and organizations could and should be mentioned! What was in many ways initially influenced by a North American/mental health context has greatly expanded to become the international and interdisciplinary field of member care. Similar developments have happened with many other multi-disciplinary groups around the world, with one example among hundreds being the recent formation of the Movement for Global Mental Health (www.globalmentalhealth.org).

\*\*\*\*

*As I reflect upon my journey in member care over the last twenty-five years, one of my main conclusions is that the timing and grace of God coupled with careful cooperative planning, have characterized the development of member care.*

\*\*\*\*

Recently I put together a PowerPoint presentation to try to highlight some of the major contributions to member care. It was not easy—there were so many materials. I suspect that for every contribution that I identified, there were likely four other significant contributions that could have also been included. Many of these contributions would come from people in and from the A4 Regions (African, Asian, Arabic-Turkic. and Latin American areas). What would be so helpful at this point is a book devoted entirely to member care history around the world. What a worthwhile project, and perhaps even the subject of a few dissertations!

For more information and perspectives on member care history, see these three articles: "Some Historical Notes on Member Care" by Ruth Tucker and Leslie Andrews in *Missionary Care* (1992); and "The Annual Conference on Mental Health and Missions: A Brief History" by John Powell and David Wickstrom, and "Missionary Care and Counseling: A Brief History and Challenge" by Laura Mae Gardner in *Enhancing Missionary Vitality* (2002).

As I reflect upon my journey in member care over the last twenty-five years, one of my main conclusions is that the timing and grace of God coupled with careful *cooperative planning*, have characterized the development of member care. Prayer and partnership have been essential. Phill Butler in *Well Connected* (2006) lists fifteen core principles that have been essential for effective partnership in missions. The first five principles for example, include having a mutual, challenging vision; developing trust, openness and mutual concern; having a committed facilitator; understanding partnerships as an ongoing process not just an event; and identifying achievable objectives (pp. 16-18). I have seen first hand over the years how these principles have been key for forging member care partnerships at all levels—international, regional, and specific project-focused partnerships. I have also seen how their neglect has had the reverse effect. Developing member care well has clearly involved doing partnerships well. And at the core of partnerships are relationships—solid relationships, healthy relationships, resilient relationships, love-based relationships. Such relationships last through thick and thin and help us to develop as good practitioners.

# PEARLS
## Enhancing and Enriching Good Practice

*Determination and sacrifice by mission/aid workers in spite of encountering major obstacles.*

*A growing awareness of how member care is needed for effective workers and operations.*

*Training in basic health care is offered specific to the setting in which workers serve.*

*Sending churches are increasingly involved in the care and support of their workers.*

*The global church embracing a biblical and history-based theology that validates suffering.*


# PERILS
## Encumbering and Endangering Good Practice

*Hearing the voices—and cries—of our colleagues but then doing little to really help.*

*Program evaluation is not done to review the relevance of our services.*

*The places and people that need the most help often necessitate the most risk.*

*Belief that we need stronger backs and not lighter loads to do our work well, or vice versa.*

*Belief that mission/aid workers are basically expendable and that attrition is unavoidable.*

CHAPTER 2

# Listening to Our Global Voices

OUR COLLEAGUES AROUND THE WORLD HAVE SO MUCH TO SHARE WITH US ALL.
WE WANT TO CAREFULLY LISTEN TO THEM AND TO LEARN FROM ONE ANOTHER.

———————————

This chapter is divided into two sections. The first section includes several first-hand accounts of the challenges of mission/aid workers from around the world. The second section summarizes some core studies on adjustment issues for mission/aid workers.

## OUR A4 VOICES

Several mission/member care leaders share below about their experiences—the joys and sorrows, issues and insights—of working in difficult settings[1]. Their voices, and at times their cries, collectively recount the struggles and sacrifices of mission/aid workers, along with their incredible resiliency, the organizational responsibilities for care, helpful member care programs, and discrepancies in resource allocations. These are just a sampling of the multitude of voices within the mission/aid community. I am especially interested in those senders/workers who are relatively new to the mission/aid world from the "Global South(s)" (Corwin, 2010), and have grouped these together in terms of what I call the *A4 Regions*: Δfrican, Δsian, Latin Δmerican, and Δrabic-Turkic. I specifically included photos that reflect the nobility and challenges of A4 people. These photos speak volumes in and of themselves! Have a look at the brief examples in Box 1 as a prelude to the longer *A4* accounts that follow.

## Box 1. Four Examples of Worker Struggles

1.  A single medical worker in Asia working with refugees. During times of stress this year I find myself struggling to maintain a balanced eating pattern. It seems we are always on call, and it is hard to turn away such needy people. There are days when I go to the refrigerator and look for things to eat and yet I am aware that I am not even hungry. This really bothers me because I hate to see myself falling into the trap of eating to cope with stress. I wish our base had a person with a pastor's heart who was willing to listen to our concerns and offer advice and encouragement.

2.  An organizational leader in India coaching first-term staff. Culture shock is the biggest struggle as our new staff pursue learning a different language and culture. This usually is hard on their sense of identity and sifts through those who can stay on long-term from those who cannot. Loneliness and isolation are two words to describe the first year. Depression is frequently a part of the stress they feel as they try to cope with their new and demanding work.

3.  A couple teaching in the Middle East. As Westerners, we must fight the fear of being unfairly labeled as politically subversive or as enemies of the established religion, and consequently be deported from the country. Paranoia is something that can keep one from sharing and helping. We often feel forced to lead divided and overly busy lives. Our "free time" is spent making visits, doing studies, and housing visitors. Faith compels us to be people-oriented and compassionate, willing to "waste time" on individuals. The problem is there isn't enough time!

4.  A middle-aged administrator in Europe. What are the issues that led my wife and me to resign? First, I had labored here for over three years without having the slightest contact from other leaders from our organization in this country. No one asked how I was doing, what I was doing, or why. The isolation from full-time workers, from fellowship, and from avenues of dealing with the problems here, were the primary factors. Oddly, in discussing these issues with another leader, he seemed perplexed that they would even be issues. Such mentality prompted a letter to our international director in which I expressed my concern for more in-depth and comprehensive pastoral oversight of staff and leaders. Too little is understood and too much is presumed!

Adapted from "Understanding and Managing Stress" in *Missionary Care* (1992)

## VOICES FROM AFRICA[2]

### *Pathetic Cries and Crucial Progress. Central Africa, Naomi Famonure[3]*

Africa is a fascinating continent, rich in natural resources and abounding in cultural diversity. It is also a continent which wrestles with incapacitating problems: widespread HIV/AIDS, poverty, war, famine, financial and government corruption, and minimal infrastructures for health care and social services. In the midst of its beauty and its bleakness, the Lord is stirring the church to rise up and send out mission workers. As with any new mission movement, the African sending groups have to come to terms with the need for ongoing supportive resources to sustain their workers.

Displaced Congolese women await food distribution in Kibati, just outside the eastern provincial capital of Goma. © 2008 Les Neuhaus/IRIN, www.irinnews.org

Right now my heart is bubbling with excitement. I am writing you from Cameroon. This is the first of the regional member care consultations in Africa, and it was a huge success. Yet you needed to hear the *pathetic cry* for member care from the participants. Some leaders came for the consultation because…they are losing good workers and they can't explain why. Now they know. Here are some of the issues pointed out by the participants:

- The need for member care is the need of the hour.
- Missionaries who evangelized us from the West did not teach us how to care for our own missionaries, and where they did the structures left behind were not relevant for us.
- The challenge in Africa was the lack of proper orientation to take over the mission work.

- The church is too weak financially to care for missions.
- Children are usually not considered.
- The church in the Central African region needs to be adequately taught about missions.
- Most Bible schools and theological seminaries where pastors are trained do not have missions included on the curriculum.
- Unfaithfulness in handling church finances means that many who would have given in support of missionaries and evangelists do not give.
- Tribalism can hinder support for missionaries who are not from one's tribe, even if they are from the same local church or denomination.

Most of the participants were pastors who initially only understood member care in terms of financial and/or material support. The bottom line has always been the need for leaders to understand member care issues and to desire to address them. I think generally the awareness throughout Africa is being created, though slowly. Initially leaders thought we were advocating pampering measures for missionaries, which they fear will extinguish the life of faith in the missionary. But some understand that there is more to member care.

### Expendable Humanitarian Workers. Uganda, Viola Mukasa[4]

I'm a humanitarian worker living in a location in Africa that is in prime need of help/ missions. I've experienced many types of stress as I have worked in various mission programs. The most sustained tension that I have experienced has been related to the urgency and the amount of work to be done in a potentially explosive social and political environment. The challenge here is not only to produce expected results quickly, under tense and sometimes risky circumstances. The challenge is also to deal with the constant worry about the security and health of those within my immediate world and where I, my family, and friends fall within that world.

There is tension from having detailed knowledge of the context and locale of the humanitarian setting. I'm often quite familiar with the problem, the attitude, the threats within the community, and the fickleness of certain politicians in allowing for help. I often think about these issues—even ruminate about them—and have even worked out the "causes" behind each.

I have another line of sustained tension that comes from belonging and yet being apart. I belong to those who are helping and to those being helped, but I'm neither an expatriate nor a beneficiary. There is a tension between my life as a national, with blood and other deep ties to those around me, and my life as an aid worker coming from the outside to help those threatened by death. It is as if I am being followed by a ghost which constantly reminds me that the needy person—for example, the displaced person in the transit camp—could have been me.

Oh yes. And there are all kinds of other tangible reminders of my own vulnerability and mortality, as I witness the life and death experiences that link me very closely to those I'm trying to save.

The fact that emergency aid work does not directly influence conflicts, but instead responds to the devastation they cause, greatly affects national humanitarian workers. It colors our attitude and often limits our enthusiasm. We can only do so much. The consequences of the conflict affect us strongly because they mirror not only what could have happened but what could still happen to us and others close to us.

Further, both national and international humanitarian workers have a difficult working environment which allows little time to process personal experiences and manage stressful situations and issues. In such situations, I'm just glad for the speed with which we must execute our work. Responding quickly to others helps keep most of my anxieties out of focus and has made me tougher. These anxieties can overwhelm a worker, so we need to develop some emotional armor in order to last.

Since I am a committed Christian, a core part of my survival strategy is to keep in touch with God by communicating with Him and referring to His Word…It's also easy to become pessimistic as we wonder why God allows wars and suffering. To keep sane, I constantly have to pray for grace and wisdom, refer to God's commands in scripture, do my assigned duties to the best of my ability, and let God be God. I also need the support of those around me and from the organization for which I work.

### *Health Promoter 1. Reflection and Discussion*
### ADJUSTMENT ISSUES FOR MISSION/AID WORKERS

**Stress** is the response of the entire person spiritually, emotionally, physically, socially to internal and external demands. Too much for too long results in: physical tension and emotional discomfort relational strains and lower cognitive functioning and sometimes addictive behaviors spiritual and relational struggles.

**Burnout** is the incapacitating result of emotional distress and behavioral dysfunction due to chronic, unresolved stress. **Compassion fatigue** is a special type of burnout resulting from dealing with people's problems. **Brownout** is a mild from of burnout and a precursor to it.

**Culture shock** is the incapacitating experience of: anxiety, confusion, value dissonance, discouragement, and identity challenges that result from trying to get one's needs (and wishes, preferences) met in unfamiliar or unavailable ways in a new culture(s).

**Post traumatic stress disorder** can occur after exposure to an extreme stressor(s) (with the threat of death/serious injury to self or other) accompanied by intense fear, helplessness or horror. The stressor can be persistently re-experienced in intrusive and distressing recollections, dreams, or flashbacks; psychological and physiological distress when reminded of the stressor; avoidance of things associated with the stressor; and persistent symptoms of increased arousal such as difficulty falling asleep, irritability, hyper-vigilance, and difficulty with concentration.

**Applications:**
1. Which of these adjustment issues above have you experienced?
2. What are some other serious adjustment issues for mission/aid personnel?
3. In which of the *A4* accounts do you see evidence of burnout or PTSD?

## VOICES FROM ASIA[5]

### *Grave Consequences. India, Dr. Manoj*[6]

The recent deaths of many young missionaries in different parts of the country have been very shocking. More so, because the causes of the deaths are malaria, enteric fever and other common treatable and preventable causes. Today when medical science has advanced so much, it is sad that these young budding lives have been lost through what could have been ignorance, neglect, or delayed/improper treatment. As a health professional, I would recommend that every missionary sent to the field, especially to the remote areas, be given a proper training in basic health and be oriented to the health realities of their locations, in addition to other areas of preparation.

### *Darkness and Developments. India, JJ Ratnakumar*[7]

One has to visit our country to understand the spiritual battle that goes on to deliver the people from bondage.[8] Coupled with the presence of the evil spirits, the caste system cripples society. As the importance and status of a man or woman is decided at birth, some people will never be able to enjoy equality. The cultural bondage very often enters even the Christian churches, preventing people from worshiping under the same roof. The present estimate is that there are over 18,000 unreached postal pin codes out of about 28,000 pin code areas. (A pin code consists of about 35,000 people). As mission leaders struggle to meet the growing needs of the country, frontline missionaries face some of the following difficulties:

Women fetch safe drinking water from rising flood waters where a tube well has not sunken, Bangladesh. © 2008 Shamsuddin Ahmed/IRIN, www.irinnews.org

- Poor living conditions make their daily living miserable
- Children getting separated on account of education
- Increasing needs of the missionary as the family grows in size
- Persecution affecting the ministry and the morale
- Diseases that keep them away from the ministry
- Very little support; limited resources to execute their plans on time
- Inadequate training to face the challenges on the field and ministry
- Loneliness that drive them "mad"
- Constant attack of the evil one while they are with out Christian fellowship
- The pressure from the society, especially on the "first-generation Christians"
- Very little reserves to face crises
- No one to listen, understand, empathize or counsel
- No encouragement at the needed time from senders and supporters
- Lack of rest resulting in burn-out

Our organization, Missionary Upholders Trust (MUT), is one of the main and pioneering member care organizations in India. Specific projects include rest houses, medical help, retreats, calamity relief, shelter for retired missionaries, marriage enrichment, interpersonal skills training, and member care consultation for organizations. For more information, visit www.mutindia.org.

## *Personal Adjustments. China, Anonymous*[9]

We had no idea at all of what to expect going deep into this region of the country. The weather was cold, but bearable. Once the sun went behind the mountain the temperature dropped quickly too. The attitude of that place is about 3,000 meters above sea level. Water boiled at about eighty-three degrees Celsius, and so meat and nuts remained hard after being cooked. The only way was to use a pressure cooker. Sometimes these cookers exploded due to poor quality. The University guest-house we stayed in did not provide a refrigerator. As the temperature remains cold throughout most of the year we just placed a basket outside our window as an alternative fridge. We placed meat into it and cooked them when we needed them. At times, the weather warmed up and the meats turned bad. That explained how we got constant diarrhea.

In the new region we were in, the local speakers spoke a local dialect that sounds like the hissing of a snake. I mean they use lots of "Ss" in a sentence. As an overseas Chinese I faced different struggles in language learning. The locals could not understand why I did not know the language, when I looked just like them. In fact, often they were a little angry when I politely asked them to repeat a certain phrase they had just spoken. They thought I was trying to be funny, or worse to be sarcastic. Although they were more open to me than to the westerners, they also expected me to know and function within their worldview.

## *Stronger Backs. China, Brother Yun*[10]

The past fifty years of suffering, persecution, and torture of the house churches in China were all part of God's training for us. He has used the government for His own purposes, molding and shaping His children as He sees fit. That is why I correct Western Christians who tell me: we have been praying for years that the Communist government in China will collapse, so Christians can live in freedom. Instead of focusing our prayers against any political system, we pray that regardless of what happens to us, we will be pleasing to God. Don't pray for the persecution to stop! We shouldn't pray for a lighter load to carry, but a stronger back to endure! Then the world will see that God is with us, empowering us to live in a way that reflects His love and power. This is true freedom! Hundreds of Western missionaries spilled their blood on Chinese soil in the past. Their example has inspired us to be willing to die for the Lord wherever he leads us with His message.

*Health Promoter 2. Reflection and Discussion*
SHORT QUESTIONNAIRE ON STRESS

Here is a brief tool to assess aid worker stress. It is used by the International Federation of the Red Cross and Red Crescent Societies and many other organizations and workers (*Managing Stress in the Field*, 2001, http://www.ifrc.org/cgi/pdf_pubshealth.pl?stress.pdf). Try assessing your own stress levels too.

Instructions: Rate each of the following items in terms of how much the symptom was true of you the last month.

0 = Never   1 = Occasionally   2 = Somewhat often   3 = Frequently
4 = Almost always

____1.   Do you tire easily? Do you feel fatigued a lot of the time, even when you have gotten enough sleep?
____2.   Are people annoying you by their demands and stories about their daily activities? Do minor inconveniences make you irritable or impatient?
____3.   Do you feel increasingly critical, cynical or disenchanted?
____4.   Are you affected by sadness you can't explain? Are you crying more than usual?
____5.   Are you forgetting appointments, deadlines, personal possessions? Have you become absent-minded?
____6.   Are you seeing close friends and family members less frequently? Do you find yourself wanting to be alone and avoiding even your close friends?
____7.   Does doing even routine things seem like an effort?
____8.   Are you suffering from physical complaints such as stomach aches, headaches, lingering colds, general aches and pains?
____9.   Do you feel confused or disoriented when the activity of the day stops?
____10. Have you lost interest in activities that you previously were interested in or even enjoyed?
____11. Do you have little enthusiasm for your work? Do you feel negative, futile, or depressed about your work?
____12. Are you less efficient than you think you should be?
____13. Are you eating more (or less), smoking more cigarettes, using more alcohol or drugs to cope with your work?

Total Score: (Add up scores for items 1-13)

31

Interpretation: No formal norms are available for this measure. Based on the content of the items, a score of 0-15 suggests the delegate is probably coping adequately with the stress of his or her work. A score of 16-25 suggests the worker is suffering from work stress and would be wise to take preventive action. A score of 26-35 suggests possible burnout. A score above 35 indicates probable burn out.

Based on "The Relief Worker Burnout Questionnaire" in *Coping with Disaster* (1999) by John H. Ehrenreich

## VOICES FROM LATIN AMERICA[11]

### *Paying the Price. Brazil, Marcia Tostes*[12]

In the beginning of the movement, missionaries were sent, almost as one sends a parcel. In some ways it seems that it was the price that zealous, though missions-inexperienced, Christians had to pay to build a foundation. These early missionaries—like the current ones—needed a lot of faith to be able to overcome things like the lack of financial support, the unknown, culture shock, and difficult communication between the home country and the field. Many of those that were sent in that beginning persevered, and they are on the field until today, twenty years later. But some were seemingly not strong enough, and had to return. Nowadays there are still many missionaries being sent out without adequate care. These people, and those connected with them, continue to pay a high price.

### *Frontline Issues. PM International, Pablo Carrillo*[13]

Many struggles that the missionary faces on the field are a direct result of minimal missions understanding in the Latin church. For example, the lack of finances for missionary support in some cases is because the church is not totally convinced of the missionary task. In other cases it stems from the entrepreneurial approach to missions whereby the local church demands results, numbers, and a return in the investment. That puts pressure on the missionary to perform. Fortunately realistic approaches to building relationships and obtaining "results" are becoming a more frequent approach to the way Latins are doing missions. Orientation about missions and visits to the field by the church leadership are some practical solutions.

Another recent issue is that of children's education on the field. As the Latin American mission movement develops, so do the families that comprise it. In general, most of the workers have mainstreamed their children in local schools or in some cases in schools which use a more international language such as French or English. One of the problems faced by our families is the lack of support in order to be able to place their children in the better schools...

One of the most significant problems has been that of convincing some of the local churches to provide medical insurance for their missionaries. Many choose to go with no medical insurance. There are many risks in sending people to politically unstable and volatile countries even with full medical and life insurance. However these hard decisions must be seriously considered by the church and the candidates before leaving for the field.

*Health Promoter 3. Reflection and Discussion*
FAMILY ADJUSTMENT SCENARIOS

Scenario One: What could be done to help this family?

A Middle Eastern family is having trouble dealing with stress while going through the orientation program of its agency. The program takes place in North Africa, and requires that the participants move to a new city every two to four weeks over a three month period. The parents are concerned that they have been moving around too much, both pre-field and now during orientation, and that their two children are suffering as a consequence. The oldest is an eight-year old girl who has started wetting the bed three times a week at night, and the youngest is a boy, aged two, who is not eating much food.

Scenario Two: How would you help this boy?

A five-year old Argentine boy (missionary kid) does not want to go to his primary school in Kyrgyzstan, which he has been attending for two months. He is in pre-school and complains that some of the kids make fun of him by sticking out their tongues at him and saying that his drawings are ugly. During the last month the boy often whines and complains as he rises to get ready for school. When he returns from school he is often hard to make contact with and acts mean towards other family members.

Scenario Three: How would you try to help this couple?

A couple with no children that has been working in Indonesia for the past five years is having marital problems. The husband is Korean and the wife is Singaporean. The work is doing well but the workload has affected their relationship. Or so they say it has. Both acknowledge that they have come from "dysfunctional" families, in which there was alcoholism and poor parental modeling of conflict resolution. They have seen a counselor on furlough and attended a marriage retreat on the field, but no lasting changes have occurred. The wife's relationships with local women are significant, and she is having a significant impact in their lives. The husband has few close relationships outside of his work and is wondering if he is going through a mid-life crisis. Their sending agency decides to let them continue on the field and to do the best they can until they can get some more help somewhere.

A man holds a sign in search of a missing person, Ayacucho, Peru. © 2004 ICRC/B. Heger

## VOICES FROM THE ARABIC-TURKIC WORLD

*Faith in the Fire.*

A number of leading Muslim background believers (MBBs) met together in 2001 with representatives from some sending agencies who work with them. They explored what it meant to practice Christian spirituality in Islamic contexts while respecting and contributing to their own cultures/societies. Together they have recommended significant principles for ministry within these societies (excerpts below). The MBB churches expressed their deep gratitude to the global church for the ongoing prayer and support. For additional research/ discussion see: *From Seed to Fruit: Global Trends, Fruitful Practices, and Emerging Trends Among Muslims* (2008), edited by Dudley Woodberry; and Fran Love and Jelete Eckheart (2000), *Ministry to Muslim Women: Longing to Call Them Sisters.*

A Lebanese boy and his mother try to cope with continuous air raids.
Beirut. ©2006 Haitham Moussawi/IRIN. www.irinnews.org

The church in Muslim contexts (including those who labor among them) should strive to communicate the gospel incarnationally, and disciple in ways that honor and embrace whole families, for instance:

- Pray for the family.
- Provide new MBBs with a scriptural view of the family.
- Pursuing reconciliation with families is an important first goal in discipleship.

- Encourage and train a new MBB to share his faith with his family when appropriate.
- MBB children need priority care; they do not benefit from fellowship in the same way as adults.
- Train children in how to live for Christ; do not train with fear, but with faith
- Encourage daily family Bible reading, devotions, quiet time.
- Trust God for our children's safety.
- Counter (non-Christian) religious education from schools.
- Encourage MBB to persevere through persecution.
- The global church must embrace a theology of suffering in order to be faithful to scripture and stand alongside believers in Muslim contexts.
- The global church must identify scripturally sound ways to join in the fellowship of His suffering, avoiding heresies or syncretistic tendencies valuing prosperity, safety, and/or security above biblical truth and testimony.
- Practical means must be found to stand with MBBs at all times, including times of persecution.
- The global church must avoid the temptation to unnecessarily remove MBBs from their culture. Extraction results in "cultural suicide" and removes the most effective witness for Christ.
- Networks must be developed which will give support to embattled MBBs.

### Servants in the Crucible, Nik Ripken.[14]

This material is excerpted from a study which involved 450 interviews in forty-eight countries. These are countries where persecution was and is an everyday occurrence. "We began interviews in places that had experienced persecution historically then moved to more current situations, having amassed insight and experience along the path. Looming on the horizon was always the challenge of Islam."

Muslim-background believers (MBBs) throughout Asia, North Africa and the Horn of Africa shared great insights. Persecution is rampant in Indonesia, Bangladesh, Afghanistan, Pakistan and others. Countries such as Saudi Arabia and other Gulf states remain the greatest challenge, but according to statistics, the persecution in those countries remains quite low, reflecting the success they have had in systematically suppressing Christian witness and faith. Obviously, there have to be believers present in order to have persecution.

In these countries the combination of family, society and government, as persecutors in partnership, is so repressive that it is extremely difficult for believers to emerge. This can be referred to as "bottom-up persecution." Bottom-up persecution appears to be the most effective form of persecution. Here one does not get the chance to hear, believe and be gathered into believing communities. The persecutors are around the meal table, in the living room and sleep in the bed next to the one seeking spiritual truth.

While the top-down persecutors (usually those in authority) attempt to enforce their will upon the believing community, bottom-up persecutors enforce their will before one ever gets to Jesus. In bottom-up persecution, one's family will not hide the believer from the authorities or bribe their children's way out of prison. It is these very parents who deliver their children to the authorities, lock them in their bedrooms or beat them into submission. In bottom-up persecution, there generally is no need to fear the government, because those seeking the truth will not survive the negative attention of their father, their uncle or their oldest brother (page 9).

*Health Promoter 4. Discussion and Reflection*
VICTORIOUS FAITH IN THE MIDST OF PERSECUTION

The interviews in *Servants in the Crucible* show that there are common life experiences and practices among believers that are crucial to help them in the midst of persecution. Here are nine summary points to ponder. How are these experiences/practices part of your life? How can they be developed in the lives of mission/aid workers and those whom they serve?

- They have a personal relationship with Jesus Christ.
- The discipline of prayer is central to their lives.
- They know how to talk with God.
- They have memorized large portions of the Bible.
- Indigenous hymns, choruses and songs are central to their daily life and worship.
- Those incarcerated for their faith know that they have the support of the believing community; they are prayed for, and the community is caring for their families.
- They know that their persecution is normal and that it is for Jesus' sake.
- They have claimed their freedom and lost their fear.
- They have a genealogy (kin and community examples) of faith.

## OUR EMPIRICAL VOICES

In this section I summarize examples of the research on mission/aid personnel regarding their stressors and struggles. I begin with an overview of an extensive study sponsored by the World Evangelical Alliance (WEA) called Reducing Missionary Attrition Project. The first part of this study (ReMAP I) focused on missionary attrition (why mission personnel leave the field) and the results/analyses are discussed in depth in the book *Too Valuable to Lose: Exploring the Causes and Cures of Missionary Attrition* (1997). The second part of this study (ReMAP II) addresses missionary retention (why mission personnel remain on the field) and the findings are published and discussed in depth in the book *Worth Keeping: Global Perspectives on Best Practice in Missionary Retention* (2007). Following the ReMAP overviews (the first written by me and the second by Detlef Blöcher), I summarize several studies over the last twenty-five years that look at mission/aid worker adjustment.

## ReMAP I: ATTRITION FOR MISSION WORKERS[15]

### 3P Attrition

The ReMAP I study found the overall annual attrition rate, for all types of attrition, to be 5.1 percent for the 453 sending societies that were surveyed. When items such as normal retirement and possible transfer to another agency were ferreted out, the bottom line figure becomes 3.1 percent—attrition that is "undesirable" because it is premature, preventable, and likely permanent. Think of this as the *3Ps of the 3 percent*, to help remember the findings.

In real person terms, and at the time of this study, this may mean that some 12,000 staff are "lost" each year out of the global pool estimated to be over 400,000 (both Catholic and Protestant; Barrett, 1998). With the current figure of foreign missionaries estimated at 400,000 (Johnson, Barrett, and Crossing, 2010) the attrition figure could still be as high as 12,000 per annum, although the more recent ReMAP II study reported a somewhat lower attrition rate. The magnitude of *3P attrition* is sobering. Such undesirable attrition also spills onto others, negatively impacting thousands of family members and friends in the home/host communities.

### More Results

So why do staff leave the field? In the ReMAP study, the main reasons were, in order, normal retirement (9.4 percent), children's issues, change of job, health problems, lack of home support, problems with peers, personal concerns, disagreement with agency, lack of commitment, and lack of call (4.1 percent). Note that those surveyed in this study were mission administrators such as personnel directors, rather than the actual workers themselves. Workers also have their own perspectives, of course, that can be different.

Thirty bodies await burial in wasteland outside Tyre, Lebanon. The bodies had lain ten days unclaimed in the burned-out shells of cars and in other places around war-ravaged villages in south Lebanon. © 2006 Hugh Macleod/IRIN, www.irinnews.org

Several important comparisons were also made between different groups of staff:

- Staff from the Newer Sending Countries (NSCs—e.g., Korea, Brazil, Nigeria) were a bit more at risk for "preventable" attrition than those from the older sending countries (OSCs—e.g., the UK, USA, Australia).
- Reasons for overall annual attrition between NSCs and OSCs were very different: for NSCs the top reasons were reported to be lack of home support (8.1 percent), lack of call (8.0 percent), inadequate commitment (7.3 percent), disagreement with agency (6.1 percent), problems with peers (5.7 percent), health problems (5.1 percent); for OSCs, the top reasons were normal retirement (13.2 percent), children (10.1 percent), change of job (8.9 percent), health problems (8.4 percent), problems with peers (6.0 percent), personal concerns (5.2 percent).
- In general the larger and older the sending society, the lower the preventable attrition rate.
- Those working in the same culture vs. cross-culturally had about the same preventable attrition rates.
- Workers in pioneer/CP settings had lower preventable attrition rates than those in relief and development settings.

To continue, the most important factor in preventing attrition was reported to be the worker having a clear call. This was then followed by having a supportive family, healthy spirituality, cultural adaptation, good relationships, pastoral care, and financial provision. Interestingly, a key component of pastoral care was the "regular communication" that occurred for field workers, which was rated even higher than pastoral visits or pre-field training (which are also important).

### Some Suggestions

I appreciate the "codes of best practice" which have developed standards for the management and care of overseas workers (e.g., Evangelical Fellowship of Canada, 2002; Global Connections, 2009; People In Aid, 2003). These documents offer agreed-upon criteria for evaluating our member care approaches, and we would do well to thoroughly review them. Dave Pollock's "Flow of Care" model (2002), outlining member care needs and responsibilities from recruitment through retirement, is also helpful.

But how do we put these items into practice? And how do we reduce our attrition rates? There's no way around it: We in mission/aid must commit ourselves to more comprehensive, culturally-sensitive approaches to sustain and nurture our personnel over the long-haul. Who will do all this? Caring leaders (church and agency) who make time for their people. People like personnel development specialists, pastors, strategy coaches, and cross-cultural trainers, who are available to support and further equip our workers will also contribute. And finally colleagues and friends—you and me—whose mutual encouragement provide the backbone for effective member care programs. Box 2 lists several applications to reduce attrition.

### Summary Perspectives

Attrition, historically, has been part of the cost the church has paid for penetrating the areas of darkness (internally and externally!). People working in challenging settings are vulnerable, and inevitably get hurt. Our weaknesses as people and as sending agencies also make us vulnerable. So let's put attrition in perspective. Whether it is considered preventable or unpreventable, desirable or undesirable, *worker* attrition happens as we work together following the One who underwent the deepest attrition for the salvation of the world.

*Box 2. ReMAP I Applications*

The findings from ReMAP I also direct us towards helping mission/aid personnel to:

- Clarify and grow in their sense of call
- Prepare realistically through good pre-field selection and training approaches
- Cultivate their walks with the Lord
- Stay connected with supportive friends and family
- Care for their children's educational and developmental needs
- Improve interpersonal, conflict resolution, and ministry-related skills
- Raise finances for long-term involvement
- Maintain good communication with leaders and peers
- Understand various service opportunities and career development possibilities
- Connect with leaders/mentors who can help them negotiate the cross-cultural world
- Receive helpful member care resources throughout the course of their lives
- Go through exit interviews with follow-up for greater closure on their experience

# REMAP II: RETENTION FOR MISSION WORKERS[16]

*Detlef Blöcher*

How do member care and missionary longevity go together? The ReMAP II study on missionary retention and agency practices provides an extensive database to address this question. Mission executives from twenty-two countries were asked to assess their agency's practices and actual performance regarding member care and to provide retention data for their mission personnel. 601 agencies with some 39,611 long-term, cross-cultural missionaries participated in the study. Older sending countries (OSC) of Europe, North America and the Pacific and newer sending countries (NSC) of Africa, Asia and Latin America were analyzed separately to explore the differences in their mission movements. Also the practices of high retaining agencies vs. low retaining agencies were compared (that is, how long staff stay with an agency), including the allocation of finances and time for member care, and the provision of preventative and crisis care and many other factors. The methodology and more results are presented in *Worth Keeping* (2007).

### Member Care in Old (OSC) and New (NSC) Sending Countries

Time. OSC agencies invest about 8 percent of their total organizational time (on the field and in the home office) in member care. NSC agencies spend about 14.5 percent, which is almost twice as much—an impressive rate, probably reflecting the relational fabric of their home cultures as well as their strong commitment to their missionaries.

Finances. OSC agencies spend just 4.3 percent of their total finances/budget on member care and NSC agencies nearly 10 percent. These percentages are lower than those for the member care "time" category above, because agency budgets also include project expenses, capital investments etc. whereas member care is mainly budgeted more narrowly and in terms of personal allowances and travel expenses.

Prevention and Crisis Care. A third (OSC) to a fifth (NSC) of the overall member care resources are spent on the broad areas of prevention and personal development. This means that the majority of resources are invested in crisis intervention: nearly 70 percent in OSC and 80 percent in NSC. These findings indicate that member care is still more reactive in nature and crisis-oriented for helping *wounded* missionaries. Preventative member care in general is still very underdeveloped!

### High Retention Agencies and Low Retention Agencies

NSCs. In terms of preventable attrition, high retaining NSC agencies invest 9 percent of their total finances on member care. This is twice as much as in low retaining NSC agencies (4 percent investment). More specifically, high retaining NSC agencies also spent twice the amount (about 23 percent) of their total member care on prevention than do low retaining NSC agencies (11 percent). *Taken together, this means that high retaining NSC agencies spent four times as much of their total organizational effort (time and finances) on personal development and support of their missionaries (that is, preventive care) than low retaining NSC agencies!* This huge distinction marks their dissimilarity in how they care for their missionaries.

OSCs. As would be expected, high retention OSC agencies invest more time (about 25 percent more) and more finances on member care than low retaining OSC agencies. However, although they both devote roughly the same amount of staff time to prevention, the high retaining OSCs devote 50 percent more time on crisis response and restoration. This finding draws our attention to the significance of good crisis intervention and professional counseling as means for restoration as well as the need to continue to develop prevention/development resources. Yet the study merely investigated the amount of member care resources, but at the end of the day it is its quality that makes the difference.

### Agencies with High and Low Member Care Investment

Agencies with high investment in member care (defined as >20 percent of their total organizational staff time) had a third less annual attrition in the years 2001-2002 (5.2

percent for OSC, 3.0 percent for NSC) than low member care agencies (defined as <5 percent of their staff time): 7.3 percent for OSC and 3.6 percent for NSC. Attrition here involved both potentially preventable as well as unpreventable attrition. The definition of unpreventable attrition included factors such as: normal retirement, death in service, return to passport country at the end of project, appointment to leadership position in the mission, completion of pre-determined length of service, and certain health reasons.

Further, NSC agencies with a high investment in member care (>20 percent) rated their organizational performance 32 percent higher (on average) than NSC agencies with little member care. In particular there were higher ratings for clear vision and purpose statements, clear plans and job descriptions, leaders as example, supportive teams, administrative support on the field, annual review, pastoral care on the field level, interpersonal conflict resolution, and regular financial support.

OSC agencies with high member care investment rated their organizational practices 5-13 percent higher than OSC agencies with little member care. There were also higher ratings for field supervision, language learning, language and culture training for new missionaries, ongoing cultural studies, assignment of missionaries to gifting, work-rest balance, leadership, annual performance review, development of new gifts, pastoral care, health care, annual vacation, regular financial support, strengthening of the missionaries' spiritual life, debriefing during home assignment and reentry program. However, there is actually a U-shaped correlation between member care and retention: too little and too much member care are both related to lower levels of retention. Perhaps too much member care can actually hinder the development of resilience for mission workers and/or may detract from other important matters such as careful selection and pre-field orientation.

## Box 3. Other Findings from ReMAP II

- In general, small agencies have very low retention rates and high attrition rates. Small agencies have significantly less structure and care facilities. Box 3. Other Findings from ReMAP II
- Very small mission agencies across NSC and OSC lose people at a rate of 33 percent per year. Larger agencies lose 6 percent for OSC (3.5 percent for including normal retirement) and 1.3 percent for NSC.
- Retention correlates highly with missionaries' educational standards, although this is not always the case in NSC (e.g., Nigeria and India).

- Retention is highly correlated with candidate selection. Factors rated highest for all categories of NSC and OSC included: calling, doctrinal statement, agency principles, mature Christian character, character references, and endorsement by pastor.
- Physical health examinations were highly correlated with retention in NSC and OSC.
- Pre-field training time is highly correlated with retention for NSC and OSC. In general, missiological training appears to be more beneficial than theological training.
- High retaining agencies expect three times more missiological training than low retaining agencies.
- Issues of spiritual life received the highest ratings of all the question groups, for both NSC and OSC. Experience with spiritual warfare was moderately correlated with retention.
- Overall, personal care issues correlated highly with retention in NSC and OSC.
- Effective missionary team ratings were more highly correlated with retention for NSC than for OSC.
- Personnel given space to shape their ministries was rated highly and correlated with retention.

## CONCLUSIONS

*Worth Keeping* (2007) is filled with 400-plus pages of findings, analyses, and recommendations from the ReMAP II study. A few more of them are reported in Box 3. Overall ReMAP II shows the impressive investment of the New Sending Countries (NSC) in member care. It also clearly demonstrates the strong positive correlation between member care and missionary retention and in particular preventative member care: little member care means more attrition, and more member care means less attrition. Member care helps mission workers in so many areas: to grow spiritually and in their personal development, learn new skills, give and receive mutual support, develop a consultative leadership style, practice open communication, build trusted relationships, increase their flexibility to go through transitions and adjustment.

Missionary longevity is not an end in itself, and it makes little sense unless one is also faithful/productive in ministry. Hard places require dedicated, experienced and committed missionaries who have mastered the language, carefully adjusted to the local culture, living out an incarnational lifestyle in trusted relationships day by day. This calls for long-term commitment and long-serving mission workers. It requires well trained workers, quality sending groups (agencies and churches) with an effective member care system. Member care needs to be rooted in the organizational ethos and values, and thus shape all of the operations and procedures of sending groups.

A father holds his injured child while surveying damage to the devastated city of Balakot, Pakistan. © 2005 Edward Parsons/IRIN, www.irinnews.org

### *Box 4. Research on Mission Workers*

Gish, 1983 (*Journal of Psychology and Theology*, reprinted in *Helping Missionaries Grow* (1988)

**Sample**: 547 field missionaries in several countries and with several organizations

**Stressors**: (reported by 40 percent-plus to be moderate to great):

- Confronting one another when necessary
- Crossing language and cultural boundaries
- Time and effort maintaining donor contact
- Amount of work
- Work priorities

Carter, 1999 (*Journal of Psychology and Theology,* adapted in *Enhancing Missionary Vitality* (2002)

**Sample**: 306 missionaries, mostly North Americans working in 13 fields

**Additional stressors to those identified by Gish 1983 above (reported by 40 percent-plus as moderate to great):**

- Seeing needs I am unable to meet
- Self expectations
- Time for personal study of the Word and prayer
- Freedom to take time for myself
- Family responsibility vs. ministry
- City driving

---

Parshall, 1987 (*Evangelical Missions Quarterly*, reprinted in *Helping Missionaries Grow* 1988)

**Sample**: 390 American missionaries working in thirty-two countries, with thirty-seven mission societies

**Spiritual stressors:**

- Maintaining devotional life
- Maintaining a sense of "victory"
- Managing feelings of sexual lust

O'Donnell, 1995 (in *International Journal of Frontier Missions*)

**Sample**: 110 mission personnel (seventy Western and forty non-Western), one agency, working mostly in Asia

**Struggles (reporting high or extreme stress):**

- Type of work for married men—53 percent
- Marital issues for married women—45 percent (caution—small sample size)
- Relationships with colleagues for single women—40 percent
- Personal struggles for men—40 percent

Quality of team life: (clarity of goals, quality of communication, time together as a group, team cohesion, sense of mutual support, time with leader, time spent on stated goals, team morale)

Rated on a five point scale with 3 = adequate; average rating for eight areas was 2.75

Most helpful resources: friends' encouragement, devotional life, prayer partnerships

---

Schaefer *et al*, 2007 (*Journal of Traumatic Stress*)

**Sample**: 256 missionaries working in Europe/West Africa, from USA-based mission organizations

- Number of severe traumatic events was significantly higher in unstable settings (West Africa)
- Higher number of traumatic events was strongly associated with: greater PTS and functional impairment, increased depression and greater resilience (positive adaptation)
- Lower resilience associated with increased distress levels
- Number of traumatic events strongly associated with risk and protective factors
- Strong sense of purpose was associated with higher rates of traumatic events

## *Box 5. Research on Humanitarian Aid Workers*

*Room for Improvement* 1995 (adjustment and care issues for British aid workers)

**Sample**: 200 emergency and relief workers from the UK, working in several organizations

**Stressors (mentioned by more than 40 percent of the group):**

- Managers—workload, organization, communication
- Non-managers—organization, security, witnessing suffering
- Men—security, workload
- Women—organization, expatriate colleagues, lack of privacy, security, communication
- Work hours—half worked more than sixty hours/week, over 25 percent more than seventy hours/week)
- Security concerns—armed military presence, driving in the dark, dangers in evacuation; about half said security guidelines were not adequate and enforced

**Strategies to reduce stress:**

- Talking about problems, socializing (86 percent had someone with whom to talk about problems)
- 26 percent admitted drinking more than usual
- Almost half did not get a performance evaluation during or after their posting
- About 90 percent received some type of debriefing at the end of their term
- (75 percent said they also had the opportunity to talk about the emotional aspects of their posting)

International Committee of the Red Cross, 1996 (Bierens de Haan, debriefing ICRC field workers)

**Sample**: 2350 delegates interviewed at the ICRC Geneva headquarters

- 32 percent (756) received debriefing to detect psychological disturbance; 7 percent (165) diagnosed as suffering from stress such as "cumulative stress or traumatic stress." "Findings suggest that if staff resistance to violent emotions and stress is to be increased, interpersonal conflicts and problems of lack of leadership arising in the field must be taken as seriously as critical incidents and multiple traumatization linked to war."

---

Holtz, Salama, Cardozo, and Gotway, 2000 (*Journal of Traumatic Studies*)

**Sample**: (Mental health outcomes, seventy expatriate and local human rights workers in Kosovo)

- Elevated measures of: anxiety (17.1 percent), depression 8.6 percent), post-traumatic stress disorder (7.1 percent)
- Workers at risk for elevated anxiety symptoms had worked with their organization longer than six months, those who had experienced an armed attack, and those who experienced local hostility

Eriksson, Foy, and Fawcett, 2003 (*Centers for Disease Control; Antares Foundation Conference*)

**Sample**: (World Vision staff, 101 participants in thirty-five nations; average field time about eight years)

**Top Five "Chronic" Stressors:**

- Separation from family (68 percent rated moderate to extreme stress)
- Travel difficulties, threatening checkpoints, rough roads (56 percent rated moderate to extreme stress)
- Team conflicts (53 percent moderate to extreme stress)
- Feeling helpless to change people/place problems (52 percent rated moderate to extreme stress)
- Environmental stress like excessive heat, cold, noise (46 percent rated moderate to extreme stress)

**Organizational Stressors**: Lack of direction from management (31 percent), lack of recognition for work (31 percent), asked to work outside one's professional training (24 percent), criticism of work by agency authorities (20 percent)

**Exposure to Trauma**: 62 percent had direct/personal exposure to trauma, 67 percent had witnessed a traumatic event, 84 percent know someone who has experienced a traumatic event, 23 percent felt their life was in danger. Events most frequently associated with life threat: being threatened by a person with serious physical harm, being chased by a group or individual, being near gunfire, being shot at, seeing a dead body.

**Consequences and Personal Vulnerability**: Up to 25 percent in the "risk range" on measures for depression, PTSD, and burnout; vicarious trauma exposure and chronic stress related to burnout and depression; significant relationship between past trauma (family of origin mostly), social support, positive health behaviors, organizational factors, and measures of adjustment.

## FINAL THOUGHTS

We have surveyed some of our human and empirical voices in the mission/aid and member care community. Not many of the voices have been comforting. Several though have offered hope concerning what good member care can offer. People working in mission/aid not only *need* support but they also *want it* and they also *give it* to one another. Social support from all kinds of sources is one of the greatest protective factors available for workers. Workers who grow together, intentionally during projects and over the long-haul, are likely to be the most resilient. May we continue to listen to and learn from our international voices, including our A4 and empirical voices. And may we continue to find new, creative ways to provide and develop the types of member care that can make all the difference in a worker's life.

# PEARLS
## ENHANCING AND ENRICHING GOOD PRACTICE

*New treasures and old treasures are provided/developed for effective member care.*

*Launching member care further to help deal with the world's greatest challenges.*

*Leaders receive member care and support member care in their organizations.*

*Psychosocial support is provided for workers and for survivors of calamities/conflicts.*

*The mission/aid community embrace the biblical core of member care to/from all peoples.*


# PERILS
## ENCUMBERING AND ENDANGERING GOOD PRACTICE

*Distractions via many opportunities and losing focus on the needs of mission/aid workers.*

*Not taking advantage of the incredible resources available via the internet, coaching, etc.*

*Member care priorities do not include human rights advocacy for persecuted Christians.*

*Not connecting with the international sectors regarding their staff support/management.*

*The commitment to true love wanes and relational malaise replaces relational resiliency.*

# CHAPTER 3

# Embracing Future Directions[1]

WHERE DO WE WANT TO GO IN THE MEMBER CARE FIELD? AND WHERE DO WE NEED TO GO? WE HAVE SUCH AN INCREDIBLE ARRAY OF SPECIAL TREASURES IN MEMBER CARE TO HELP US GO FORWARD. WE MUST CONTINUE TO PROVIDE SUCH TREASURES AND DEVELOP MANY NEW ONES FOR BOTH THE MISSION/AID COMMUNITY AND THE WORLD IN NEED!

---

In March 2006, I was privileged to help launch a member care working group that met initially in Asia as part of the first *"Ethnê to Ethnê"* conference. The conference was attended by some 350 leaders from the international Evangelical mission community. It focused largely on networking in order to effectively work among Unreached People Groups (UPGs). UPG is a missiological term that refers to ethno-linguistic groups who do not have a viable, Christian community/church (representing about 25 percent of the earth's 6.7 billion people). More information is available at www.ethne.net.

Our purpose in the working group was to: "…discuss, envision, and discern ways to provide and develop member care resources, on behalf of mission/aid workers who are serving among UPGs. What structures, approaches, and issues do we need to consider in order to help these workers remain healthy and effective?" Added to these purposes over time were questions about *quality control* to encourage the development of skills for member care workers as well as *evaluation research* to review and refine the effectiveness of our services.

One of our guiding principles as a working group was to consider both current and new resources/directions for supporting the *diversity* of mission/aid workers among UPGs. This principle is reflected in Christ's conclusion to the Kingdom parables. "Therefore every scribe that has become a disciple of the kingdom of heaven is like the owner of the house that brings from his treasure new things and old things" (Matt. 13:52). Many of these "treasures" are directly relevant for all of types Christian workers in the world today, estimated to include 400,000 "foreign missionaries" and 11.8 million national workers, along with many more that do not fit into these two broad categories such as "tentmakers" (Johnson, Barrett, and Crossing, 2010).

The need for old/new treasures must also take into account the significant shifts in demographics among the world's 2.1 billion "affiliated Christians," especially the growing majority of Christians in/from the diverse Global South(s) and the proportional decline in Christians in/from the diverse Global North(s) (Corwin, 2010; Johnson and Kim, 2006). These treasures must also support the efforts to resolutely and responsibly deal with the world's greatest problems, including the need to eradicate poverty (e.g., the 910 million urban slum dwellers), provide universal education, promote gender equality, combat HIV/AIDS, foster environmental sustainability, etc. (United Nations Millennium Development Goals, http://www.un.org/millenniumgoals).

The member care field therefore, while maintaining its core focus on supporting the diversity of mission/aid personnel, must expand into new international and cross-sector areas. Each of us for example, would do well to stay current with at least one related health area and/or global issue that we are particularly passionate about (including organizations, practitioners, resources etc. related to the area/issue). We will need courage to face new challenges to enhance human well-being and combat evil in its many forms. And we will need a solid, practical theology that sees God at work throughout the variety of human efforts and "treasures" around the world.

Here are twelve such treasures among many—current and future resources/directions—that I believe are crucial for member care. The final treasure, "*Ethnê to Ethnê Member Care*," pulls together all the other treasures listed in this chapter as well as the material in Part One of this book.

## TWELVE TREASURES OF MEMBER CARE

**Treasure 1.** Sending Churches and Support Teams—The church has a core, biblical role in both sending and supporting workers. Historically this has often not been the case as often sending agencies (as a missiological structure of the church) have undertaken much of the member care responsibility. Sending churches can and do support workers in the areas of logistics, finances, prayer, communication, reentry, etc. The sending church along with "support teams" need to be trained to send well and to serve their workers well. Neal Pirolo's book, *Serving as Senders*, is a superb resource which is available in twelve languages (www.eri.org). Note though that some new ways of "going" do not reflect the usual approaches to "sending" (e.g., Asian Christians going to the Middle East for employment; Chinese workers with various levels of training/support heading "West" with the gospel; Christians living in Western countries who minister to UPG neighbors; Christians working in secular NGOs and United Nations offices/field settings; people creatively providing resources to UPGs via the internet). We will thus need to consider additional ways to support these "goers," including the roles for the sending churches, sending agencies, member care groups, and a variety of support teams working together.

**Treasure 2.** CEOs/Leaders—Loneliness and discouragement occur for most people in leadership. They, like all mission/aid personnel, need supportive member care. They are also in key places to provide encouragement and care to others as well as to open doors for member care as "gatekeepers" into their organization. One resource for supporting mission leaders is the "LeaderLink" training offered in various locations around the world by Cross Global Link (www.crossgloballink.org). Another example is the India Mission Association's retreats for CEOs and spouses (www.imaindia.org). In addition to its positive impact on leaders, these retreats have also helped open the doors to member care in India—leaders are gatekeepers, and what they experience can be passed on to staff. K Rajendran's account about his struggles as a leader in South Asia reflect just some of the many challenges of mission leaders (see Chapter 8, *Doing Member Care Well*, 2002). Some excerpts: "It is 12:45 midnight. I toss in bed, pleading for sleep to overtake me…We are asking many questions… These questions meander through my mind and nearly overtake me…I almost panic. It is now 2:30 am…Many CEOs and other leaders have many similar sleepless nights" (pp.77-79). For some additional reflections on the types of issues that concern mission leaders—and that can keep them awake at night—see Paul McKaughan's article "Challenges for a Constantly Changing Mission Context" (2010).

**Treasure 3.** Relief/Aid Workers—Psychosocial support is increasingly being recognized as a necessary and ethical organizational resource for workers in Complex Humanitarian Emergencies (CHEs). This support includes briefing, stress management, debriefing, and practical help for relief workers as well as equipping them with trauma/healing skills to help survivors (e.g., see the account in Randy Miller's interview with a World Vision relief worker, "Staying Sane and Healthy in an Insane Job" (1998) and the many accounts in *Sharing the Front Lines and the Back Hills*, edited by Yael Danieli, 2001). Many disaster scenarios provide opportunities to interact with and help UPGs, leading to ongoing joint programs in community development. It is especially important to consider the reality of "neglected emergencies"—the ones that get overlooked due their chronic, seemingly unsolvable problems and overall lower profile— including "fragile states affected by ongoing conflict, poverty, corruption, and weak infrastructure (Gray, 2008, Moeller, 2008). One timely resource is the radio program and materials created to help survivors and caregivers in both natural and human-made disasters (www. seasonsofcaring.org). See also two publications in particular from the International Federation of the Red Cross and Red Crescent Societies: *Managing Stress in the Field* (2001) www.ifrc.org/publicat/catalog/autogen/4773.asp and *Psychological Support: Best*

*Practices* (2001) www.ifrc.org/publicat/catalog/autogen/4516.asp. The following quote, from the later publication, highlights the relevance of equipping relief/aid workers with psychological skills. It also reflects some of the emotional consequences that can affect workers themselves.

> The distinction between psychological needs and other priorities in relief opera-
> tions is an artificial one, as psychological needs permeate and affect all other
> aspects such as shelter, food distribution, and basic health care. Provision of
> traditional relief aid is, therefore, not sufficient. *Neglecting emotional reactions*
> *may result in passive victims rather than active survivors* (italics mine). Early
> and adequate psychological support can prevent distress and suffering from
> developing into something more severe, and will help the people affected cope
> better and return more rapidly to normal functioning (p. 5).

**Treasure 4.** The Diaspora of Peoples— There are geographic "movements" of people all over the globe. Our human interconnections are significantly shifting too through globalization and digitalization. Christians would do well to track with such changes, and seriously consider ministry to those who are now much more accessible. Two types of physical "movement" involve people who cross borders for economic reasons or who flee for safety as part of internationally or internally displaced peoples (e.g., see the many short accounts throughout the *Handbook for the Protection of Women and Girls*, 2008 by the United Nations High Commissioner for Refugees http://www.unhcr.org/protect/PROTECTION/47cfae612.html). What an opportunity for the church to connect with these people, many who are in our own physical and/or digital "neighborhoods." For more updates on the needs of refugees, the poor, etc., visit the Web site of World Vision International (www.wvi.org) and the UN High Commissioner for Refugees: (www.unhcr.org).

**Treasure 5.** Persecuted Humans— Tens of thousands of Christians (and those from other religions) are affected by discrimination and human rights violations, including religious liberty violations, as a result of their religious and political beliefs and/or ethnicity. There are major physical, economic, and psychological consequences to violating humans through persecution (e.g., Companjen's, *Hidden Sorrow, Lasting Joy, 2000*). We must find ways to better support Christians and all people who suffer in this way (see chapters 19 and 45 in *Doing Member Care Well*, 2002 on pressure/persecution and advocacy). John Amstutz commented in Humanitarianism with a Point. "...the place of hospitality and kindness toward followers of Jesus Christ is no small matter, particularly those who are being persecuted for their faith in Him…. [It is time] to speak clearly and fully of the essential need of intentional humanitarianism—member care— toward those who have chosen to suffer loss for Christ in these nations" (*Doing Member Care Well*, 2002 p. 39). See the materials from the Religious Liberty Commission (www.worldevangelical.org),

Amnesty International (www.amnesty.org), and at the United Nations High Commissioner for Human Rights, including the *Universal Declaration of Human Rights* (www.un.org/rights). Finally, consider Wilfred Wong's perspective as a human rights advocate regarding persecution and the growth of the church.

> There is nothing new about the persecution of Christians. Such actions have taken place since the birth of the church 2,000 years ago. More Christians have been imprisoned, tortured and killed for their faith in the 20th Century than at any other time in the church's history.... But it's not all doom and gloom. One reason why there is persecution in so many different countries today is because the church is expanding its frontiers throughout the world. More than at any other time in the history of Christianity we can truly regard the church as a global community. It is because the church is growing in places traditionally hostile to the Gospel that in many of these locations the backlash of persecution occurs. Governments or religious extremists feel threatened by the spread of Christianity and try all sorts of methods to stop its growth, ranging from murder and genocide...to more subtle measures such as the introduction of restrictive laws on church registration... (2002, pp. 477-478).

**Treasure 6.** Special Support for A4 Workers—There is an increasing number of Christian workers from the *A4 Regions*. A4 senders/workers desire to provide/develop quality member care approaches that fit their own sending groups, personnel, and cultures. Their experience in member care is also relevant for those from other sending nations [e.g., see the article on the India organization, Missionary Upholder's Trust (*Ethnê-Member Care Update* 11/08; www.ethne.net/membercare/updates)]. The commitment to quality care for A4 workers is clearly stated and modeled for all of us in these excerpts from the *Declaration* by the Philippine Missionary Care Congress of October 2005. (You can find the entire *Declaration* in the *Global Member Care Briefing* from February 2006, www.membercare.org).

> ...we will foster a culture of care among our churches and mission organizations compliant with the model and mandate of Christ to love and serve each other; we will endeavor to raise awareness about Member Care that would catalyze the Filipino church to harness capacities in order to ensure the flow of care towards those who were sent out; ...we will share knowledge, resources, and personnel; cooperate in stewardship of God's resources with each other and with the global member care community so that potentials are maximized and excesses are minimized in serving cross-cultural Christian workers;...we will seek out good practice models of Member Care that are biblically founded, and harness the existing strength of the Filipino culture for missionary care;

we endeavor for the cross-cultural Christian workers' personal growth that includes the nurture of each of their family members; …we will raise more church leaders and ministers particularly focused on Member Care, adequately equipped and tooled to serve the needs of the Filipino missionary including their families and home-based personnel; …we will personally engage in caring for Filipino cross-cultural Christian workers—celebrating their joys, sharing in their sorrows, supporting their needs and supplicating for their victory in seeing the unreached peoples coming to Christ (*Global Member Care Briefing*, February 2006; www.membercare.org).

---

**Box 1. Examples of Member Care Materials Relevant for the A4 Regions**

**Chinese**: www.Chinamembercare.com
**Arabic**: www.sites.google.com/site/arabicmembercare/
**Bahasa Indonesia**: www.sites.google.com/site/indonesiamembercare/
**Spanish**: www.cuidadointegralcomibam.blogspot.com
**Korean**: www.wearesources.org

**Resources in many languages (also see the listing in chapter four):**

**Reality Dose**: www.sites.google.com/site/mcaresources/realitydose
**Christian Recovery International**: www.christianrecovery.com
**World Federation of Mental Health**: www.wfmh.org
**World Health Organization (emergencies)**:
www.who.int/mental_health/resources/emergencies

---

**Treasure 7.** Training and More Training— Member care is not just a "specialist" function—something to be only provided by "professionals." Rather it is essential to further train and equip various member care workers (MCWs), leaders, senders, and mission personnel themselves with "special" member care skills. These skills help to sustain workers for the long-haul. Training includes such areas as: counseling, crisis care/debriefing, organizational systems/dysfunction, interpersonal skills, personnel development, and family/marriage. One course in particular that continues to make its international rounds is the one week intensive "Sharpening Your Interpersonal Skills" (www.itpartners.org). Another course offered primarily in Africa is based on the book by the same title: *Healing the Wounds of Trauma; How the Church Can Help* (2007), and also translated into over 100 languages spoken in Africa. Offering member care-related courses via the internet (e.g., www.headington-insitute.org) and via workshops at conferences are also good ways forward. Currently there is no global calendar of training and related events like conferences for the member care community (there was for a few years until mid-2006). Hopefully such a calendar will be restarted in the near future.

**Treasure 8.** Secular Connections—There is so much mutual benefit from connecting with the international health, humanitarian, business, human resource, media, and educational sectors. How do they manage/support their staff and how to they help/ protect humans in need of aid and developmental resources? How do they maintain "good governance" in light of corruption and dysfunction? One key document dealing with the management and support or aid workers is the *People in Aid Code of Good Practice* (2003, www.peopleinaid.org). Its seven principles and various "key indicators" (criteria for determining the extent to which the principles are being followed) have also served as helpful guides to many organizations in mission/aid. See also the Web sites for the Society for Human Resource Management (www.shrm.org), AtHealth (www. athealth.com), the International Society for Traumatic Stress Studies (www.istss.org), World Health Organization (www.WHO.org), the World Federation for Mental Health (www.wfmh.org), Families in Global Transition (www.figt.org), Humanitarian Policy Group (www.odi.org.uk/hpg), Transparency International (www.transparency.org), and AlertNet (www.alertnet.org).

**Treasure 9.** Coaching—Coaching is just one of many developing areas for further supporting workers (some other areas include spiritual direction, conflict mediation, and leadership development). It focuses on both personal and professional development. Strategy-related coaching has been around for many years (e.g., "Coaching Missionary Teams" by Tim and Becky Lewis, 1992). But coaching as a core component of member care is also rapidly developing. Coaching can occur via face to face and the variety of telecommunications such as Skype and Webcams. Keith Webb describes coaching in the mission context:

> Coaching is an ongoing conversation that empowers a person or team to fully live out God's calling—in their life and profession. The goal of coaching is to develop a person or team to more effectively reflect, correct, and generate new learning. It's learning new ways to learn, listening to the heart and the Holy Spirit, and taking action to reshape their lives around that learning...Coaching focuses on learning rather than teaching. Coachees (those who are coached) are in the driver's seat. Coachees choose their own growth goals. Coachees reflect deeply about their current situation. Coachees think through their

options. Coachees decide their next steps. All the while, the coach actively listens and asks reflective questions, supportively challenging limited beliefs and behaviours. Advice-giving is kept to a minimum so that the coachee can discover Holy Spirit-inspired solutions (*Ethnê-Member Care Update*, November 2006, pp. 3-4; note: later published in *Evangelical Missions Quarterly*, volume 44, 2008, pp. 284-291).

Gary Collins sends out regular newsletters with many coaching and counseling helps. The newsletters are concise, user-friendly and archived on his Web site.(www. garyrcollins.com). See also: International Coach Federation (www.coachfederation. org), Christian Coaches Network (www.christiancoaches.com), and the Institute for Life Coach Training (www.lifecoachtraining.com).

**Treasure 10.** Internet and Telecommunications—We want to develop skills to use the Internet well. It is now a main tool for many who want to stay in touch with the member care field and colleagues, exchange resources etc. Some of the skills needed include using voice over internet technologies (VOIP), podcasting, running Web sites, and using webcams for consultation. Thomas Friedman is well-known for his observations on how the world is becoming increasingly "flat"—that is, the greater accessibility to other people and resources and the greater possibility to equalize opportunity/development. In *The World is Flat* (2007), he describes "the convergence of ten major political events, innovations, and organizations….and the multiple new forms and tools for collaboration that this flattening has created" (p. 51). The tenth "flattener" in particular refers to advances in our "digital, mobile, personal, and virtual" capacity:

> …engines can now talk to computers, people can talk to people, computers can talk to computers, and people can talk to computers farther, faster, more cheaply, and more easily than ever before. And as that has happened, more people from more places have started asking one another the same two questions: Can you hear me now? Can we work together now? (p. 198-199).

But note that in spite of these incredible changes and communication advances, many people— member caregivers and service receivers—do not have inexpensive, reliable, and easy access to the internet, or to computer technology, much less a stable environment in which to live! So the internet is currently a real luxury item for many— and possibly not even a "culturally-relevant" means of communication.

**Treasure 11.** Resiliency—Member care seeks to develop strong people who balance the need for support/growth with the reality of sacrifice/suffering. Good member care helps develop resiliency—the inner strength, consistent practices, and social supports necessary to successfully deal with and grow through life's challenges. Resiliency is necessary of course to work effectively in UPG settings, many of which are very demanding. Both the experiences of "barely surviving and actively thriving" are realities for Christian workers. Resiliency is developed through hard experiences and via the courageous examples we see in the people who receive the services of mission/aid workers. Here is a brief quote from *Stress and Trauma Handbook: Strategies for Flourishing in Demanding Environments* (2003). The quote is from the chapter by Cynthia Eriksson *et al*. It summarizes research on the adjustment of World Vision aid workers from over thirty countries:

> ...for each of the mental health risk adjustment measures (depression, post-traumatic stress disorder, and burnout) 30-50 percent of staff scored in the moderate to high-risk range. This is a significant number of people who are working and 'surviving' while experiencing considerable emotional distress. These staff may not be incapacitated by these symptoms presently, but we cannot deny the effects that depression, burnout, and PTSD can have on relationships, work, and personal health. An NGO's commitment to people includes the welfare of beneficiaries around the world, but it also includes the well-being of staff who commit their lives to serving and saving others." (p. 95)

This 30-50 percent figure is likely similar for many organizations with staff serving in more volatile areas. I believe it is also important to consider the impact of the emotional distress and behavioral dysfunction that occur leading up to the actual diagnosis/development of the three disorders mentioned in this research. Workers are vulnerable, yet still able to provide effective services in spite of their heavy stress loads. The disorders which sometimes do result reflect the realities (consequences) of humans who serve God in difficult places.

## FINAL THOUGHTS

**Treasure 12.** *Ethnê to Ethnê* Member Care
I would like to now pull together the previous member care treasures as well as the material in Part One of this book as we have explored member care in mission/aid. Let's consider a preeminent and unifying treasure called *Ethnê to Ethnê Member Care* (E2MC). Concisely stated, in E2MC we are:

- prioritizing resources/directions
- that are visionary/practical
- to further provide/develop member care
- for/by all people groups.

61

**The Vision**: As Christians we believe there is a purpose to human history, and that there will be a conclusion to this age. We see how God is actively involved in history to redeem humans from every nation, people group, and language (Rev. 5: 9, 10). It is an "ethnê to ethnê" strategy, in which believers from different people groups reach out to other people groups, until "all of the earth is filled with the knowledge of the glory of the Lord." The vision is thus for all ethnic groups to be involved in *cross-ethnê* mission/aid.

**The Commitment**: Member care is a service ministry which supports this historical and biblical vision. As an international movement of quality people who provide and develop quality resources, the member care community is committed to helping mission/aid workers grow in the personal character, professional competencies, and life skills necessary to work effectively. This includes workers from *all* ethnê.

**The Strategy**: Now let's consider an amazing corollary to this commitment: I want to suggest that this also means that we are committed to seeing quality member care workers (MCWs) from *all* ethnê raised up and trained, including those within/from the Unreached People Groups (UPGs) and the A4 regions (Africa, Asia, Arabic-Turkic, and America-Latina). And these MCWs work both within their own cultures *and* cross-culturally. So the focus is twofold: supporting the diversity of people involved in Christian mission/aid; and training others from various cultures to be quality care providers. Member care, then, is also very much an "ethnê to ethnê" strategy.

**The Directions**: E2MC is very challenging. What can help the member care community as it moves in this direction? It will be important to set up opportunities for colleagues from different cultures to interact with each other (forums, conferences, writing, networks etc.). It will also be important for colleagues with member care training/experience in different cultures/countries, to facilitate learning and practice as "multicultural bridges." Multi-cultural Southerners/Easterners who have sojourned for extended periods to the North/West and vice versa, will play key roles. Such multicultural learning is a core part of providing and developing member care well. And it is a two-way street.

**Growing and Going**: E2MC requires the best or our conceptual thinking and research skills; extensive practical experience; a commitment to use transcultural principles (concepts common across cultures, especially ethnic and organizational "cultures"); and lots of personal connections and ongoing relationships with colleagues. Said another way, we as a member care community are heading increasingly towards the reality of "boundaries without borders"—that is we are aware of our personal cultural/disciplinary identities and member care competencies (boundaries) as we intentionally work with those having different geographic/ethnic identities and member care concepts (borders). E2MC challenges us to grow *deeply as persons* as we go *broadly as practitioners* to all peoples.

**Love**: Above all, the core of E2MC involves the trans-ethnê, New Testament practice of fervently loving one another—like encouraging one another each day; bearing one another's burdens; and forgiving one another from the heart. By this all people will know that we are His disciples (John 13:35). The Great Commission and the Great Commandment are inseparable. Our love is the final apologetic. It is the ultimate measure of the effectiveness of our member care.

*Health Promoter 1. Reflection and Discussion*
DOING E2MC WELL

Suppose you were going to write or edit a book called *Doing E2MC Well: Perspectives and Practices from Around the World*. If there were three sections in the book, what would you title them? What would be a few chapter topics and types of authors to include?

A young boy drinks rain water at the displaced camp in Eldoret Kenya.
© 2008  Manoocher Deghati/IRIN www.irinnews.org

# RESOURCES

CHAPTER 4

# Resources for Good Practice

"THESE ARE THE ONES THAT HAVE HELPED RESTORE TO ME
THE MISLAID TREASURES OF GOD."
—PHILLIP YANCEY, *SOUL SURVIVOR*, 2001

---

This chapter provides materials to encourage your personal and professional growth. As good practitioners we want to continue to develop our character (virtues and resiliency) and competence (skills and knowledge). We grow together with others. We have clear and strong ethical commitments to do good and to provide quality services. We go broadly and grow deeply as we follow the Good Practitioner and the Heart of Member Care, Jesus Christ.

Materials in this Chapter:

- Learning to be Safe
- CHOPS Adjustment Inventory
- Flourishing in Demanding Environments
- Self –Care and Lifestyle Balance Inventory
- Team Feedback Form
- Sixty-Plus Books for a Member Care Library
- Healing the Body: Part One

* * * * * *

# Learning to be Safe
### Kelly O'Donnell

Staying safe is something we learn about from the day we are born. We don't eat every plant we find in a field, we don't cross streets without looking, we watch our money belts/handbags etc. Learning about how "life works"—the dangers, the practicalities, and the wonders—is also an ongoing and essential part of our organizational lives as well. There is continuity, in other words, for staying safe throughout our lives—including before, during, and after our mission/aid work.

To illustrate these thoughts, let's have a look at the paraphrased opening lines of a short story by the Uruguayan author, Horacio Quiroga This story is taken from his 1918 book, *Cuentos de la Selva* (Jungle Stories). The eight stories in this book are nature-metaphors in which the flora and fauna reflect the realities of our human world.

### The Blind Doe

There once was a beloved doe. Her mother taught her how to survive. Before the doe could venture on her own, she had to repeat each day at sunrise the "Lord's Prayer" of the Deer. She needed to learn it well in order to survive. Here are the four parts of the prayer in English:

I:   Smell well before you eat because some plants are poisonous.

II:  Watch and wait before drinking to make sure there are no crocodiles in the river.

III: Every half hour lift your head and smell the wind to recognize the scent of the tiger.

IV:  Always look between the weeds when you eat field grass to see if there are vipers.

---

### Reflection and Discussion

1. How can you apply these principles and instructions to your life right now? What might some of the flora and fauna represent for you?

2. If you were to write a similar "prayer" for your life, what would be some main components?

3. List a few important ways that these principles/warnings apply to the mission/aid sectors.

\* \* \* \* \* \*

# CHOPS Adjustment Inventory
*Kelly and Michèle O'Donnell*

In Matt. 10:16 Jesus sent His disciples out as "sheep in the midst of wolves." This exercise explores ten "wolves"—which we refer to as stressors—that cross-cultural workers frequently encounter. We use the acronym "CHOPS" as a way to help identify and deal with these stress-producing "wolves."

**Directions: Using a separate piece of paper, write down some of the stressors that you have experienced over the past several months.** Refer to the 10 stressors and some of the examples mentioned below. Put these under a column labeled "Struggles." In a second column, "Successes," list some of the helpful ways you have dealt with stress during the last several months. Next, under a "Strategies" column, jot down some of your ideas for better managing stress in the future. You may also want to do the same for/with some of the important people in your life, such as individuals and groups found at the bottom of this page (use additional paper). Discuss your responses with a close friend or a counselor. Note that each stressor can be a source of stress and/or a symptom of stress.

| Struggles | Successes | Strategies |
|---|---|---|
| *Cultural* (getting needs met in unfamiliar ways: language learning, culture shock, reentry) <br><br> *Crises* (potentially traumatic events, natural disasters, wars, accidents, political instability) <br><br> *Historical* (unresolved past areas of personal struggle: family of origin issues, personal weaknesses) <br><br> *Human* (relationships with family members, colleagues, nationals: raising children, couple conflict, struggles with team members, social opposition) <br><br> *Occupational* (job-specific challenges and pressures: work load, travel schedule, exposure to people with problems, job satisfaction, more training, government "red tape") | | |

| | | |
|---|---|---|
| *Organizational* (incongruence between one's background and the organizational ethos: differing with company policies, work style, expectations) | | |
| *Physical* (overall health and factors that affect it: nutrition, climate, illness, ageing, environment) | | |
| *Psychological* (overall emotional stability and self-esteem: loneliness, frustration, depression, unwanted habits, developmental issues/stage of life issues) | | |
| *Support* (resources to sustain one's work: finances, housing, clerical/technical help, donor contact) | | |
| *Spiritual* (relationship with the Lord: devotional life, subtle temptations, time with other believers, spiritual confrontations) | | |

Answers apply to (circle): self, spouse, child, friend, department, team, company, other.

---

### Questions about Stress

1. How do you know when you are experiencing stress? How does it affect you physically, spiritually, emotionally, relationally, mentally?
2. When was the last time that you went through a significant period of stress? What was it like?
3. How did Jesus deal with stress? There are 25-plus things He did to mange His levels of stress.
4. What things do you do to deal with stress? What helps? What does not help?

**Note**: The CHOPS Inventory is available in several languages. See the link for Giants, Foxes, Wolves, and Flies in the Tools/Training section at: www.MemberCareAssociates.org.

\* \* \* \* \* \*

# Stress and Trauma Handbook:
## *Strategies for Flourishing in Demanding Environments*

Excerpts from the *Introduction* by John Fawcett, ed., World Vision, 2003

In the context of complex humanitarian emergencies and the rigors of life in developing nations, aid workers arrive on the scene expecting to enhance life, not just to neutralise pain. Humanitarian work is, after all, a celebration of life, not homage to death and despair. ...International aid is a challenge to the power not only of hunger, war, and poverty, but to cynicism. Faith-driven or secular, the workers who bring aid...are the living embodiment of a human conviction that wrongs not only *must* be righted, but that they *can* be righted (p.1).

Humanitarian personnel work in increasingly dangerous environments... aid workers often find themselves targets and suffer accordingly...(p. 1). But protection against the major impacts of traumatic stress is not only possible—it is critical for all humanitarian and welfare agencies...A significant method of protecting staff against serious stress injury is to work on improving organisational factors such as management capacity and team functioning (p.2).

...the objective of stress and trauma management is not merely to protect local and expatriate staff but to encourage them to grow, flourish, and sow the seeds of well-being among colleagues and communities in which they work and live...One of the most effective ways both to protect and to flourish is to maintain excellent social relationships within and outside the work environment (p.5). Our findings suggest that strong relationships afford the best protection in traumatic and stressful environments (p.6).

...the most stressful events in humanitarian work have to do with the organisational culture, management style and operational objectives of an NGO or agency rather than external security risks or poor environmental factors. Aid workers, basically, have a pretty shrewd idea what they are getting into when they enter this career, and dirty clothes, gunshots at night and lack of electricity do not surprise them. Intra-and inter-agency politics, inconsistent management styles, lack of team work and unclear or conflicting organizational objectives, however, combine to create a background of chronic stress and pressure that over time wears people down and can lead to burnout and even physical collapse (p. 6).

...the full organisational benefit of attention to stress and trauma management will be gained when learnings and techniques are applied to groups or teams. Programme objectives and organisational plans will be more achievable where aid workers have strong social relationships, are members of cohesive teams, are blessed with consultative leadership, and are adequately skilled to do the job for which they have been employed (p.6).

Effective stress management is a holistic practice, requiring more than piecemeal attempts at prevention and protection (p.7). Protection and prevention are always more cost effective than treatment, especially considering that a person who experiences severe burnout may never be able to return to front-line field work. But organisations and management who view stress management merely as a way to protect existing assets by erecting containment measures miss the point.

Containment is not what humanitarian life is about. Life, which international aid work affirms every day, is about growth, learning and transformation. A comprehensive organisational stress management strategy will identify outcome objectives relating to flourishing rather than containment. The vision…is that of humanitarian workers enabled to experience their own growth and development as they care for themselves and the great needs of those to whom they are responding (p. 10).

✷ ✷ ✷ ✷ ✷ ✷

# Self Care and Lifestyle Balance Inventory
© *Headington Institute, www.headington-institute.org*

Please note that this scale is not a clinical diagnostic instrument and is provided for educational purposes. It merely examines some of the more effective physical, psychological and spiritual methods of staying balanced and preventing burnout. If you have any concerns about your state of emotional health, you should consult with a mental health professional.

**Instructions:** In the last month, how often has the following been true for you? For each question, write the number that best fits your experience on the line before the question.

1. I have at least one full day off work each week.
   (0) Never / (1) Seldom / (2) Sometimes / (3) Often / (4) Always

2. I take some time for myself to be quiet, think, meditate, write and/or pray.
   (0) Never / (1) Seldom / (2) Sometimes / (3) Often / (4) Daily

3. I work for less than ten hours a day.
   (0) Never / (1) Seldom / (2) Sometimes / (3) Often / (4) Daily

4.  I do aerobic exercise (walking, running, swimming etc) for at least 25 minutes at a time.
    (0) Never / (1) Seldom / (2) Once a week / (3) Twice a week / (4) 3 or more times/week

5.  I do something I find fun (e.g., play a game, go to a movie, read a book etc).
    (0) Never / (1) Seldom / (2) Sometimes / (3) Often / (4) Daily

6.  I practice muscle relaxation, Pilates, yoga, stretching, meditation or slow breathing techniques.
    (0) Never / (1) Seldom / (2) Sometimes / (3) Often / (4) Daily

7.  I share how I am feeling with at least one friend or my partner.
    (0) Never / (1) Seldom / (2) Sometimes / (3) Often / (4) Daily

8.  I sleep well and get at least seven hours of sleep a night.
    (0) Never / (1) Seldom / (2) Sometimes / (3) Often / (4) Daily

9.  I am careful about what I eat and eat a balanced diet.
    (0) Never / (1) Seldom / (2) Sometimes / (3) Often / (4) Daily

10. I drink at least 1.5 liters of water (approx. 3 pints) a day.
    (0) Never / (1) Seldom / (2) Sometimes / (3) Often / (4) Always

11. I laugh without malice or cynicism.
    (0) Never / (1) Seldom / (2) Sometimes / (3) Often / (4) At least once a day

12. When I leave work at the end of the day I can disengage and leave the pressures of work behind.
    (0) Never / (1) Seldom / (2) Sometimes / (3) Often / (4) Always

13. I listen to my body's signals and recognize when I am becoming tired, rundown and vulnerable to illness.
    (0) Never / (1) Seldom / (2) Sometimes / (3) Often / (4) Always

14. There are people who care about me that I trust, to whom I can talk if I want.
    (0) Never / (1) Seldom / (2) Sometimes / (3) Often / (4) Always

15.	I do something I find creative or expressive (e.g., writing, cooking, gardening etc).
(0) Never / (1) Seldom / (2) Sometimes / (3) Often / (4) Daily

16.	I feel I have the training and skills I need to do my job well.
(0) Never / (1) Seldom / (2) Sometimes / (3) Often / (4) Always

17.	I set and maintain healthy boundaries for myself by standing up for myself, saying "no" when I need to, and not letting others take advantage of me.
(0) Never / (1) Seldom / (2) Sometimes / (3) Often / (4) Always

18.	At work I take a brief break at least every two hours, and switch tasks regularly so that I don't become too drained.
(0) Never / (1) Seldom / (2) Sometimes / (3) Often / (4) Always

19.	I spend time with groups of people I trust and to whom I feel close who are part of a community of meaning and purpose (e.g., a church group, a group of volunteers, work colleagues).
(0) Never / (1) Seldom / (2) Sometimes / (3) About once a week / (4) More than once a week

20.	My ability to communicate with others is…
(0) Very poor / (1) Poor / (2) Fair / (3) Good / (4) Excellent

21.	I feel good about how I spend my time and energy in relation to what is really important to me in life.
(0) Never / (1) Seldom / (2) Sometimes / (3) Often / (4) Always

22.	I believe in myself and generally give myself positive messages about my ability to accomplish my goals – even when I encounter difficulties
(0) Never / (1) Seldom / (2) Sometimes / (3) Often / (4) Always

23.	I set realistic goals for my life (both short term and long term) and work towards them consistently.
(0) Never / (1) Seldom / (2) Sometimes / (3) Often / (4) Always

24.	I take good vacations (at least one two-week vacation every year).
(0) Never / (1) Seldom / (2) Sometimes / (3) Often / (4) Every year

25. I drink alcohol, smoke, or use other recreational drugs
    (0) Three or more times every day / (1) At least once every day / (2) Three to six times a week / (3) Less than three times a week / (4) Never

TOTAL SCORE: _____

## Interpretation Guidelines

**0-25:** A score in this range suggests that your self care skills and lifestyle balance strategies may be poor, and that you could possibly benefit from developing a plan to change your lifestyle and improve your self-care.

**26-50:** A score in this range suggests that your self care skills and lifestyle balance strategies may be poor to average, and that you could possibly benefit from developing a plan to improve your self-care.

**51-75:** A score in this range suggests that you may have moderately good self-care skills and lifestyle balance strategies in place.

**76-100:** A score in this range suggests that you may have good self-care skills and lifestyle balance strategies in place.

＊ ＊ ＊ ＊ ＊ ＊

# Team Feedback Form
*Kelly and Michèle O'Donnell, adapted from Chapter 30,*
*Doing Member Care Well (2002)*

The purpose of this form is to help you look at how your overall team/department is doing. It is intended to stimulate mutual feedback between you and your leader and between group members when done as a joint exercise. Your assessment will hopefully lead to constructive changes for you and your work.

**Directions:** Use the five point scale below to rate the following fifteen areas. Feel free to make additional comments for any of the items. Note—virtual teams may want to adjust some of the items.

1--------------------2--------------------3--------------------4--------------------5
Strongly Disagree                Basically Agree                Strongly Agree

1. The objectives of my team/department are clear to me.
   Rating_____Comments:

2. The objectives were formed with ample discussion and prayer.
   Rating_____Comments:

3. I am involved in the decision making process in my work area.
   Rating_____Comments:

4. We meet often enough as a group.
   Rating_____Comments:

5. There is a good sense of team spirit in our work.
   Rating_____Comments:
6. The communication process is adequate within our group.
   Rating_____Comments:

7. I understand what is expected of me.
   Rating_____Comments:

8. I receive timely and sufficient feedback on my work.
   Rating_____Comments:

9. I feel respected and encouraged by my leader/supervisor.
   Rating_____Comments:

10. I feel encouraged and respected by my colleagues.
    Rating_____Comments:

11. I regularly try to encourage and support my colleagues.
    Rating_____Comments:

12. My communication with my leader/supervisor is adequate.
    Rating_____Comments:

13. I have sufficient time to fulfil my responsibilities.
    Rating_____Comments:

14. I am growing as a person as a result of my work involvement.
    Rating_____Comments:

15.  Overall I am satisfied with and enjoy my work.

Rating_____
Comments:

---

**Scores:**

**Individual**: Your overall rating (total divided by 15); also note your 3 highest and 3 lowest scores

**Group**:  Overall score for your group (total scores divided by 15 then divided by the number of raters)

**Note**:  Also explore how to improve the work done *together,* rated on a scale of 1-5 with comments:

We trust…We plan…We discuss…We own…
We commit…We perform…We review…We grow…

\* \* \* \* \* \*

# Sixty-Plus Books for a Member Care Library
*Kelly O'Donnell*

There is a growing body of materials being written in the member care field. This material is helping us to improve our member care programs, policies, and practices. Here is a compilation of sixty-plus materials, primarily books in English that are a core part of my member care library. These publications are categorized into the eight specialty domains of member care, and a category of "general member care." I also list materials and Web sites listed primarily related to humanitarian aid and psychosocial support. Note that there are many other excellent materials that are not included here. For more information on many of these materials and additional references, see the original article in Chapter 50 of *Doing Member Care Well* (2002) and the materials indexed at: www. crossculturalworkers.com. For more updates/resources visit: www.globalmembercare. com; www.membercareassociates.org; www.ethne.net/membercare; www.membercare. org; and http://sites.google.com/site/membercaravan

**Pastoral/Spiritual** *(see annotated list by Scott Shaum in the February 2010 Update at www.ethne.net/membercare)*

1. *Devotional Classics: Selected Readings for Individuals and Groups (1990)*—Foster and Smith
2. *Too Soon to Quit: Reflections on Encouragement (1994)*—Lareau Lindquist
3. *Formed by the Desert: A Personal Encounter with God (1997)*—Joyce Huggett

**Physical/Medical**

4. *Where There is No Doctor: A Village Health Care Handbook (1992)*—David Werner
5. *Culture/Clinical Encounter: Intercultural Sensitizer for Health Professions (1996)*—Rena Gropper
6. *Principles and Practices of Travel Medicine (2001)*—J. Zuckerman and A. Zuckerman
7. *Travelers Guide to Good Health (revised 2007)*—Ted Lankester

**Training/Career (and reentry)**

8. *Naturally Gifted: A Christian Perspective on Personality, Gifts, and Abilities (1991)*—Gordon and Rosemary Jones
9. *Reentry: Making the Transition from Missions to Life at Home (1992)*—Peter Jordan
10. *The Reentry Team (2005)*—Neal Pirolo
11. *On Being a Missionary (1995)*—Thomas Hale

**Team Building/Interpersonal**

12. *Cross-Cultural Conflict: Building Relationships for Effective Ministry (1993)*—Duane Elmer
13. *Building Credible Multicultural Teams (2000)*—Lianne Roembke
14. *Peacemaking: Resolving Conflict and Building Harmony in Relationships (2001)*—Rick Love
15. *The Five Dysfunctions of a Team (2002)*—Patrick Lencioni
16. *Teamwork (1995; revised 2003)*—Gordon and Rosemary Jones
17. *Snakes in Suits: When Psychopaths Go to Work (2006)*—Paul Babiak and Robert Hare
18. Materials from Ken William's *Sharpening Your Interpersonal Skills* www.ITPartners.org

### Family/TCK

19. *And Bees Make Honey: An Anthology...by Third Culture Kids (1994)*— Jill Dyer, Roger Dyer
20. *Raising Resilient MKs: Resources for Parents, Caregivers, and Teachers (1998)*—Joyce Bowers
21. *Third Culture Kids: Growing up Among Worlds (2009, 2nd ed.)*— Dave Pollock, Ruth Van Reken
22. *Kids Without Borders: Journals of Chinese MKs (2000)*—Polly Chan
23. *Fitted Pieces: Parents Educating Children Overseas (2001)*— Janet Blomberg, David Brooks
24. *Families on the Move: Growing Up Overseas and Loving It (2001)*— Marion Knell
25. *The Family in Mission: Understanding and Caring for Those Who Serve (2004)*—Leslie Andrews
26. *The Global Nomad's Guide to University Transition (2010)*—Tina Quick
27. *Celebrating Children: Equipping People Working with Children and Young People Living in Difficult Circumstances Around the World (2003)*—Glenn Miles and Josephine-Joy Wright

### Financial/Logistical

28. *Understanding Voluntary Organizations (1990)*—Charles Handy
29. *Friend Raising: Building a M Support Team that Lasts (1991)*—Betty Barnett
30. *Stop, Check, Go; A Short-Term Overseas Projects Checklist (1996)*—Ditch Townsend
31. *Code of Good Practice for the Management and Support of Aid Personnel (2003)*—People In Aid
32. *Human Resource Management (2007 rev.)*—Robert Mathis and John Jackson
33. *Member Care for Missionaries: Practical Guide for Senders (2002)*— Marina Prins, Braam Willemse
34. *Governance Matters: Faith-based not-for-Profit Organization (2004)*— Les Stahlke, Jennifer Louglin

### Crisis/Contingency

35. *Safety First: Protecting NGO Employees in Areas of Conflict (2003, 3rd ed.)*—Save the Children
36. *Operational Security Manual in Violent Environments (2000; revision 2010)*—Konrad Van Brabant

37. *Stress/Trauma Handbook: Strategies for Flourishing in Demanding Environ (2003)*—John Fawcett

38. *Psychosocial Support: Best Practices from Red Cross/Red Crescent Programs (2001)*—IFRC

39. Materials from Mobile Member Care Team's Web site on crisis/debriefing www.mmct.org

40. *Tear Soup: A Recipe for Healing after Loss (2003)*—Pat Schwiebert and Chuck DeKlyen www.griefwatch.com

41. *Supporting Staff Responding to Disasters*—Debbie Lovell-Hawker www.peopleinaid.org

42. *IASC Guidelines on Mental Health/Psychosocial Support in Emergency Settings* www.who.int/mental_health/emergencies

43. *Recovering from Traumatic Stress: A Guide for Missionaries (2010)*—Stephanie Laite-Lanham and Joyce Pelletier

### Counseling

44. *Christian Counseling: A Comprehensive Guide (1990; updated version 2006)*—Gary Collins

45. *Healing the Wounds of Trauma: How the Church Can Help (2007)*—Hill, Hill, Baggé, Miersma

46. *New Guide to Crisis and Trauma Counseling (2003)*—Norm Wright

47. *Ad-Mission: The Briefing/Debriefing of Teams of Ms/Aid Workers (1999)*—Graham Fawcett

48. *Debriefing Aid Workers and Missionaries*—Debbie Lovell-Hawker www.peopleinaid.org

49. *Honourably Wounded: Stress Among Christian Workers (2001 rev.)*—Marjory Foyle

50. *Enhancing Missionary Vitality: Mental Health Serving Global Missions (2002)*—John Powell, Joyce Bowers

51. *Where There is No Psychiatrist: A Mental Health Care Manual (2003)*—Vikram Patel

### General Member Care

52. *Helping Missionaries Grow: Readings in Mental Health/Missions (1988)*—Kelly and Michèle O'Donnell

53. *Serving as Senders: How to Care for Your Missionaries (1991)*—Neal Pirolo

54. *Missionary Care: Counting the Cost (1992)*—Kelly O'Donnell

55. *Too Valuable to Lose: Exploring the Causes/Cures of Attrition (1997)*— William Taylor

56. *Thriving in Another Culture: A Handbook for Cross-Cultural Missions (1998)*—Jo Anne Dennett

57. *Doing Member Care Well: Perspectives/Practices from Around the World (2002)*—Kelly O'Donnell

58. *Sharing the Front Line and the Back Kills: Peacekeepers, Humanitarian Aid Workers and the Media in the Midst of Crisis* (2002)—Yael Danieli

59. *Understanding HR in the Humanitarian Sector: Handbook 1 (2004)*—James Henry, People in Aid

60. *Enhancing Quality in HR Management: Handbook 2 (2004)*— James Henry, People in Aid

61. *Body Matters: A Guide to Partnership (2005)*—Ernie Addicott

62. *Well Connected: Releasing Power, Restoring Partnerships (2006)*— Phill Butler

63. *Worth Keeping: Perspectives on Good Practice in Retention (2007)*— Rob Hay *et al*

64. *Approaches to Staff Care in International NGOs (2009)*— Benjamin Porter, Ben Emmens www.peopleinaid.org

65. *Global Member Care: The Pearls and Perils of Good Practice (2010)*— Kelly O'Donnell

\* \* \* \* \* \*

# Additional Materials and Web Sites:

100 Books for Humanitarians (annotated list, organized into several categories) www.onlineclasses.org/2010/06/17/100-best-books-for-humanitarians/

*Refugees* magazine, special issue on staff and recipient safety/security called Too High A Price? United Nations High Commissioner for Refugees, (volume 4, Number 121, 2000).

Red Cross Red Crescent magazine, How Safe Are We? (Issue one, 2004)

Materials from People In Aid (www.peopleinaid.org) on trauma care, debriefing, health care, etc.

Special Issue on member care (Feb 2003) and retention (June 2004): *Connections*, www.wearesources.org

Society for Human Resources Management offers materials, conferences and updates related to the international field of human resources
www.shrm.org

Mental Health Workers Without Border offers a free handbook to download on how relief workers can provide community-based trauma care
www.mhwwb.org

International Federation of the Red Cross offers free helpful publications, available at:
www.ifrc.org
a. A short booklet for workers called "*Managing Stress in the Field*" (English Spanish, French)
b. *Best Practices for Psychosocial Support* includes brief case summaries in several humanitarian disasters

World Health Organization has regular updates on many health issues/programs
www.who.org

Centers for Disease Control has good information on public health issues and materials related to disasters. e.g., "Health Information for Humanitarian Workers" and "Traumatic Incident Stress"
www.cdc.gov

Office for the Coordination of Humanitarian Assistance (OCHA) is the United Nations body to help joint efforts in times of human and natural disasters.
www.ochaonline.un.org

Reuters Alertnet service provides updated information on crisis areas in the world
www.alertnet.org

Aid Workers Network links relief/development staff to share support, ideas;
www.aidworkers.net

Humanitarian Practice Group provides various materials for free.
www.odi.org.uk

National Center for PTSD has material and helps on crisis care and PTSD.
www.ncptsd.org

International Society for Trauma and Stress Studies has four short pieces linked to its home page on mass trauma, helping children, the indirect effects of trauma etc.; also conference and training info
www.istss.org

✳ ✳ ✳ ✳ ✳ ✳

# Healing the Body

## Member Care and the Body of Christ: Part 1
### Kelly O'Donnell

*Hoc est corpus meum quod pro vobis datur.*
Luke 22:19

What would you do if you had an eight hour layover at the *Barajas* International Airport in Madrid, Spain? Well, this is what I did. Rather than simply waiting for my next flight, I jumped on the metro and headed for *El Prado,* one of the finest museums for European art from the 12th-19th centuries. As I strolled through the ornate, expansive halls, I was particularly struck by the many images of Jesus Christ among the over 1,300 paintings on display.

This painting is one of my favorites and depicts the *Last Supper.* It was painted around 1560 by the Spaniard Juan de Juanes. As I look at it again now, I am thinking about the Body of Christ—of Christ giving his life for us—the central theme of this painting. It is beautiful!

Yet I am wondering...wondering why throughout history those who say they are followers of Jesus continue to break His body through their lies, stealing, and gross mistreatment of others. There are so many ways to lie and steal, including subtle and seemingly "little or inconsequential" ways! These are sad stories. But there are so many wonderful stories too—stories of people who truly love and who are willing to go to great costs to honor and serve others, His dear Body—of which the mission and the member care community are members—is meant to be whole, and not broken. What a mixture church history is of the mostly laudable and the sometimes loathful!

81

*"What are those wounds between your arms?"*
*"Those with which I was wounded in the house of my friends."*
(Zech. 13:6)

---

**Reflection and Discussion**

The Body of Christ is amazingly beautiful. People through the ages, like the apostles depicted in the above painting, are in awe of it. One of the apostles however (in a yellow garment) appears to be backing away, and would soon further betray the Body.

1. Think of some ways to apply the above comments and this 16th century painting to the contemporary mission/member care community.
2. List a couple practices that promote health and prevent wounding in the body of Christ.
3. What does it mean to have the "brand-marks of Jesus" as per Paul's statement: "From now on let no one cause trouble for me, for I bear on my body the brand-marks of Jesus." (Gal. 6:17)

# PART TWO
## Wise as Doves and Innocent as Serpents?
## Promoting Health in Mission/Aid

*"Men never do evil so completely and so cheerfully as when they do it from religious conviction."*

BLAISE PASCAL

Wise Doves in Innocent Snakes by Jeff Nentrup. © 2006 Kelly O'Donnell

IN PART TWO OF *PEARLS AND PERILS* WE EXPLORE TWO IMPORTANT AND OVERLOOKED AREAS FOR HEALTH IN MISSION/AID. They are the role of human *dysfunction* (problems from significant weakness/wrongness, e.g., leadership abuse, psychological disorders, moral failure, harassment) and the role of *discipline* (correction to restore people/organizations which violate others e.g., independent reviews, counseling, recovery programs, remedial training, and dismissals).

We overview the nature dysfunction in Chapter 5, discuss the need to upgrade our friendships and trust in Chapter 6, and highlight five essential areas to develop for personal/organizational health in Chapter 7. These areas in Chapter 7 include interpersonal skills, conflict and discipline, grievances and whistle-blowing organizational assessment, and human resources management, concluding with a summary of ten core principles for dealing with dysfunction.

## "Better a broken helmet than a broken head."
### FAMILY PROVERBS

We finish, as in all three Parts in *Pearls and Perils,* with several materials to stimulate your personal and professional growth in member care (Chapter 8). Throughout Part Two you will find "Health Promoters" which are short exercises to help you think through and apply the material.

I write from the perspective of a psychologist in the faith-based sector. My understanding of dysfunction has been greatly shaped by materials from the behavioral/health sciences and the teaching from the New Testament. Much of the material in Part Two has been significantly expanded from the article Wise as Doves and Innocent as Serpents?

(2007, *Evangelical Missions Quarterly*, Volume 43, pages 40-49). This article is also available in twelve languages at: http://mcaresources.googlepages.com/realitydose

Finally, these chapters are informed by the difficult lessons that several colleagues and I have learned over the years as we have dealt with dysfunction and more recently serious deviance. Some additional comments related to these lessons as well as the content of Part Two are included in the *resiliency* entries on the *CORE Member Care* weblog (December 2009-January 2010; www.COREmembercare.blogspot.com). Further developing our capacity for both *strengthening* and *safeguarding* the diversity of workers and sending groups are two sides of the same coin for promoting health and good practice in mission/aid.

> *"Virtue does not have to be so painful,*
> *if it is sensibly organized."*
>
> CHARLES HANDY

# PEARLS
## ENHANCING AND ENRICHING GOOD PRACTICE

*Recognizing the characteristics of dysfunction can safeguard workers and senders.*

*Professional and impartial input is essential to ascertain facts and deal with dysfunction.*

*Pursue the full truth and full transparency when disclosures about dysfunction are needed.*

*Moral courage, prudence, and tenacity along with experience and skill are needed to deal with dysfunctional systems.*

*Seek beauty and the support of true friends to counter the effects of dysfunction.*


# PERILS
## ENCUMBERING AND ENDANGERING GOOD PRACTICE

*Dysfunction damages our relational and operational resiliency unless we bravely deal with it.*

*We overlook our virtuous convictions and vulnerable colleagues in order to protect ourselves.*

*The internal dissonance we feel from our mistakes is usually resolved by self-justifications.*

*Affinity groups like mission/aid senders are especially vulnerable due to high levels of trust.*

*Leaders/workers err by assuming they can handle dysfunctional people/systems on their own.*

# CHAPTER 5

# Unmasking Dysfunction

DYSFUNCTION IS INSIDIOUS. IT'S DECEPTIVE AND DESTRUCTIVE TENTACLES INFILTRATE INTO OUR RELATIONSHIPS AND OPERATIONS. WE CAN COUNTER IT BY BETTER UNDERSTANDING IT, EXPOSING IT, AND EMPHASIZING HEALTHY PRACTICES SUCH AS GENUINE TRANSPARENCY AND VERIFIABLE ACCOUNTABILITY.

What a mess! A humanitarian organization is losing lots of its staff—again. Good folks are leaving and some good folks are staying. Many are emotionally broken and disillusioned. Sides are formed. Some say the departing staff members are insubordinate and not a good fit for the organization. Others believe there are significant personal and organizational problems that are not being addressed. Mutual friends try to stay neutral, and are baffled. The governing board wants to maintain the work, but is also confused about what is going on. The written policies for grievances, dismissal, or discipline are vague and outdated. No safe forums exist to share personal and work-related concerns as a group. No exit interviews are done. No independent review happens. A few well-meaning folks, mindful that this is considered to be a "Christian" ministry, plead for reconciliation. Something is definitely not right, but no one seems capable or willing to do anything. And over the next several months, the toxins continue to take their toll, as unresolved relational discord, dysfunction, and distraction spread maliciously to others. What a mess!

## Health Promoter 1. Reflection and Discussion

Healthy organizations have clear policies and procedures that are recognized, understood, and reviewed. Transparency and good communication are also indicators of health. Yet even with these "protective factors" in place, there might still be serious dysfunction and a "mess." How can this happen and give a few examples.

In this chapter I review two important areas for promoting health in mission/aid. They are recognizing human *dysfunction* (problems resulting from significant weakness and "wrongness," including serious deviance) and using appropriate *discipline* (correction helping to restore people and organizations, including dismissals). Upgrading our skills in these two areas is fundamental for good practice and managing staff better. How do we help people and organizations that negatively affect others—and sometimes many others—over time? What type of help or discipline is appropriate? And what is our responsibility to safeguard the well-being of our staff and organizations? I want to look realistically at the "relational reality" in mission/aid (i.e. the quality of our interpersonal relations) so we can learn from our impasses, struggles, and even distortions. My intent in this article is not to blame ourselves but rather to build "relational resiliency" (i.e., relationships that are healthy and enduring in spite of challenges).

****

## *Dysfunction disables our people and purposes, but most importantly from a Christian viewpoint, it dishonors God (Rom. 2:21-24).*

****

Most of us have been part of both healthy and dysfunctional work settings. The healthy ones are personally rewarding and we feel we are contributing and growing, and challenged and respected. The dysfunctional ones on the other hand drain us, stealing our time, focus, effectiveness, and even our emotional and physical health. Much of my work in member care is devoted to helping organizations develop healthy practices. Conflict management in particular takes up a lot of time for me and many of us, especially for those in management roles. Research also supports what we all seem to know from painful experience: relational struggles in the mission/aid sectors stress us out (Gish, 1983, Carter, 1999, Fawcett, 2003). Conflicts, even if managed well, do not always lead to personal growth and closer relationships. This is especially the case when dysfunction is involved. Dysfunction *disables* our people and purposes, but most importantly from a Christian viewpoint, it *dishonors* God (Rom. 2:21-24).

Stephen Behnke, the Director of Ethics for the American Psychological Association asserts, "A large part of what we do in psychotherapy is to try to understand people's motivations for distorting reality" (2008, p. 33). This assertion, balanced by a solid appreciation of health and strengths, is also true for organizational contexts in the mission/aid sector. Bennis, *et al*, in their insightful book called *Transparency* (2008) offer these observations:

Pride in belonging to a high-performing or a high-status group and the cozy sense of belonging to a tight-knit organizational "family" can be genuine sources of professional satisfaction. The paradox is that there is a dark side to belonging—the almost reflexive temptation to spin information in ways that protect the group's shared pride, to make the group look better than it really is, or even simply to preserve the group. All these make it easier for group members to suppress information or distort it (pp. 35-36).

Understanding and managing distortions of reality, especially where neglect and exploitation of others occur, is a key part of *good governance*, acting responsibly, and being professional. It represents the pragmatic and health focus of this chapter and Part Two.

### Health Promoter 2. Reflection and Discussion

What recognized ways exist in your groups/organization to help review your "relational reality"? What helps/hinders the development of your "relational resiliency"?

### What is Dysfunction and How Does It Affect Us?

"Dysfunctional" is a good term that when used carefully can help us understand people and organizations better. By dysfunctional I mean a consistent pattern of relating to oneself and others that is hurtful or "toxic," characterized by such things as authoritarianism, closed/secretive communication, high control, and denial of what is actually happening (see Box 1). Such dysfunction can be compounded when no one sees it clearly, when it is imbedded in more functional behaviors, or when no one wants to or can do anything about it. It can be further compounded by the various ways that all of us from different cultural, theological, generational, and organizational backgrounds understand "relational discord," especially how to be both "respectful and honest" when discussing concerns. Three foundational readings, among many, that have helped shape my understanding of dysfunction are: *The Addictive Organization,* 1988 by Anne Wilson Schaef and Diane Fassel; Frances White's article, *The Dynamics of Healthy Missions,* 1992; and my favorite book on dysfunction, written for "children": *Millie and the Mudhole,* 1992 by Val Reddix.

**Box 1. Signs of Organizational Dysfunction
(based on Hay, 2004; Aterburn, Felton, 1998)**

**Poor leadership and management as evidenced by:**

High control, withholding information, rigidity, legalism, intolerance of questioning, punitiveness, blaming others, not admitting one's problems, keeping up the image of the organization at all costs, high priority on giving money to the organization, limited accountability, influential people with pervasive character deficits, narcissistic traits, bruised backgrounds or addictive behaviors, poor history of staff retention/relationships

**Lack of satisfaction and optimism in staff as evidenced by:**

Feeling one is "dispensable," lack of work/life balance, lack of opportunities for development and learning, not being able to talk openly about the "reality" of the situation, fear of harassment and retaliation, not expressing one's feelings unless they are positive, not doing anything outside ones "role," not being able to trust, not having the freedom to make "mistakes," high turnover rates, job changes, and absenteeism

At the individual level, dysfunction can also involve certain personality traits/ disorders (McIntosh and Rima, 1997; Hotchkiss, 2002; and Mclemore, 2003). People can appear to be odd-erratic, dramatic-emotional, or anxious-fearful. Clinically speaking, serious disorders of personality are marked with "an enduring pattern of inner experience and behavior that deviates markedly from the expectations of the individual's culture, is pervasive and inflexible, has an onset in adolescence or early adulthood, is stable over time, and leads to distress or impairment" (*Diagnostics and Statistics Manual-IV*, p. 629). I dutifully note that the "distress and impairment" will usually also negatively affect others. Esther Shubert (1992) describes these serious personality problems in mission settings:

When people with personality disorders slip through selection without adequate evaluation, their presence on the field is usually surrounded by contention, dissention, disagreements, and exhaustion on the part of other missionaries and field executives who try to support them emotionally and spiritually....The concept of a personality disorder which does not fall within the continuum (of

normal-neurotic-psychotic) is a foreign concept to many mission executives...
(we) can be reluctant to admit that committed Christians can have psychological
problems that are not solved by spiritual modalities...we would like to think
that anyone with a willing spirit can serve...it is hard for us to acknowledge the
poor prognosis of severe personality disorders...we have difficulty distinguish-
ing between a "spiritual call" and ...a "psychological agenda"...there is some
expense involved in quality psychological testing and selection (p. 80).

## Health Promoter 3. Reflection and Discussion

What behaviors in your experience would you consider to be dysfunctional?
Examples from my work include: manipulation, lying, stealing, ignoring, ridi-
culing, discrediting, withholding information, blaming/shaming, scapegoating,
demoting, dismissing, etc. Note that organizational and personal health can be
described in opposite terms of how dysfunction is described (e.g., honesty vs.
lying, affirming vs. discrediting).

How can focusing on healthy practices be more constructive than focusing
on the negative?

In the face of interpersonal tensions, we tend to see ourselves as all or mostly right
and the other party as being all or mostly wrong. We conveniently resolve our cognitive
dissonance and maintain our self-worth by justifying ourselves and creating fictional
explanations that absolve us of responsibility (Tavris and Aronson, 2007: *Mistakes Were
Made But Not By Me.*). In cases of protracted, major conflict, friends can become *fiends*.
Leaders become *lepers*. Organizations become *ogre-nizations*. Inappropriately labeling
others' *differences* as being dysfunctional, although a "normal" tendency for us all, is
clearly a dysfunctional coping strategy itself!

From a Christian perspective, we are to be grace-oriented disciples rather than
judgment-oriented derelicts. Who are we to call down fire from heaven on our colleagues
and organizations, similar to what James and John wanted to do to the cities that rejected
them (Luke 9:54)? As the psalmist says, "If the Lord numbered our sins, who could stand
in God's presence" (Ps. 130:3)? And as Paul the Apostle warns, "Who are we to judge one
another's servant, for before his/her own master he/she will stand or fall" (Rom. 14:4).
Relational problems, more often than not, are a two-way street. We are all both weak
and wrong at times. Further, we are influenced far more by our environments and by
our own propensity to evil, than we may be comfortable to admit, as Phillip Zimbardo
points out in *The Lucifer Effect* (2007—see also his informative twenty minute speech
on this topic at http://www.lucifereffect.com/aboutphil_media.htm).

The above assertions may sound good and "balanced" most of the time. But we must also be concerned about the other side of the distortions—downgrading clear dysfunction and referring to obvious deviance as merely being "differences." This will become apparent usually if skilled, unbiased people will take the time to inquire. Otherwise most of us will back away from what is seen as a complex, confusing story with two or more sides, rather than there being a cohesive core of truth that is being distorted/overlooked. So surely we must not make a mountain out of a molehill; yet neither should we make a molehill out of a mountain! The tricky part is trying to discern who has *the* clear or clearest perception of what constitutes a mountain or a molehill. It is also tricky since most issues are not so black and white. As Proverbs reminds us (16:2, 18:17): All the ways of a person are right in one's own eyes, but the Lord weighs the motives; and the first to plead one's case seems just, until one's neighbor comes and gives input.

****
*By dysfunctional I mean a consistent pattern of
relating to oneself and others that is hurtful or "toxic,"
characterized by such things as authoritarianism,
closed/secretive communication, high control,
and denial of what is actually happening*
****

However, there are likely many examples in all of our experience, and certainly in the Christian Scriptures, when serious wrong doing must be identified, and whereby some form of discipline is clearly needed (Matt. 18:17, I Cor. 5:11; 2 Thess. 3:6,14). Ken Williams says in *Sharpening Your Interpersonal Skills* that "Scripture teaches us that in some cases our relationship with others must be secondary to the issue. We need to know when to put the issue first, even if it means the relationship is harmed or broken" (2002, p. 114). Similarly Cloud and Townsend state in *Safe People:* "The necessity of separation is a grim reality…But the truth is that some relationships are not workable if someone is not willing to change and reconcile" (1995, p. 197). At times there can be good reasons why someone should not want to change and reconcile. Where do such behaviors lie on the continuum between the appropriately healthy or prophetic on one end and the inappropriately deviant or toxic on the other end?

The problem is further complicated when there is not proper accountability in place, or when there is not enough relational history with a person or an institution to really confront it and require verifiable changes. Again I want to be clear that I am not talking about how to handle situations where folks simply differ or where both the normalcy of conflict and the need to work it through in helpful ways are understood. Rather I am referring to instances where there is significant personal and organizational dysfunction. So in other words organizations and people, whether they are aware of it or not, and whether they are willing to admit it or not, are having an ongoing "toxic" influence on people. And as a result, unless we have the necessary life skills, training, and professional support (which would include being well-versed in the behavioral science areas of systems, recovery, and clinical disorders; and well-grounded in mediation practices and in the breadth of Christian scripture for dealing with conflict and dysfunction) we can end up being "wise as doves" as we interact with others who may be "innocent as serpents." *Truth without grace may be brutal, but grace without truth can be lethal.*

Manipulated "truth" which undermines trust and healthy relationships, is particularly lethal. For instance, currently in the business and financial world there is much emphasis in being transparent and accountable. Yet transparency and accountability can be elusive—and manipulated for one's own purposes. "And lack of transparency," as Bennis *et al* state in *Transparency* (2008), "is usually no accident. It is often systematically built into the very structure of an organization" (pp. 2-3). Even as a drop of toxin in a glass of water contaminates the water so can a seemingly "small" dysfunctional behavior such as covering up, adjusting, or withholding an important fact pollute an otherwise transparent process (Ec. 10:1). Zachary Karabell highlights this in *The Myth of Transparency (2008, paraphrased)*:

> Transparency is understood to be a key part of good governance. The ideal seems to be that the more a company discloses about what is happening within it, the less chance there will be for misconduct, and the greater chance there will be for effective performance. Yet companies can still be deceptive and commit fraud even if they disclose what they are required to do so legally. Two recent examples are Enron and Parmalat. They disclosed all kinds of data per statutory requirements in the United States and Europe. However both companies deceived the public about what was really going on in their businesses. **The issue was certainly not simply transparency. Rather it was telling the truth** (p. 47).

Situations are not always so bleak fortunately. A positive example of transparency is seen in the response of organizations like Frontiers, as they openly informed their constituency of their misguided role, in spite of their due diligence, in losing $350,000 US Dollars in the infamous New Era Scandal of the 1990s.

> I was devastated. Absolutely devastated. We had won the trust of hundreds of donors, who had given generously to help us obtain this matching offer. We had taken their generous gifts, and unwittingly put them into a fraudulent scheme. And there was little chance of getting their money back. Trust had been shattered. First, WE had violated the trust of our donors—by making

these gifts, our donors had placed their confidence in us; they found that this trust had been misplaced. Second, a man with criminal intent had exploited OUR trust. We had placed our reliance upon the integrity, ability, and character of a person and an institution—that reliance had been a very serious mistake. Third, because so many Christian charities were involved, donor confidence in Christian ministries had been badly shaken. Our reputation, and the reputation of the broader charitable community, had been severely damaged. These were very, very, dark days...Trust involves truth...it means breaking bad news when you have it...Being a truthful witness also means avoiding generalization, spin, or overstatement (David Harriman, *Trust Me! Trust Me! Building Trust in Development* (2006), pp. 4,5,7).

It is very challenging to try to help in dysfunctional matters and settings—to "unmask the darkness" (Eph 5:11, *The Message*). A common mistake of leaders/consultants is to overestimate their ability to understand and deal with dysfunction, including being able to ascertain the "facts" and offering effective discipline or mediation. It takes concerted joint, professional effort, not simply self-confidence and noble intentions, or even martyrs and machismo! Unfortunately, people usually do not have the time, skills, or objectivity to do a proper investigation. A corollary mistake, usually learned the hard way, is to think that "devout" Christians or "nice" people would never act so negatively. Another mistake is to believe that one is immune to: fear and intimidation by others; covering up and opting for convenience; conflicts of interest and partiality; and/or being discredited and wounded in the process of helping. Kate Adie's concluding remarks in her autobiography as a BBC war correspondent, sadly, can also be applicable to pathogenic agents within the mission/aid sector: "Occasionally you get a little too close to stories and your fellow man tries to swat you out of existence." (*The Kindness of Strangers,* 2002, p. 425).

****

*A common mistake of leaders/consultants is to overestimate their ability to understand and deal with dysfunction, including being able to ascertain the "facts" and offering effective discipline or mediation.*

****

Dysfunction and especially its more deviant varieties can maim one's work and sanity. People need to protect themselves for sure. But on the down side, will people pragmatically acquiesce to self-interest and forsake both their virtuous convictions and their vulnerable colleagues? Unfortunately, this is often the case. When confronted by some perceived pathogenic agent, and when push comes to shove, we tend to first protect our own persons as well as the people closest to us, then our positions and possessions, then our purposes, and eventually our principles, often in that order. But of course we convince ourselves and others that we are acting primarily in a highly "principled" manner. There is nothing too noble about the default practice for self-protection here, although it may actually serve the adaptive function of keeping us relatively safe in order to live and work another day. When is such pragmatism the most sensible way forward and allowing perhaps the "greater good?" And when is it a fatal flaw? As Barak Obama has observed, "the blood of slaves reminds me that sometimes our pragmatism can be moral cowardice (*Audacity of Hope*, 2008, p. 98).

### Health Promoter 4. Reflection and Discussion

List some additional skills needed to confront dysfunction well and to avoid overestimating one's ability to deal with it. What type of "street wisdom" (e.g., experience, perspectives, and interventions) might be necessary in order to deal with dysfunction?

The sad fact is that many times we can be seriously duped and disabled by both personal and systemic dysfunction. No one is immune. We are not able to "unmask the darkness." Box 2 describes the insidious process of dysfunction.

### Box 2. Four Tasks of Dysfunction

**Deny**. The first task of dysfunction is to conceal itself. "Don't ask about problems, don't tell about problems" is a pervasive, core, unwritten rule. In short, deny reality.

**Downplay**. If that does not work, then the second task becomes getting folks to minimize it by downplaying its negative impact, stating that the group/person is going through a "normal" stage of adjustment; or simply acting as if it is not so important. Relational unity/conformity takes precedence over relational truth/connection.

**Distract**. If that does not work then the third task is to distract from the real issues, "feign pain" and get sympathy, or admit that something is "not exactly right" and perhaps refer to problems as being largely a matter of having different perspectives/preferences. Changing the subject or talking "about things" in abstract or convoluted ways is also effective. There is little commitment to acknowledge real issues and little capacity to address them.

**Discredit.** If that does not work, then the fourth task, which can actually occur simultaneously with the previous three, is to discredit those who point it out, no matter how sensitively they try to do so. An atmosphere of fear and subtle intimidation are usually part of dysfunctional/authoritarian systems. Fear of reprisal prevents people from speaking up and advocating for healthy change.

This is not easy to say, but in my experience the majority of Christian workers in the mission/aid community cannot adequately identify and deal with dysfunction. This is true whether it is subtle or more explicit such as with major deviance like fraud and major organizational misconduct. Serious dysfunction in particular can be just too hard to believe, too disconcerting to imagine, too upsetting to our worldview, and too inconvenient for our lifestyles. The joint report by Transparency International *et al* on *Preventing Corruption in Humanitarian Assistance* (2008) corroborates this point:

> These findings suggest that many humanitarian workers have a narrow view of what constitutes corruption, seeing it primarily as a financial issue, rather than abuse of power…including nepotism/cronyism, sexual exploitation and abuse, coercion and intimidation of humanitarian staff or aid recipients for personal, social or political gain, manipulation of assessments, targeting and registration to favour particular groups, and diversion of assistance to non-target groups (p. 2-3).

Likewise, Babiak and Hare's volume on psychopathy at work, *Snakes in Suits* (2006) affirms the serious vulnerability of colleagues and organizations to the deceptive/exploitative ways of highly deviant people (psychopaths). This is especially true for those in "affinity" groups as in the mission/aid community, where "Christian" corruption and "Christian" criminality are possibilities that must never be ruled out.

> Affinity groups—religious, political, or social groups to which all members share common values or beliefs—are particularly attractive to psychopaths because the collective trust that members of these groups have in one another. Those who perpetrate affinity and similar frauds rely on the common belief system of the group members for cover…As long as the psychopath can accurately espouse these beliefs while in the presence of group members, the true motives are less likely to be discovered. Religious belief groups, open to new members joining from all lifestyles, readily assume that those who join them hold similar beliefs and values and tend to focus on professed beliefs and

values and to forgive past transgressions. These noble qualities, however make them easy targets for manipulation by unscrupulous fraudsters.…This type of fraud is disturbing because of the ease with which a social predator infiltrates, cons, and manipulates affinity groups. It is also a testament to the power of impression management, and to the tendency of many to be influenced by style more than substance (pp. 90-92).

These psychologist-authors continue their warning about the vulnerability of members of affinity groups, especially religious ones. "The result is a 'fox in the henhouse,' with predictable results. Religious groups are particularly vulnerable…Even sophisticated members of financial and business groups—such as investment clubs—often are no match for the charm and seduction of a good-looking, well-dressed, and apparently well-connected psychopath" (Carozza, 2008, p. 43). And if the above comments are not unsettling enough, Babiak and Hare also state that few people are willing to take the risks to confront such serious deviance. Another way to say it is that few people have the desire, capacity, and at times the moral audacity necessary to confront "member tares."

Unless caught and prosecuted for breaking the law, psychopaths suffer little consequence from the physical, emotional, psychological and financial abuses they leave behind. The sad fact is that few victims—coworkers, partners, and spouses—report them to the authorities (or to their friends for that matter) because of the shame they feel for being conned. Even in large firms, such as banks and brokerage houses, frauds and scams are sometimes not reported for fear of damaging the reputation of the firm. Psychopaths know and use this to their advantage. Others are too intimidated by fears or reprisal or litigation to speak up, being thankful that the psychopath is no longer in their life but has moved on to some other unfortunate person or firm (p. 88).

There are, fortunately, many examples of successfully dealing with major deviance such as fraudsters. But it takes much tenacity and skill and often amidst much trepidation and being ignored or discredited. Harry Markopolos and associates, who tracked Bernie Madoff's fraudulent investment scheme for years, is one high-profile example. In this case, as we state on our 25 January 2010 weblog entry (www.COREmembercare. blogspot.com), it took professional skill and a trio of virtues (perseverance, honesty, courage—*virtrios*) to successfully confront the trio of evils (corruption, cover-ups, cowardice—*trimangles*). The fuller story however, is chronicled by Markopolos in his book *No One Would Listen* (2010). The investigations did not happen until it was 40 billion dollars too late, due primarily he says to incompetence and arrogance among the government agencies that should have investigated.

Cynthia Cooper's experience is also instructive. This courageous woman was the primary investigator and whistleblower that helped uncover the largest fraud (prior to Madoff) in corporate history—Worldcom (Carozza, 2008).

> Listen to your instinct. If something doesn't feel or seem quite right, it might not be. If people are acting out of character or appear to be working to head you in the wrong direction, step back and ask yourself why. Auditing can often be a plodding process of developing facts checking and re-checking theories and connecting the dots. Continue to ask for support and dig until you are satisfied that you've gotten it right. Don't allow yourself to be intimidated by superiors...It's critical that we decipher not only the business lessons but the personal lessons (p.43).

### Health Promoter 5. Reflection and Discussion

How might we be duped or even dupe ourselves? How aware are we of our own hard-wired propensity to seriously self-justify (Tavris and Aronson, 2007)?

Further, why is it hard to confront dysfunction? (e.g., believing that dysfunction could not really exist in our organization; looking the other way in the face of obvious dysfunction; being reluctant to have one's life or ministry inconvenienced; fearing that we will be discredited; not making time to investigate facts).

Finally, how would you relate the above quotes from Babiak and Hare to Christ's warning in Luke 12:15: "Beware, and be on your guard against every form of greed?" (e.g., the many types of greed in ourselves and others, the lack of generosity)

## FINAL THOUGHTS

How can we pull together the many sobering and frankly unsettling materials presented in this chapter? Let me strongly suggest that you do four things. First, reread these materials, and take notes. Be sure to do the same with the other three chapters in Part Two. Second go through and discuss the Health Promoters with trusted colleagues. Do not simply skim over them! Each Health Promoter is carefully designed to help you 'to know wisdom and prudence and to receive instruction in wise behavior, righteousness, justice, and equity' (Prov. 1: 2-4). Third, take time to connect with something beautiful— every day. Focus on healthy things not unhealthy things (Phil. 4:8; Col. 3:2). Even just studying about dysfunction can drain us. Experiencing something beautiful, something life-giving, helps safeguard against the draining effects of such a challenging topic. Finally remember that the light is stronger than the darkness. Resilient virtue is stronger than resilient evil. Find concrete examples of how this is true for you in your life and work. The light of God shines in the darkness and the darkness cannot overpower it (John 1:5).

# PEARLS
## ENHANCING AND ENRICHING GOOD PRACTICE

*True friends are beyond price, real treasures, and even like the elixir of life.*

*Foundational trust helps us to persevere in our relationships and share deeply together.*

*Responsible openness considers the best interests of others and helps us to honor one another.*

*Strong social relationships positively impact program objectives and organizational plans.*

*Healthy relationships are worth the investment and take time to form and maintain.*


# PERILS
## ENCUMBERING AND ENDANGERING GOOD PRACTICE

*Prosperity and success can obfuscate who is a true fried and who is not.*

*Functional trust is confused with foundational trust and deep disappointments/can happen.*

*It is very hard to regain trust once it is broken.*

*Some people will probably never be able to work together well.*

*Ignoring issues and pretending that problems don't exist indicate/incubate toxic relations.*

CHAPTER 6

# Upgrading Relational Resiliency

MOST OF US HAVE LOTS OF FRIENDS AND FRIENDLY COLLEAGUES IN OUR LIVES.
SOME OF THESE PEOPLE ARE OR WILL BECOME OUR "TRUE FRIENDS." BUILDING TRUE
FRIENDS TAKES TIME, EARNED TRUST, AND A RESOLUTE COMMITMENT TO THE
WELL-BEING OF ONE ANOTHER. DON'T SETTLE FOR SOMETHING LESS.

---

Healthy friends help each other stay healthy. They speak into each others' lives, giving encouragement regularly, and offering corrective input as necessary. My close friends have been essential for me over the last several years, as I have weathered the challenges of member care work internationally. I have also greatly appreciated my healthy relationships with many colleagues and a core group of consultants. In this chapter we'll take a look in some refreshing ways about what it means to have healthy relationships. We want to all do our best to foster relational resiliency in the mission/aid community.

## HEALTHY FRIENDSHIPS

I so enjoy being with people—all kinds of people. Business people, aid personnel, Muslims, Hindus, psychologists, students, conservationists, "campesinos" and rural folks, liberals and conservatives of all types, and so on. You name it and we can almost always find something in common to help us connect. Having lived in six countries and traveled to so many places have allowed me to meet and work with so many fascinating people. My life has been truly enriched! I do my utmost to remain as prudently optimistic as possible about people and life in general.

Yet in the midst of all these special and fulfilling relationships, I am still careful who I deeply trust. Perhaps you are too? I am also much more careful about who I consider to be a true friend as opposed to a nice friendly person. I am reminded of the folk adage that says something like "everyone is your best friend until you sit in their pew." Translation: we are all smiles and share niceties with each other until we inconvenience or cross one another. Then the good vibes cease and the bad jibes can begin. Ouch! Am I mistaken or unbalanced here? I don't think so.

I often remind myself that all humans are *weak* at times as well as capable of some very *wrong* actions. One of the worst case scenarios would be that of dysfunctional people/systems that try to exploit us but act as if they are actually trying to support or help us. They take advantage of our weakness or trust with feigned sincerity in their attempt to get something from us. Other people however are gems, filled with integrity, and will do their utmost to make sure that you are understood and cared for. There are quite a range of possibilities in our relationships as I am sure we all know!

Over the years I have acquired an immense appreciation for church history, the humanities, and the wealth of instructive materials that have been written over the centuries. One example is Sirach, circa 190 BC, whose fifty chapters in the book of *Ecclesiasticus* make up a significant portion of the wisdom literature in the *Septuagint* version of the Scriptures. Chapter 6 on friendship and trust is especially relevant for managing the dysfunction of "fair-weather" colleagues with self-serving motivations.

****
*Yet in the midst of all these special and fulfilling relationships, I am still careful who I deeply trust. Perhaps you are too?*
****

Let your acquaintances be many, but for advisers choose one out of a thousand. If you want to make a friend, take him on trial, and do not be in a hurry to trust him; for one kind of friend is so only when it suits him but will not stand by you in your day of trouble. Another kind of friend will fall out with you and to your dismay make your quarrel public, and a third kind of friend will share your table, but not stand by you in your day of trouble: when you are doing well he will be your second self, ordering your servants about; but, if disaster befalls you, he will recoil from you and keep out of your way. Keep well clear of your enemies, and be wary of your friends. A loyal friend is a powerful defense: whoever finds one has indeed found a treasure. A loyal friend is something beyond price, there is no measuring his worth. A loyal friend is the elixir of life, and those who fear the Lord will find one. Whoever fears the Lord makes true friends, for as a person is, so is his friend too (Ecclesiasticus 6:6-17, New Jerusalem Bible, Reprinted with permission of Catholic Online www.catholic.org).

For me, Sirach's teaching is like a breath of fresh air. He helps us to candidly look at our relational reality. Sirach is not overly suspicious or paranoid in his cautions and he is not overly elitist or narcissistic in his exclusiveness. I can't imagine that his advice stems from an overreaction to a few bad relationships in which he was "burned" by so called friends. Perhaps many if not most cultures in the world would see Sirach's caution as being normative—realistic. I also appreciate his balance in highlighting the need and possibility for making true friends. True friends are the elixir of life!

Sirach goes on in chapter 12:8 with a similar line of counsel: "In prosperity you cannot always tell a true friend, but in adversity you cannot mistake an enemy." Enemies, to paraphrase Shakespeare in Part II of *Henry VI*, "hide their poison in sugared words." They "pray for you Sunday and then prey on you Monday" to paraphrase an example from Babiak and Hare (2006, p. 89). True friends though are trustworthy treasures.

### *Health Promoter 1. Reflection and Discussion*

How is Sirach's advice on friendship similar or different to your own perspective?

Who are your true friends? Would you consider them as Sirach did to be treasures and the elixir of life?

## FUNCTIONAL AND FOUNDATIONAL TRUST

I like to distinguish between *functional trust* and *foundational trust*. Functional trust is *assumed*, and needed so that we can work together. It believes *a priori*, within limits, in the good intentions and reliability of a colleague. It gives others the benefit of the doubt until proven otherwise, so that work-related tasks and mutual interests can be realized. Foundational trust however is much deeper and it is *earned*. It is developed over both time and over tough times together. Enduring and genuine friendships are based on such trust.

Functional and foundational trust can overlap over time, with work-related confidence in a colleague flowing into a growing friendship. Yet it is a real mistake to think that being friendly colleagues in a work context (functional trust) is the same as being true friends (foundational trust) in life. The shift from functional trust to foundational trust is slow and easily hindered. As Christians, this shift leads to deeper levels of "fellowship" (*koinonia*) as emphasized in New Testament writings (e.g., John's epistles) and to greater levels of "oneness, unity, community" (*yachad*) as emphasized in the Old Testament (e.g., Ps. 133).

"Trust shifts" from the functional to the foundational are healthy. They happen via consistent demonstrations over time that people are seriously and sacrificially committed to each other. This is especially evident during crises which force people to work together closely with mutual dependency. Further, there is the genuine willingness to put someone else's best interests over one's own, with no strings attached. There is the deep sense that people are doing their utmost to respect and understand each other. People communicate regularly, equitably, and empathically. Finally, trust shifts happen when people fulfill their promises. Where foundational trust flows, entrenched conflicts usually do not.

---

### Health Promoter 2. Reflection and Discussion

What has helped to produce *trust shifts* towards intimacy in your relationships?

What has helped to produce *trust rifts* towards alienation in your relationships?

---

I like to encourage *responsible openness* and not just *"openness"* in our work relationships. The emphasis on responsibility acknowledges that personal disclosures must consider the best interests of others and the overall group. For example, "spontaneous and authentic" comments can actually be too much for a group to handle at times, especially poorly-timed, negative ones shared by a person of influence. Further, in light of cultural variations, it is not always wise to encourage people to be "explicitly honest and open" when sharing perspectives and differences" (see Roembke's book *Building Credible Multicultural Teams*, 2000). As part of our commitment to "love truth and peace" in our relationships (Zech. 8:19), we want to honestly discuss matters in ways that honor each other, respect our cultural backgrounds/preferences, and thus help us to stay connected and productive.

I also recognize that there are different levels of *relational closeness* within a group of colleagues. Rebecca Lewis with Frontiers has mentioned four types of relationships that usually exist in a team setting. Going from the most intimate to the most antagonistic, there are:

- *Kindred people*—best friends such as David and Jonathan, Ruth and Naomi in scripture who have experienced so much together and share very closely with each other;
- *Collegial people*—workers who like each other and work together well but don't necessarily share deeply with one another;
- *Enigmatic people*—people we just don't understand and who seem to come from another planet and so we tend to avoid each other; and

- *Irritating people*—people we definitely don't like and they probably don't like us and we would be quite happy if they lived and worked far away from us.

In short, not everyone can be or needs to be best friends (like kindred people) with each other in a mission/aid setting. The implication is that developing relationships with work associates more as colleagues rather than as confidants is realistic. Another implication is that we will all need some help to work with people whom we consider to be enigmatic or irritating (and vice versa!).For example, have a look at: *Dealing with Difficult People: 24 Lessons for Bringing out the Best in Everyone*, by Brinkman and Kirschner, 2006; *A Survival Guide for Working with Humans: Dealing with Whiners, Back-Stabbers, Know-It-Alls, and Other Difficult People*, by Scott, 2004; and *The Office Survival Guide; Surefire Techniques for Dealing with Challenging People and Situations* by Puder-York, 2006. The bottom line is that it is important to sincerely appreciate the special qualities and gifts each person brings to a group/setting, and to do our best to develop mutually respectful and trustworthy relationships with everyone.

What happens though when trust between people is essentially shattered due to things like lying, abuse, serious misunderstandings, and other major hurts? It is extremely difficult to help restore trust once it is broken and especially when major strife has taken root. As Prov. 18:19 says: "A brother offended is harder to be won than a strong city, and contentions are like the bars of a citadel." If the warring parties are close to knocking each other out emotionally, including seriously discrediting one another's work and character, then someone in authority, analogous to the referee in boxing, needs to a) call a TKO (technical knock out) to stop the fight to prevent grievous injury; b) set up an unbiased inquiry; and c) meet at a later point for mediation. Note that mediation is *not* the same as an inquiry. Mediation attempts go wrong by not trying to first establish basic facts or by assuming that such facts will come out as one tries to mediate face to face. In spite of the obstacles to rebuilding trust, here are some ideas in Box 3 that eventually may help people to reconnect.

## Box 1. Ten Ideas for Recreating Trust

1.  Understanding different preferences and different "ways of being"—leadership styles, work styles, processing styles, etc—rather than simply focusing on disagreements

2.  Changing departments or teams for a better "fit" and not trying to make a relationship work that is not working—people then connect with each other better in their different settings/roles

3.  Therapy/counseling for personal growth rather than to simply fulfil an organizational requirement

4.  Professional conflict mediation that investigates facts as a prerequisite for possible reconciliation

5.  Going through an interpersonal skills course together

6.  Unilaterally humbling oneself and/or unilaterally making amends and/or unilaterally changing

7.  Experiencing a crisis together that requires close cooperation for its resolution

8.  Verifiable contrition and behavior change (over time) on the part of one or both of the parties

9.  New leaders or power structures are put into place in an organization

10. Organizational interventions that can appropriately remove and require restoration for dysfunctional people and the dysfunctional systems that they help engender

Relational health is work settings is one of the key factors that influence performance outcomes as well as being one of the key indicators of the overall health of the setting. John Fawcett in *Stress and Trauma Handbook* (2003) summarizes much of the research on factors that influence mission/aid effectiveness when he states: "Programme objectives and organisational plans will be more achievable where aid workers have strong social relationships, are members of cohesive teams, are blessed with consultative leadership, and are adequately skilled to do the job for which they have been employed" (p. 6).

In addition to Fawcett's comments, what are some of the core characteristics that would make you want to be part of a team, department, or organization? Here is how I have answered this question, below. Note the various characteristics that are directly related to healthy, resilient relationships. Note too that the opposite of these characteristics is what ushers in toxicity and malaise in our relationships. Everyone loves to work in settings like these, but remember, like healthy families, they take a lot of work and sacrifice to develop and maintain!

- Mutual respect among staff
- Fair pay/compensation and fair play especially in light of power differentials
- Opportunities to make contributions
- Opportunities for advancement and personal growth
- Sense of purpose and meaning
- Management with competence and integrity, including sharing information
- Safeguards to protect individuals (staff and customers) from injustice
- Responsibility for actions: owning mistakes, not blaming others or covering up
- Honesty in communication and public disclosures: not slanting the truth or exaggerating
- Accountability for personal/work life: seeking out feedback and ways to improve, not ignoring or pretending

## *Health Promoter 3. Reflection and Discussion:*
## THE CHALLENGES OF RELATIONAL RESILIENCY

### WHEN DO WE TURN THE OTHER CHEEK?

One day in winter, as St Francis was going with Brother Leo from Perugia to St Mary of the Angels, and was suffering greatly from the cold, he called to Brother Leo, who was walking on before him, and said to him: "Brother Leo, if it were to please God that the Friars Minor should give, in all lands, a great example of holiness and edification, write down, and note carefully, that this would not be perfect joy."

A little further on, St Francis called to him a second time: "O Brother Leo, if the Friars Minor were to make the lame to walk, if they should make straight the crooked, chase away demons, give sight to the blind, hearing to the deaf, speech to the dumb, and, what is even a far greater work, if they should raise the dead after four days, write that this would not be perfect joy."

Shortly after, he cried out again: "O Brother Leo, if the Friars Minor knew all languages; if they were versed in all science; if they could explain all scripture; if they had the gift of prophecy, and could reveal, not only all future things, but likewise the secrets of all consciences and all souls, write that this would not be perfect joy."

After proceeding a few steps farther, he cried out again  with a loud voice: "O Brother Leo, thou little lamb of God! If the Friars Minor could speak with the tongues of angels; if they could explain the course of the stars; if they knew the virtues of all plants; if all the treasures of the earth were revealed to them; if they were acquainted with the various qualities of all birds, of all fish, of all animals, of men, of trees, of stones, of roots, and of waters—write that this would not be perfect joy."

Shortly after, he cried out again: "O Brother Leo, if the Friars Minor had the gift of preaching so as to convert all infidels to the faith of Christ, write that this would not be perfect joy." Now when this manner of discourse had lasted for the space of two miles, Brother Leo wondered much within himself; and, questioning the saint, he said: "Father, I pray thee teach me wherein is perfect joy."

St Francis answered: "If, when we shall arrive at St. Mary of the Angels, all drenched with rain and trembling with cold, all covered with mud and exhausted from hunger; if, when we knock at the convent-gate, the porter should come angrily and ask us who we are; if, after we have told him, 'We are two of the brethren,' he should answer angrily, 'What ye say is not the truth; ye are but two impostors going about to deceive the world, and take away the alms of the poor; begone I say'; if then he refuse to open to us, and leave us outside, exposed to the snow and rain, suffering from cold and hunger till nightfall—then, if we accept such injustice, such cruelty and such contempt with patience, without being ruffled and without murmuring, believing with humility and charity that the porter really knows us, and that it is God who maketh him to speak thus against us, write down, O Brother Leo, that this is perfect joy. "And if we knock again, and the porter come out in anger to drive us away with oaths and blows, as if we were vile impostors, saying, 'Begone, miserable robbers! to the hospital, for here you shall neither eat nor sleep!'—and if we accept all this with patience, with joy, and with charity, O Brother Leo, write that this indeed is perfect joy.

"And if, urged by cold and hunger, we knock again, calling to the porter and entreating him with many tears to open to us and give us shelter, for the love of God, and if he come out more angry than before, exclaiming, 'These are but importunate rascals, I will deal with them as they deserve'; and taking a knotted stick, he seize us by the hood, throwing us on the ground, rolling us in the snow, and shall beat and wound us with the knots in the stick—if we bear all these injuries with patience and joy, thinking of the sufferings of our Blessed Lord, which we would share out of love for him, write, O Brother Leo, that here, finally, is perfect joy.

"And now, brother, listen to the conclusion. Above all the graces and all the gifts of the Holy Spirit which Christ grants to his friends, is the grace of overcoming oneself, and accepting willingly, out of love for Christ, all suffering, injury, discomfort and contempt; for in all other gifts of God we cannot glory, seeing they proceed not from ourselves but from God, according to the words of the Apostle, 'What hast thou that thou hast not received from God? And if thou hast received it, why dost thou glory as if thou hadst not received it?' But in the cross of tribulation and affliction we may glory, because, as the Apostle says again, 'I will not glory save in the cross of our Lord Jesus Christ.' Amen."

Excerpted from Chapter 8, pp. 17-18, *The Little Flowers of Saint Francis* (1330), Brother Ugolino.

Applications: How might this story promote both virtue and dysfunction? Where might discipline fit in here?

## FINAL THOUGHTS

Good relationships take work. They are formed and relational resiliency is strengthened as we weather the ups and downs of life together. Our good relationships (our lack thereof) are also a core part of the message that we communicate in our work in the faith-based mission/aid community.

Also key is the quality of one's relationship with his/her immediate supervisor/manager. This relationship has a major influence on the longevity and satisfaction of organizational staff. For example take some time to review the unconventional and very helpful findings from Buckingham and Coffman's 1999 research-based book, *First Break All the Rules: What the World's Greatest Managers Do Differently*. You can also see a short review of this book and the 12 core questions used in the research at www.bizsum.com (type the author/book name in the search engine to access the review).

True friendships refresh us like a place of peace and great beauty. As Sirach would say, they are life's treasures, elixirs, and beyond price. Those who truly love others will make true friends because "as a person is, so is his/her friend."

# PEARLS
## ENHANCING AND ENRICHING GOOD PRACTICE

*True love is tough love and thus with dysfunction both verifiable contrition and verifiable change are needed over time.*

*Skilled managers with integrity are needed to effectively implement good policies.*

*High interpersonal skill levels throughout the organization are fundamental for health and effectiveness.*

*The New Testament gives us many warnings and instructions about dysfunction and deviance.*

*Moral courage, investigative skills, and professional input in a group context are needed to deal with dysfunction well.*

# PERILS
## ENCUMBERING AND ENDANGERING GOOD PRACTICE

*Significant dysfunction is often mistaken for or conveniently categorized as relational differences.*

*Requiring or working towards reconciliation prematurely when there is major dysfunction can do much harm.*

*People in vulnerable places are reticent to confront peer and organizational misconduct, especially in settings where there is an ethos marked with fear, control, impunity, and retaliation.*

*Fraudsters and other deviants can thrive in the faith-based sector when groups inadequately screen, relax regulations, are overly mercy-oriented, and have limited experience with corruption.*

*You can feel like you are going crazy when you confront and deal with dysfunction, and your time, health, and energy levels can be woefully taxed.*

CHAPTER 7

# Supporting Good Governance and Good Management

OUR ORGANIZATIONAL CULTURE (ETHOS) AND PERSONNEL PRACTICES GREATLY IN-
FLUENCE THE QUALITY OF STAFF LIFE AND THE EFFECTIVENESS OF OUR OPERATIONS.
HOW HEALTHY ARE AN ORGANIZATION'S CULTURE AND PERSONNEL PRACTICES?
HOW DO WE PRACTICE TRANSPARENCY AND ACCOUNTABILITY ACROSS ALL LEVELS OF
OUR SENDING GROUPS AND THROUGHOUT THE MISSION/AID COMMUNITY?
HOW HELPFUL ARE OUR GUIDELINES FOR DEALING WITH THINGS LIKE CONFLICT,
GRIEVANCES, ORGANIZATIONAL MISCONDUCT, AND DYSFUNCTION?
LET'S EXPLORE SOME KEY STRATEGIES FOR PROMOTING AND SAFEGUARDING
THE HEALTH OF SENDING GROUPS AND WORKERS.

---

Healthy people form healthy organizations, and vice versa. This is no terse comment but a vital reality. One of the greatest challenges of maintaining a healthy organization is to manage conflict and dysfunction well. Conflict results when there is a perceived divergence of interests between people and when no alternative seems to exist that will satisfy everyone's preferences (see Pruit *et al* 2004, *Social Conflict: Escalation, Stalemate, and Settlement*, p. 35). I have learned the hard way that people in conflict do not often play fair and that in some cases significant dysfunction (not just differences in opinion or personality) must be addressed.

Probably like many of us, I default towards being a helper who stays neutral, preserves unity, increases mutual understanding, arrives at a "win-win" outcome, who helps people agree to disagree and believe the best in each other. This approach is usually sensible of course. However there are times when this approach is inadequate and ill-advised, and confrontation and discipline are required. This is tough love that necessitates verifiable contrition and verifiable change. Otherwise innocent people, now and in the future, get hurt. And justice is not done. Robert Schreiter's sobering comments on the challenges of reconciliation at the societal level are also applicable at the interpersonal and organizational levels.

Truth-telling, struggling for justice, working toward forgiveness: these are three central dimensions of the social process of reconciliation. In all situations I know, they are never undertaken on a level playing field; the consequences of oppression, violence, and war are not predisposed to honesty, justice, and even good intentions in all parties. Nor are the processes, for the most part, orderly. And they never seem complete, in fact, we usually experience them as truncated, prematurely foreclosed, high-jacked by the powerful. We can find ourselves acquiescing to half-measures, half-truths, compromised solutions (Schreiter, 2005, p. 4).

Managing conflict and dysfunction well, in all of its varied forms, seldom results in total justice or the total eradication of problems. So at the interpersonal and organizational levels, how do we upgrade our conflict and dysfunction management skills in a way that leads to both justice and health? In this chapter, I offer commentary on and examples for professional resources that help promote *good governance and good management practices* in five areas. These resource areas are listed in Box 1. One hopefully obvious point I would like to make is that any resource, no matter how good it is, can be potentially abused by a dysfunctional system or person.

---

### Box 1. Core Resource Areas for Organizational Health

- Interpersonal skills development
- Guidelines for conflict, discipline, and restoration
- Guidelines for grievances and whistle-blowing
- Organizational assessment: staff feedback, internal/external auditing, and board governance
- Human resources management.

---

## FIVE RESOURCE AREAS FOR HEALTHY ORGANIZATIONS

### 1. Interpersonal Skills

First I want to highly recommend the *Sharpening Your Interpersonal Skills* course developed by Ken Williams with Wycliffe (www.ITpartners.org). This week-long course is taught around the world and the materials have been translated into over ten languages. It provides clear, foundational training to help apply Scriptural principles in preventing and working through some of the more typical problem areas. It also helps to build or refresh basic listening, problem solving, and communication skills (see example in Box 2). Good and widespread interpersonal skills are essential for healthy staff and healthy organizations!

This course however is not designed to help deal with serious personal and systemic dysfunction. The skills needed to deal with dysfunction must be developed through life experiences and additional focused training. But this course will help further build the *relational competencies* needed for *relational resiliency* and doing our work well with others. Ken Williams reminds us in the *Introduction*, that the development of interpersonal skills is not the only goal. Rather "Love is the goal of this workshop, that we love God and love one another more" (2003, p. 2). He then goes on to share twenty-four passages of scripture related to love, which clearly set a foundation for the interpersonal principles and skills that are taught in the course.

---

### Box 2. Pre-Conflict Check: When You Can Anticipate a Conflict Situation

Ken Williams, *Sharpening Your Interpersonal Skills* (2002, p. 113; Used by permission.)

**1. Preparing My Heart**

_____Have I honestly considered why I'm doing this?

_____Have I acknowledged my negative feelings and begun working on resolving them?

_____Have I surrendered any wrong attitudes and motivations to God?

_____Have I asked Him to prepare the other person's heart and to be willing to find a solution with which we can live?

_____Is there anything else I need to talk over with God first?

**2. Preparing What to Say (How to Begin)**

_____Do I have the essential *issue* clearly in mind, and am I able to clearly state it?

_____Am I prepared to honestly and lovingly share my feelings in this matter?

_____Do I have a clear understanding of what I would like to see happen?

**3. Preparing for the Context**

_____Have I decided on the best time to bring up the issue?

_____Have I decided on the best location?

---

### 4. Post Conflict Check and Comments

_____Did I clearly and specifically present the issue, in dialogue?

_____Were we able to keep the conversation to one present issue?

_____Did I appropriately control and express my feelings?

_____Did I avoid attacks, mind reading, prophesying and counter attacks?

_____Did I effectively present ideas for possible solutions?

_____Did I listen well without interrupting, giving feedback and adequate opportunity to express feelings, perceptions and solutions?

_____Did we find a mutually acceptable solution, resulting in a minimum of unresolved feelings/misunderstanding?

_____If we couldn't agree, did I do everything possible to preserve our relationship?

_____Have we set up a time for ongoing dialogue, if needed?

## 2. Conflict, Discipline, and Restoration Guidelines

Second, I want to encourage mission/aid organizations to develop clear, written guidelines for handling conflict. Be sure to include the place of personal and relational restoration and discipline, along with justice issues, rather than solely having an end goal of reconciliation (White and Blue, 1985 and Baker, 2005). Earl and Sandy Wilson *et al's* book *Restoring the Fallen* (1997) is an in-depth case study on deception, moral failure, and healing. It is written by an "offender" and the support team that provided him with the tough accountability and care that were needed for restoration. Their experience together, as reflected in the quotes below, are helpful to guide true restoration.

> Unfortunately, there seems to be an unwritten rule that if you believe in forgiveness… then you should not be tough or confrontative. This is a dangerous approach, particularly in those instances where patterns of sin and deceit have existed for a long time. The perception of the problem by those in need of restoration is usually so distorted that they may never truly come to grips with the issues.(be careful not to simply) reframe the offense…into a "spiritual problem"…it is quite simple for the offender to accommodate to such a reframe: just have a religious renewal experience, and then the "problem" will dissolve…True restoration is achieved through a process of discipline that recognizes both grace and responsibility as it seeks to guide the person back to a God-centered life." (pp. 117, 200, 15).

Organizations would greatly benefit from comparing each other's internal guidelines and practical experiences in conflict, discipline, and restoration. What works and what does not work? One example is the *Guidelines for Restoration* developed for Wycliffe International in cases of moral failure/serious problems (available in the main article on the Reality DOSE site: http://MCAresources.googlepages.com). These guidelines, written by Laura Mae Gardner, include three broad steps to be implemented with an attitude of "corrective grace." Step one, *Discipline*, can involve a change of status, loss of position, and informing others for accountability. Step two is *Recovery* which seeks a sincere willingness and demonstration over time of repentance, restitution, rehabilitation, and a willingness to re-earn credibility. *Restoration* is step three, based on the person having returned to a consistent place of health and then possibly given a place of responsibility.

Keep in mind that any guidelines are only as helpful as the skill levels of the managers who use them. I also note, sadly, that when guidelines are bypassed or inadequate, we may tend to make them up to our own advantage rather than with impartiality and in the best interests of everyone in mind. As one colleague has shared with me, somewhat skeptically, "Poor organizational management is all about the other "golden rule" in which the person with the most gold, rules."

Organizational guidelines, in the hands of managers who are capable and full of integrity, must also stand the test of conflict/discipline situations that are ambiguous and/or where there is lots of toxicity, and where there can be bias and partiality that can potentially interfere with establishing the facts and justice. Again I say that any tools and guidelines, no matter how well-written, are only as helpful as the person or persons who are implementing them. Those in positions of influence and responsibility must play fair when applying discipline/restoration guidelines. They must acknowledge any conflicts of interest and biases, be open to objective external input, and be aware of areas where their competencies and information may be limited. Accountability at all levels of an organization is needed, including for those charged with the challenging and sometimes thankless task of implementing discipline/restoration.

****

*Keep in mind that any guidelines are only as helpful as the skill levels of the managers who use them.*

****

Peacemakers International is a US-based Christian organization offering training materials for conflict management and providing mediation services (www.peacemaker.net). Their goal is to equip and assist Christians and churches to respond to conflict biblically. *Relationship Commitments* is one of their main documents to help people in a Christian community (primarily churches in a North American context) relate together in a way that honors God and promotes authentic relationships. It covers peacemaking and reconciliation, marriage and divorce, counseling, confidentiality, mutual accountability, and protecting children from abuse. They also have a *Peacemakers Pledge*, reproduced below in Box 3, which they encourage Christians to adopt in order to maintain good relationships.

### Box 3. Peacemakers Pledge
PEACEMAKERS INTERNATIONAL

As people reconciled to God by the death and resurrection of Jesus Christ, we believe that we are called to respond to conflict in a way that is remarkably different from the way the world deals with conflict.[1] We also believe that conflict provides opportunities to glorify God, serve other people, and grow to be like Christ.[2] Therefore, in response to God's love and in reliance on his grace, we commit ourselves to respond to conflict according to the following principles:

Glorify God — Instead of focusing on our own desires or dwelling on what others may do, we will rejoice in the Lord and bring him praise by depending on his forgiveness, wisdom, power, and love, as we seek to faithfully obey his commands and maintain a loving, merciful, and forgiving attitude.[3]

Get the Log out of Your Eye — Instead of blaming others for a conflict or resisting correction, we will trust in God's mercy and take responsibility for our own contribution to conflicts—confessing our sins to those we have wronged, asking God to help us change any attitudes and habits that lead to conflict, and seeking to repair any harm we have caused.[4]

Gently Restore — Instead of pretending that conflict doesn't exist or talking about others behind their backs, we will overlook minor offenses or we will talk personally and graciously with those whose offenses seem too serious to overlook, seeking to restore them rather than condemn them. When a conflict with a Christian brother or sister cannot be resolved in private, we will ask others in the body of Christ to help us settle the matter in a biblical manner.[5]

Go and be Reconciled — Instead of accepting premature compromise or allowing relationships to wither, we will actively pursue genuine peace and reconciliation—forgiving others as God, for Christ's sake, has forgiven us, and seeking just and mutually beneficial solutions to our differences.[6]

By God's grace, we will apply these principles as a matter of stewardship, realizing that conflict is an assignment, not an accident. We will remember that success in God's eyes is not a matter of specific results, but of faithful, dependent obedience. And we will pray that our service as peacemakers will bring praise to our Lord and lead others to know His infinite love.[7]

[1] Matt. 5:9; Luke 6:27-36; Gal. 5:19-26.

[2] Rom. 8:28-29; 1 Cor. 10:31-11:1; James 1:2-4.

[3] Ps. 37:1-6; Mark 11:25; Jn. 14:15; Rom 12:17-21; 1 Cor. 10:31; Phil. 4:2-9; Col. 3:1-4; James 3:17-18; 4:1-3; 1 Pet. 2:12.

[4] Prov. 28:13; Matt. 7:3-5; Luke 19:8; Col. 3:5-14; 1 John 1:8-9.

[5] Prov. 19:11; Matt. 18:15-20; 1 Cor. 6:1-8; Gal. 6:1-2; Eph. 4:29; 2 Tim. 2:24-26; James 5:9.

[6] Matt. 5:23-24; 6:12; 7:12; Eph. 4:1-3, 32; Phil. 2:3-4.

[7] Matt. 25:14-21; John 13:34-35; Rom. 12:18; 1 Pet. 2:19; 4:19.

Adapted from: *The Peacemaker: A Biblical Guide to Resolving Personal Conflict* ©1997, 2003 by Ken Sande. Peacemaker® Ministries, www.Peacemaker.net.

This pledge seems especially relevant in situations where there is skilled support, good will, and little to no dysfunction. For example, we have endorsed this pledge as a reference point for approaching any relational differences within our group, Member Care Associates. However, I personally would like to see additional written commitments that would include principles (statements and biblical passages) which: a) instruct us on managing dysfunctional systems/people (e.g., 1 Cor. 5) and, b) warn us about abusive people (member tares) and abusive situations (member tears). Box 4 lists several New Testament terms to describe such agents of abuse. I call them "Member Tares." Christians and Christian communities, when taught these principles, could be less vulnerable to the debilitating effects of deviance and dysfunction. The principles would thus be included as part of the core, positive focus of building up people, as in "The authority the Master gave me is for putting people together, not tearing them apart" (2 Cor. 13:10, *The Message*).

Helping anyone in a conflict situation is challenging. Negotiation and mediation skills are paramount. For example, see chapter 12 on "Best Practices in Negotiation" by Lewiski *et al* (2007), which highlights areas like being aware of unspoken intangibles/motives, managing relational coalitions, and the relative/subjective nature of fairness and rationality. One potential snare is that helpers may unwittingly or intentionally misuse power themselves—stepping into a conflict situation with "spiritual authority" and disempowering those in the situation by being highly directive, not making adequate inquiry, or even pronouncing harsh judgments. Further, keep in mind that mediation efforts that primarily seek reconciliation, as has been pointed out, is not an initial or even advisable goal when there is deviance-dysfunction (e.g., see material and suggestions from the Reconciliation Network, 2005).

Protection and discipline along with truth and justice, however, *are* appropriate goals. Confusing forgiveness with accountability, as Stahlke and Laughlin strongly warn against in *Governance Matters* (2003, p. 34), is even considered by them to be one of the "seven deadly sins" of faith-based non-profit organizations. As healthy adults, we want to be informed and alert, but not afraid. We do not need to continue to be bitten by snakes or wolves, much less devoured by them! In short, I want to strongly advocate that being *truthseekers, safeguarders,* and *peacemakers,* with a view towards both mercy/ justice, is a balanced, biblical, and healthy way forward.

---

**Box 4. New Testament Warnings: Member Tares**
NEW AMERICAN STANDARD BIBLE, THE MESSAGE

Ravenous wolves.
*(Matt. 7:15)*

False christs. Anti-christs.
*(Matt. 24:24; I John 2:18)*

Evil men. Imposters. Deceivers.
*(2 Tim. 3:13)*

Frauds. Snakes. Reptilian sneaks.
*(Matt. 23:29, 33)*

False brethren. So-called brother—wicked man.
*(Gal. 2:4; I Cor. 5:11-13)*

False prophets. False/pseudo apostles. False teachers.
*(Matt. 7:15; Matt. 24:1, 24; 2 Cor. 11:13; 2 Pet. 2:1)*

Professional liars. Deceitful/crooked workers. Imposters.
*(1 Tim. 4:2; 2 Cor. 11:13; 2 Cor. 11:20)*

Deceived hypocritical liars with seared consciences and depraved minds.
*(1 Tim. 4:2; 2 Tim. 3:8)*

---

Hidden reefs, waterless clouds, fruitless trees, wild waves, wandering stars.
*(Jude 12-13)*

Don't be naïve. Don't be naïve. Don't be naïve.
*(Matt. 10:1) (Mark 14:37) (2 Tim. 3:1)*

## 3. Guidelines for Grievances and Whistle-blowing

Third, I suggest that organizations have clear guidelines for handling grievances and for "whistle-blowing." This includes non-retaliation commitments to those who confront serious problems in an organization. These guidelines are part of good management practices and are in addition to those for conflict resolution. With regards to grievances, mission/aid organizations should also consider the role of an "ombudsman." This is a trained and designated person who acts as an independent, neutral, confidential and usually informal intermediary to represent and help negotiate the interests of both staff and the organization.

For more information go to these Web sites:

- www.web.mit.edu/ombud/index.html
- www.web.mit.edu/negotiation/toa/TOAintro.html
- www.ombuds-blog.blogspot.com.

As for whistle-blowing, one helpful resource is the *Policy on Suspected Misconduct, Dishonesty, Fraud, and Whistle-Blower Protection* by the Evangelical Council for Financial Accountability in the USA (see Box 5). This White Paper is a suggested policy that takes into account the legal protection offered by the 2002 Sarbanes Oxley Act in the USA for those who report possible or actual organizational misconduct. It also urges that a variety of safe reporting mechanisms be set up that are understood and used by staff. It includes sample policies for both large and small organizations to adapt for their purposes. Note too that similar legislation to protect whistleblowers was passed in the United Kingdom in 1998, as part of the Public Interest Disclosure Act. See http://www.opsi.gov.uk/acts/acts1998/ukpga_19980023_en_1.

*Box 5. Policy on Suspected Misconduct, Dishonesty, Fraud, and Whistle-Blower Protection*
EVANGELICAL COUNCIL FOR FINANCIAL ACCOUNTABILITY, WWW.ECFA.ORG

Recent scandals in the for-profit and nonprofit worlds have highlighted the importance of integrity within an organization. Fraud prevention has recently been addressed in new legislation and accounting standards. This new level of fraud awareness applies to nonprofit organizations just as much as it does to for-profit organizations, and it is therefore important that nonprofit organizations establish a means for employees to report concerns about misconduct, dishonesty, or fraud. Such a reporting structure should be recorded and communicated to employees in a written policy on suspected misconduct, dishonesty, and fraud.

**Whistle-blower protection**
One of the two provisions of the Sarbanes-Oxley Act of 2002 that applies to nonprofit organizations (the other provision relates to document destruction) is the legal protection of whistle-blowers. The Act makes it illegal for a corporate entity to punish whistle-blowers who risk their careers by reporting suspected illegal activities in an organization. No form of punishment, including firing, demotion, suspension, harassment, failure to consider the employee for promotion, or any other kind of discrimination, is allowed.

Punishing a whistle-blower in any way is a criminal offense. Even when an employee's claims are unfounded, the nonprofit may not reprimand him. To receive whistle-blower protection, an employee does not have to demonstrate misconduct; a reasonable belief or suspicion that violation of a federal law exists is sufficient.

As a result of this legislation, it is important that nonprofit organizations develop procedures for receiving and handling complaints. Nonprofits need to create and implement a formal process to receive and investigate complaints and prevent retaliation. As a part of this process, a confidential and anonymous mechanism should be established to receive employee complaints. These needs for whistle-blower protection can be incorporated into a general policy on misconduct, dishonesty, and fraud.

**Important policy components**

Typically, the audit committee has ultimate responsibility for the processes that define the confidential communication system relating to significant employee concerns. Fraud prevention and whistle-blower policies should:

1.  Provide confidentiality and anonymity to the submitter. Both the perception and the reality of safety are necessary to encourage people to speak up about sensitive topics.

2.  Enable anyone who may have information about wrongdoing to make a report. This includes employees, vendors and suppliers, internal and external auditors, consultants, advisors, and board members.

3.  Facilitate the reporting of all varieties of wrongdoing. Many Federal and state laws prohibit retaliation for reporting illegal acts.

4.  Give submitters choice and convenience. A phone call to truly skilled listeners elicits the most complete set of facts about a case. However, the preferences driven by age and background may dictate allowing people to use the web or write a letter. Make the service available at all times, and support foreign languages if some organization employees are non-native English speakers.

5.  Focus on obtaining a full set of facts from the submitter. More information is better than less. Experienced and well-trained listeners are better equipped to obtain the information necessary to begin solving problems before they become emergencies.

6.  Adhere to a compliance approach, with checks and balances built into the case review and closure steps. The process must include systematic follow-up and tracking capabilities. Instill a culture of accountability that precludes the potential for management to sweep problems under the rug.

7.  Put the information into the hands of people who can and will act on it. Invest the time up front to determine specific roles and responsibilities. Establish rules for action and oversight. Retain each and every report, even those that appear to lack substance, so that no bits and pieces are lost.

8.  Have options for investigation and resolution. If you use a third-party hotline, the provider must not be the same firm as the one doing the investigating. It is an inherent conflict of interest to listen objectively and at the same time seek additional revenue from investigation activity. Investigation is not the role of audit committee members; use staff personnel who are unrelated to the submitter who are experienced in conducting investigations.

9. Freely publicize the existence of the confidential reporting service. Communicate the safety and availability of the process, and give permission to use it. The whistle-blower policy should be included in the organization's employee handbook and policy manual, discussed in the organization's newsletters, presented in training of new employees, and periodically (at least annually) be communicated to all current employees.

10. Protect the whistle-blower. Nonprofits should take every step possible to protect the confidentiality of the whistle-blower. Organizations must ensure that no director, officer, or employee who in good faith reports a violation will suffer harassment, retaliation or adverse employment consequence.

Mission/aid workers, whether they are employees, volunteers, or independent contractors, need to be aware of their rights/status under the law. Organizations are responsible to explain these laws to their members and to abide by them. The main caveat however regarding legislation and organizational policies is aptly summarized by Bennis *et al* in *Transparency: How Leaders Create a Culture of Candor* (2008): "But legislation alone cannot make organizations open and healthy. Only the character and will of those who run them and participate in them can do that….If a culture of collusion exists instead of a culture of candor, participants will find ways around the rules, new or old, however stringent" (p. 8). Legislation is only as good as the people that apply it.

### 4. Organizational Assessment

Fourth, sending organizations need to be resolutely committed to getting feedback from and staying connected to their staff. Rob Hay with Redcliffe College in the United Kingdom provides a list of key questions adapted from the ReMAP II study on mission staff retention. Results of the ReMAP II study are in the excellent book that he co-edited, *Worth Keeping* (2007). Organizations and their staff can use this short survey below (Box 6) to monitor their levels of health and toxicity. What types of problems significantly affect us and our workers? What are our strengths and weaknesses as a sending structure and institution?

Leaders and staff must be willing to look beyond the individual level of analysis, and assess the whole area of organizational health and dysfunction. Lencioni's comments about health teams apply to organizations as well: "Members of great teams improve their relationships by holding one another accountable, thus demonstrating that they respect each other and have high expectations for one another's performance" (2002, p. 213). Finally, I note that most workers want not only good feedback tools, but also good managers with whom they can talk.

## Box 6. Organizational Life
ADAPTED BY ROB HAY

This is an exercise that can be done individually or preferably as a group. Spend a few minutes reflecting on some of your organizational practices. For each of the following questions, enter a score between 0 and 6 where: 0 = not done, 1 = not done well, up to 6 = very well done (as evidenced by time, effort, and effectiveness).

Add up your scores and enter the total in line A, then divide A by B and enter in C. Which scores are highest, and which are lowest? What is being done well, and poorly? How can the quality of work and life be improved?

1. _____Vision and purpose are shared and understood throughout the agency
2. _____Plans and job descriptions are communicated clearly to staff
3. _____There is a free flow of communication to and from the leadership
4. _____There is effective communication between sending base and field
5. _____Staff are included in major decisions related to the field
6. _____Policies are well documented and understood
7. _____Most leaders are a good example of the agency's beliefs and values
8. _____Most leaders identify problems early and take appropriate action
9. _____Good on-field supervision is provided (quantity and quality)
10. _____Leaders conduct an annual performance/ ministry review with each staff person
11. _____There are documented procedures for handling complaints from staff
12. _____Effective on-field orientation is in place for new staff
13. _____Staff are assigned roles according to their gifting and experience
14. _____Staff are given room to shape and develop their own ministry
15. _____Staff are committed to their ministry
16. _____Staff are committed and loyal to the agency
17. _____Staff are generally not overloaded in the amount of work they do
18. _____Staff regularly evaluate and seek to improve the agency's ministry
19. _____Staff are actually achieving the agency's goals and expectations
20. _____Staff are developing good relationships with the people they serve
21. _____The people our staff serve are becoming followers of Christ

22. _____The church on the field values the ministries of our staff
23. _____Staff are developing leadership among the people they serve
24. _____Staff experience a sense of fulfilment in their ministry
25. _____Staff are effective in providing each other with mutual support
26. _____Effective pastoral care exists at a field level (preventative and in crises)
27. _____Interpersonal conflicts are resolved in a timely and appropriate manner
28. _____Emphasis is placed on the maintenance and growth of personal spiritual life
29. _____Health care services for staff and their families are satisfactory
30. _____Time for an annual vacation or holiday is provided
31. _____Risk assessment and contingency planning is in place in all fields
32. _____There is financial back-up for staff with low or irregular support

A. Total    B. Divide by 32    C. Average    D. Highest and lowest scores

Another important aspect of organizational assessment involves the crucial role of financial auditing—both internal and external—and the effective governance of boards. Auditing and boards help provide the accountability to make sure that the organization's resources are being used properly and to prevent the devastating consequences of personnel/organizational "corruption"—"the abuse of entrusted power for private gain," to quote Transparency International (www.transparency.org).

Such corruption, including financial fraud, is unfortunately part of the mission/aid sector. For example, in their annual review of global Christianity, Barrett, Johnson, and Crossing assert: "Emboldened by lax procedures, trusted church treasurers are embezzling each year $25 billion from church funds, but only 5 percent ever get found out. Annual church embezzlements by top custodians exceed the entire cost of all foreign missions worldwide." (2008, p. 29). This is a staggering and sobering estimate of corruption! Their more recent estimate (Johnson, Barrett, and Crossing, 2010, p. 39, lines 56-57) lists "ecclesiastical crime" to be $32 billion and the "income of global foreign missions" to be $29 billion. Consider this data in terms the "collective minimum hourly wage for international ecclesiastical crime" being $350,000 per hour (based on twenty-four hours, seven days a week) or $1.5 million dollars per hour (based on a 40-hour work week)! Whenever unscrupulous people mix Christianity and criminality, and whenever we passively sit by and let this happen, we sadly end up with a highly deviant "Christian criminality" or what I call "crimianity." For various examples of preventing/confronting corruption, see Vian *et al's Anticorruption in the Health Sector: Strategies for Transparency and Accountability* (2010) and Anello's *Ethical Infrastructure for Good Governance in the Public Pharmaceutical Sector* (2006, World Health Organization, www.who.int.org).

Krishna Memon (2008), writing on corruption in the humanitarian sector, underscores the importance of having in place both effective auditing systems and effective management systems.

> Many in the field have debated about the extent to which internal auditors share the responsibility for fraud detection…However, the consensus among fraud auditors seems to be that although they have an important role to play in fraud prevention and detection, the primary responsibility is managements…. Auditors and fraud examiners, through interviews and review of documents, can identify and trace suspicious transactions and payments, test prices and performance, and inspect work and deliverables. Fraud indicators are but clues or hints that a particular area or activity requires detailed inquiry. That inquiry might show that all is fine, poor management or negligence, or signs of wrongdoing (p. 20).

Mernon goes on to speak of the vulnerabilities and consequences for this sector.

> Employees in international humanitarian organizations are givers. Unfortunately, a few are also takers. Management, often in crisis mode, unwittingly enables the fraudsters by relaxing regulations to quickly deliver aid….In addition to the monetary costs, staff members' fraudulent activities have long-term deleterious consequences for the reputation and credibility of humanitarian organizations. Anything that tarnishes their reputations can drastically reduce donor funding (p. 20).

It is not just the financial and reputation costs, however, but the human costs as well that must be remembered. Cynthia Cooper, in her account of the impact of the Worldcom fraud reminds us that:

> …numbers and accounts are only partly what hung in the balance. What happened touched real people. The man who lost his children's college fund., the elderly lady whose life savings disappeared, the employee living paycheck to paycheck and struggling to find another job. It also affected the families of those involved in the wrongdoing, who, on an emotional level, would endure the pain and serve prison sentences along with their loved ones (*A Dark Cloud Descending,* 2008, p. 33).

Additional information on boards and management, specifically in the faith based/non-profit sector, can be found in Stehele and Laughlin's book *Governance Matters* (2003). This book presents a model of governance based on relationships and includes a detailed example of a board governance manual that can help inform the board practices and policies for organizations. Some of the classic works on management, such as Peter Drucker's *The Essential Drucker* (2001) or the *HR Magazine Guide to Managing People* (Johnson, 2006) are also well worth considering. So also are the materials on managing off-site employees and virtual teams (e.g., *The Distance Manager* 2001, Fisher and Fisher; or *How to Manage Virtual Teams* in the July 1, 2009 issue of Massachusetts Institute of Technology's online magazine, *Sloan Management Review* www.sloanreview.mit.edu/the-magazine).

### 5. Human Resource Management

Fifth, I want to suggest staying in touch with professional practice in the field of human resource management (HRM). One need not be an HRM professional to benefit from the important resources in this field! HRM looks at how best to set up and manage systems in organizations in order to help staff meet organizational goals (Mathis and Jackson, 2003, p. 2). One way to stay current in this field is to receive the regular e-mailings from the Society for Human Resource Management (SHRM), the largest HRM organization in the world (www.shrm.org). See also the material from the Association for HR Management in International Organizations (www.ahrmio.org). Another way would be to regularly review the materials from People In Aid, based in the UK (www.peopleinaid.org). Examples include their quarterly newsletter on a variety of HRM topics, the *Code of Good Practice in the Management and Support of Aid Personnel* (2003), and many other human resource materials (e.g., *Understanding HR in the Humanitarian Sector*, 2004 and *Enhancing Quality in HR Management*, 2004). Management Sciences for Health also has many helpful materials, including a free assessment tool (HRM Assessment Tool, 2005) to review an organization's HRM components, capacity, and areas needing improvement and a practical HRM overview, "Strengthening HRM to Improve Health Outcomes" (www.mhs.org).

In addition, the Web sites in Box 7 are helpful as they include various resources related to HRM, organizational management, business ethics, and staff support.

---

*Box 7. Some Web Links and Resources for HRM and Organizational Health*

**Dingman Company,** www.dingman.com
   See the newsletters for book reviews and comments on organizational governance and management.

**Evangelical Council for Financial Accountability www.ecfa.org**

See their material on: *whistle-blower protection in and its applicability to nonprofits.*

www.ecfamembers.org/documents/PolicyOnSuspectedFraud.doc

**Global Compliance** www.glogalcompliance.com

See their material on: developing ethics and compliance in organizations.

www.globalcompliance.com/pdf/the-seven-pillars-of-an-effective-ethics-and-compliance-program.pdf

**Heartstream Resources** www.heartstreamresources.org

See the paper (and especially point 6 on "organizational care") *Caring for People in Missions.*

www.heartstreamresources.org/index.php?view=article&id=67

**Humanitarian Practice Group** www.odi.org.uk/hpg

See their material on: preventing corruption in humanitarian assistance—September 2008.

www.odi.org.uk/hpg/papers/hpgbrief32.pdf

**Independent Sector** www.independentsector.org

See their checklist for accountability in organizations.

www.mcaresources.googlepages.com/tr_1199122887038

www.independentsector.org/issues/accountability/Checklist/Checklist_Full.pdf

**Institute of Business Ethics** www.ibe.org.uk

See their material on developing ethics codes and embedding ethical values in organizational culture.

www.ibe.org.uk/publications/DevelopingSumm.pdf

**Markkula Center for Applied Ethics, Santa Clara University**
www.scu.edu/ethics

See their material on: the background and perspectives for internal whistle-blowing.

www.scu.edu/ethics/publications/submitted/whistleblowing.html

**Massachusetts Institute of Technology, Ombuds Office**
www.web.mit.edu/ombud/index.html
> See their Terms of Reference that describe how the ombuds office operates.
> www.web.mit.edu/ombud/about/MIT-Ombuds-Terms-of-Reference.pdf

**Management Sciences for Health** www.msh.org
> Management resources for NGOS and public health organizations, including HRM assessment tools.
> www.msh.org/resource-center/human-resource-management-assessment-instrument-for-ngos-and-public-sector-health-organizations.cfm

**New Era Scandal**
> See the overview and links regarding this large-scale fraud that affected many people/organizations.
> www.en.wikipedia.org/wiki/Foundation_for_New_Era_Philanthropy

**People In Aid** www.peopleinaid.org
> Code of Good Practice for Managing and Supporting Staff
> www.peopleinaid.org/code

**Public Concern at Work** www.pcaw.co.uk
> See their recent book: *Whistle Blowing Around the World: Law, Culture and Practice.*
> www.pcaw.co.uk/law/wbaroundtheworld.htm

**Reality Dose: Resources for Good Practice in Member Care**; Member Care Associates
> Materials on health/dysfunction in mission/aid (shorter version of Part Two in twelve languages).
> www.MCAresources.googlepages.com/realitydose

**Society for Human Resource Management** www.shrm.org
> Hundreds of resources along with regular newsletters, conferences and international updates on HRM.

**United Nations Global Compact** www.unglobalcompact.org
Strategic initiative for businesses: ten principles for human rights, labor, environment, anti-corruption.
www.unglobalcompact.org/AboutTheGC/TheTenPrinciples/index.html
www.unglobalcompact.org/docs/news_events/8.1/GC_brochure_FINAL.pdf

One specific HRM example, which overlaps with the previous four resource areas, deals with the importance for sending groups to put into place fair and clear policies/procedures for terminating staff. This can be such a difficult area to manage, especially when people are friends or volunteers or when employment law is involved. Sometimes no one really wants to do anything. It is too tricky or too complicated or just not "nice." Other times certain laws or organizational procedures may be so exacting that they seriously encumber the process of effectively dealing with an incompetent or otherwise non-productive staff member. A case in point may be the meticulous documentation over time needed to properly disciple or substantiate termination of an employee. The same can be true when trying one's level best to confront dysfunction or deviance within organizations and the individuals involved. Mix in the dynamics of there being political appointees who are protected by higher-ups as well as "good ol' boy" clubs which influence what gets addressed and thus the outcomes. Over time the resulting negative environment becomes a serious detriment to the quality of life and operational goals for the organization.

In spite of the above challenges, termination and discipline can still be done very well. Here are some of the key questions to consider. What are the conditions and procedures under which we ask a person to leave the work/organization for the purposes of restoration and/or for discipline? Is there a clear appeal process? How do we help those who have significant struggles yet want to keep working? Will helping a colleague in need deplete others' energy and time and distract from the organization's primary objectives? How does an organization demonstrate good governance by balancing the need to both support both staff and to safeguard its own interests? How do we safeguard against the challenges of inaction, excessive documentation, time constraints, and political maneuvering mentioned in the above paragraph? You can find a lot of help to these and other questions, plus many examples in Bliss and Thornton's *Employment Termination Sourcebook: A Collection of Practical Examples* (2006) as well as many other materials offered by the Society for Human Resource Management (www.shrm.org).

## PULLING OUR RESOURCES TOGETHER

Taken together, these five resource areas from both the faith-based and secular world, reflect Part Two's opening quote by Charles Handy in *Understanding Voluntary Organizations*: "Virtue does not have to be so painful, *if* it is sensibly organized" (1988, p. 9). We can in fact get organizational and personnel management right. In so doing we can improve the quality of life for our staff and the effectiveness of our operations. Organizational life is challenging yet it need not be so distressful!

---

### *Health Promoter 1. Reflection and Discussion*

"Organizations must create a corporate culture where dialogue and feedback are regular practice—and this should extend to every level of employee throughout the organization. Such a culture can build the foundation of an open problem-solving environment, demonstrate to employees that it is safe to raise concerns, and exhibit that the organization takes retaliation seriously." (Heard and Miller, *International Business Ethics Institute Review, 2006*, p. 1) http://hubpages.com/hub/BUSINESS-Creating-an-Open-and-Non-Retaliatory-Workplace

1. What could be done to help your organization further develop the healthy culture described above?
2. Which resources listed in this article can be the most helpful for you in your organization/setting?
3. What other resources can help an organization promote health and manage dysfunction better?

---

I have also summarized ten recommendations (Box 8) which represent the core suggestions in this chapter as well as in Part Two for dealing with dysfunction. I recommend that these suggestions in particular be reviewed and discussed in depth within one's mission/aid setting. Keep in mind that when significant dysfunction is present, I strongly encourage consultation with professionals experienced in organizational development and psychopathology, plus good personal support, as per points 4 and 8 below. For organizations, putting these suggestions into practice is a significant part of promoting health and good governance.

*Box 8. Ten Suggestions for Dealing with Dysfunction/Toxicity*
WHAT HELPS TO PROTECT AND PROMOTE HEALTH?

1. There is a continuum of responses to carefully consider. It ranges from prudently withdrawing and protecting oneself (Prov. 27:12) to prudently confronting and holding one's ground (Prov. 25:26). Act with integrity, without wavering, based on your convictions and wise advice.

2. Make room for cultural, generational, gender, and organizational variation. Difference is not deviance. Preferences are not usually pathogens. In many cultures, direct approaches may not be appreciated, no matter how diplomatic or respectful one is.

3. Impartiality and objectivity do not necessarily imply neutrality. Don't be afraid to take a stand. But beware of seeing any party as being "all bad" or "all good." Truth, packaged diplomatically, is usually a good way forward. Talking in terms of behavior patterns rather than personality problems, and situational influences rather than dispositional inadequacies, may help make the input/process more acceptable. But be realistic: certain pervasive and ongoing character or systemic issues are not amenable to change.

4. Confrontation of serious dysfunction is done as a group, with solidarity, not by oneself. Get ongoing, experienced, outside consultation, at times including legal advice. Don't simply rely on Bible verses or the advice of friends! Well-intentioned colleagues wanting to help, yet with limited understanding of dysfunction/discipline, can create even greater problems. Refer to any organizational policies for conflict resolution, grievances, and whistle-blowing. Ask yourselves: "What are our goals, what are the likely outcomes, and what are the risks?"

5. Confrontation is usually a necessary step (e.g., clinical/recovery interventions) prior to or as part of mediation and reconciliation approaches that involve dysfunction. This assumes though that there are people willing to take some risks and that there is an authority structure in place for leverage and accountability. Always include an historical review to help identify pervasive patterns. Focus on truth and justice, and do so mercifully, and don't get side-tracked or duped by anyone's contrived, embellished, or real "sincerity" or "pain."

6. Core parts of the reconciliation process in dysfunction/toxic situations include truth, justice, contrition, forgiveness, restitution, and discipline. Prematurely seeking for reconciliation is never helpful. In certain situations, the reconciliation process takes years. And without verifiable contrition and change, sometimes all we can do is "cut our losses," move on, and entrust ourselves to our faithful Creator (I Pet. 4:19). Forgiveness though, is a command in scripture to intentionally pursue (Matthew 18: 21-22).

7. Expect there to be diverging accounts of "truth" and deflecting responsibility, plus being misunderstood, manipulated, and blamed. It is a messy process. One must be willing to live with compromise, incomplete closure on important issues, minimal contrition, and partial justice.

8. If you think you are going crazy as you deal with toxicity, you probably are. Dealing with toxicity takes a high toll on our sanity. Get outside reality checks and support. Don't overestimate your ability to repel toxicity or to avoid becoming toxic yourself. Bitterness defiles. Resist it! (Heb. 12:15).

9. True trust is earned and not assumed. One needs good reasons, over time, to deeply trust others where there is a history of dysfunction. Trust is slowly built, easily broken, and slowly rebuilt.

10. Maintain a solid biblical perspective: Our Lord cares for us often by refining us through desert experiences and through injustices. He zealously loves others, even dysfunctional people, as much as He loves us; and we are all major debtors in need of unmerited mercy (Matt. 18:23-35).

## Final Thoughts

I wonder if in our sincere commitments to mercy and forgiveness if we are at times being too naïve, too vulnerable, and side-stepping good practices. I also wonder if we too easily minimize the cries for justice from battered colleagues who are exposed to dysfunction, looking the other way in order to avoid the discomfort we feel or the inconveniences and risks that any action on our part might entail. And I also wonder about our own remarkable capacity as humans for self-deception, distortions, and defensiveness when we relate and work with one another. Again I say, as emphasized in Chapter 5, that we all need help, because we are all in dire need to receive and give mercy (Gal. 6:1ff).

Above all, however, I wonder about the confounding toxins and nefarious schemes of non-human Evil—"the biggest Troublemaker in the cosmos," "the Peril of great vice," and the "serpent of old." I take much comfort in the Christian understanding of human history, when at the end of this age, the heinous, serpentine head of Evil will be irreparably and irrevocably crushed by Christ (Gen 3:15).

I really appreciate a Middle-Eastern proverb which says. "The greatest crime in the desert is to find water, and remain silent." I would like to suggest a rejoinder to this proverb: "The second greatest crime in the desert is to find *poisoned* water and remain silent" (see also Prov. 25:26). Sometimes mission/aid workers at all levels of organizations can get into trouble by blowing a whistle and confronting the poisoned water of dysfunction. This is not easy to do as we have said repeatedly. Neither is it easy to do well, nor to do well by oneself. It is often scary, risky and easy to make mistakes in spite of good intentions. There is often a high cost to pay when advocating for personal and organizational health, People need integrity and skill (Ps. 78:72) to consistently and resolutely act with moral courage both publicly and privately.

Sometimes the wisest thing to do is to back away, hope for and work slowly towards healthy change, or to move on. But there are also times when one must stand firm with a supportive community, or with a few others, or even alone. And on behalf of health and good practice one must say to dysfunction what Gandalf said to the monstrous balrog in the Mines of Moria: "You cannot pass!" (Tolkien, 1999, p. 434)

## Health Promoter 2. Reflection and Discussion

Have you had to confront "poisoned water" ? If so, what were the outcomes? What helped? What did you learn?

Have you ever felt like you and/or your colleagues were being harassed and "sifted like wheat" by a malignant force that seemed far greater than yourself (e.g., Luke 22:31)? If so, what did you learn?

Christ will irreparably and irrevocably crush evil. ©2010 Erin N. O'Donnell

# RESOURCES

CHAPTER 8

# Resources for Good Practice

"MORALITY MUST MATCH WITH CAPACITY."
DAVID BORNSTEIN, *HOW TO CHANGE THE WORLD*, 2004, P. 242

This chapter provides materials to encourage your personal and professional growth. As good practitioners we want to continue to develop our character (virtues and resiliency) and competence (skills and knowledge). We grow together with others. We have clear and strong ethical commitments to do good and to provide quality services. We go broadly and grow deeply as we follow the Good Practitioner and the Heart of Member Care, Jesus Christ.

Materials in this chapter:

- Safe People and Safe Places
- Organizational Health and Dysfunction
- Organizational Politics 101
- Good Leaders Live in Reality
- Leadership Listening
- Preventing Corruption in Humanitarian Assistance
- Healing the Body: Part Two

✳ ✳ ✳ ✳ ✳ ✳

# Safe People and Safe Places
## Organizational Ethos and Self-Disclosure

Based on "Understanding and Managing Stress" by Michèle and Kelly O'Donnell,
*Missionary Care*, 1992

An agency's culture, or ethos, significantly influences the quality of life of its people. Personnel also help shape the ethos and the quality of life within the organization.

Every cross-cultural worker needs acceptable and safe outlets (people, places, practices) to openly share personal and group concerns. Some ways of doing this include spending time with friends and confidants, getting staff feedback from questionnaires, planning meetings where ideas and perspectives can be exchanged, and providing opportunities for confidential counseling. These outlets not only help *develop* staff, but they are also are real safeguards to *prevent* poor morale, bitterness, and needless frustration.

An agency's ethos influences the types of outlets that are made available for its personnel. This in turn affects the way in which staff relate personal struggles and express feelings about departmental or organizational practices. In consulting at different faith-based contexts, we have observed various organizational styles for making self-disclosures. Agency/group ethos becomes a type of monitor, determining what and how comments can be made, especially in group situations. Most agencies/groups seem to gravitate towards one or possibly two styles in particular, although this can change over time. For more information on organizational ethos and ten "fit factors" see *Fit In!* (2007) by Mark A. Williams.

**Style 1—Spiritualization of the past.** The organization is most comfortable focusing on past issues using spiritual terms. Problems are usually only talked about when they have already been overcome. An example is the statement, "I thank God for 'victory' over my temptation to be critical about and 'rebel' against my boss."

**Style 2—Past focus.** Issues are discussed fairly openly, but usually not until they have already been resolved. They are not necessarily spiritualized, yet only shared when it is safe—that is, after the fact. Here is an example. "We were really upset about the decision to decrease furlough allowances, and were privately hoping that it would get overturned."

**Style 3—Spiritualization of the present.** Current issues and problems are discussed but referred to largely in spiritual terms. Spiritual concepts may be used as a metaphor to refer to other ideas and feelings. For instance, "This mission station needs to pray more," may mean "I am feeling really hurt that people around here seem to overlook me."

**Style 4—Present focus in vague terms.** Current problems are mentioned in indirect, general, roundabout ways. Potentially threatening material is kept at a distance. An illustration would be a team leader who states at an inter-departmental meeting, "Its interesting working around here these days" when the real feeling might be more "The Personnel Department's chronic shortage of staff is significantly undermining our team's ability to recruit needed members."

**Style 5—Present focus with contact.** This involves making genuine, usually direct comments, in which issues, feelings, and reactions are shared promptly. Feelings are seen as vital sources of information rather than stumbling blocks. The result is that everyone involved senses that real contact with each other has been made. "I so appreciate the quality of your work on this project" or "I am frustrated that this agency has an inner circle which makes all the decisions," would be examples. Style five reflects the biblical admonitions to "speak truth and pursue peace with one another" (Eph. 4:25, Zech. 8:19). The various cultural expressions of this style, including the timing, attitude, and setting for such disclosures are, of course, crucial. The goal is to edify, not candidness. Responsibility has priority over spontaneity.

---

### Reflection and Discussion

1. Which disclosure styles do you see in your life?
2. List some organizational/group practices that help or hinder self-disclosure.
3. How might you adjust your organizational/group ethos—to support safe ways to discuss/connect?

✶ ✶ ✶ ✶ ✶ ✶

# Organizational Health and Dysfunction
*Kelly O'Donnell*

**What are some of the "organizational realities" that can disrupt an organization's personnel and purposes?** Here are some thoughts from Charles Handy (1988).

*Understanding Voluntary Organizations: How to Make Them Function Effectively*

**1.** Volunteer groups are often characterized by well-intentioned ideals, an avoidance of hierarchical structure, and a lack of basic management capacity. Poor management practices in particular can seriously disrupt both virtuous objectives and collegial relationships. Virtuous behavior by groups need not be so painful, provided the group is managed properly (paraphrased pp. 8, 9).

**2.** "Group think" is a typical experience, in which a group of people "let their drive for consensus override their good sense when looking at all the options for the future" (p. 62). Only a few solutions are discussed to the exclusion of other solutions, the possible adverse consequences of preferred decisions are ignored, little effort is made to get specialist/outside advice, and there are usually no contingency plans made for failure (paraphrased, p. 62).

**3.** With time, "coalitions" interested in their own turf/agendas emerge within organizations (and movements) which can end up harming the overall purpose and contributions of the group. This can lead to infighting and enormous amount of "transaction costs"—the time and energy needed to sort out differences and keep on track (paraphrased, p. 148).

**4.** "People ought not to be encouraged or allowed to acquire the rights of statutory tenants to any part of the organization. In the voluntary world this applies particularly to management and executive committees, which have a preference for the re-election of their existing members, for co-option and for committee nomination for new members. Such ways encourage vested rights, and while there is a lot to be said for retaining wisdom and experience in the organization it need not always sit in the same place." (p. 148)

**5.** Do not be surprised by the political nature of groups and organizations. Do not be surprised by the reality of power, control, and struggles. However the use of "fear" to motivate or control is not appropriate and it does not produce long-lasting or self-sustaining behavior (p. 74).

> Because power is a forbidden topic in organizations, and particularly in volunteer organizations, there is seldom any proper discussion of two key aspects of organizational life: the place of competition and/or conflict and the role or meaning of democracy in work. If they are talked about at all it is under the heading of organization politics, and in this context 'politics' is assumed to be bad. Such myopia is misguided. Organizations are communities, societies in their own right. They cannot avoid the questions (concerning power/control) which beset all societies....To push these issues under the table is not to solve them; to brandish grandiloquent slogans— 'we are all one family' or 'conflict has no place'—only outlaws discussion of the topic without adding to an understanding of it. If organizations (such as our mission and member care organizations) are going to be effective social institutions, they need to grapple with these issues, which are not going to disappear as long as human beings live and work together (pp. 75-76).

**Reflection and Discussion**

1. Which of the above points apply most to your organizational context?
2. Any new thoughts for you about organizational politics?
3. Organizational development topics have been discussed in major member care and human resource gatherings. What types of topics for presentations would be most useful?

＊ ＊ ＊ ＊ ＊ ＊

# Organizational Politics 101: Being Astute
*Kelly O'Donnell*

**Understanding the political context of mission/aid work:**
**What can we learn from Machiavelli and friends?**

"The children of this age are more shrewd in relation to their own kind, than are the children of light. (Luke 16:8)"

"Politics" is always involved, in the broadest and best sense of the term, for determining agendas, influence, and resource allocation. **However, if in organizational life: the pressure to be** *politically-correct* **is an affront to your integrity, then being** *politically-astute* **is necessary if you want to assert your integrity... and still survive.**

Three years ago I was engrossed in a conversation with one of my closest friends. It was a cold winter's day, as we walked along the icy shores of a grey alpine lake. I was basically lamenting, with candid fervor, about why it seems so hard for good people to simply try to do good in an organizational context. "Why can organizational life be as bleak as this winter's day?", I mourned. After an hour into this somber discussion, my friend stopped, turned his gaze at me, and gently offered me two words of advice:

**"Read Machiavelli."**

My friend was referring to the 1512 work by Nicolò Machiavelli, *The Prince*. I had heard about this book—this disturbing treatise on power—but never read it. Machiavelli resolved to develop a reasoned argument for leadership that was practical and reality-based, and not simply idealistic or solely virtue-centered. Power could be "legitimately" unencumbered by ethical values. His work was arguably the beginning of the "realpolitiks" thinking that has impacted national and international governance for the last five centuries. Imbedded in his succinct admonition, my friend was telling me not to be naive, and to seriously upgrade my understanding of how the "real" organizational world works.

I took his advice. He was right. Chapter 15, reproduced below, was especially instructive. I have read and reread it many times (see especially the sentences in bold). It is less than one-page long. This short chapter is all about the use of virtue and vice by leaders. People in power, regardless of their religious convictions, can use both virtue and vice in order to preserve the state/organization and in order to maintain their position in the state/organization. In the worst case scenarios (apart from things like "murder," of course), people will "justifiably" resort to such "vices" as shaming, blaming, silencing, and scapegoating others, often with impunity, in order to protect the state/organization/oneself. There is much to learn from Machiavelli. I see *The Prince* as an important tool for the "children of light," as cited above in Luke, to help them to think and act shrewdly in this age.

I am not advocating for vice. I am advocating for reality. I am advocating for understanding the reality of how both vice and virtue are used, often in ways that can be hard to distinguish, by those who are committed to maintain power structures and productivity in organizational contexts.

### *The Prince*
Nicolò Machiavelli
Chapter 15

Concerning Things for Which Men, and Especially Princes Are Praised or Blamed (written circa 1505, published 1515, translation by W. K. Marriot 1908; reproduced from the Constitution Society, www.constitution.org)

It remains now to see what ought to be the rules of conduct for a prince towards subject and friends. And as I know that many have written on this point, I expect I shall be considered presumptuous in mentioning it again, especially as in discussing it I shall depart from the methods of other people. But, it being my intention to write a thing which shall be useful to him who apprehends it, it appears to me more appropriate to follow up the real truth of the matter than the imagination of it; for many have pictured republics and principalities which in fact have never been known or seen, because how one lives is so far distant from how one ought to live, that **he who neglects what is done for what ought to be done, sooner effects his ruin than his preservation; for a man who wishes to act entirely up to his professions of virtue soon meets with what destroys him among so much that is evil. Hence it is necessary for a prince wishing to hold his own to know how to do wrong, and to make use of it or not according to necessity.**

Therefore, putting on one side imaginary things concerning a prince, and discussing those which are real, I say that all men when they are spoken of, and chiefly princes for being more highly placed, are remarkable for some of those qualities which bring them either blame or praise; and thus it is that one is reputed liberal, another miserly, using a Tuscan term (because an avaricious person in our language is still he who desires to possess by robbery, whilst we call one miserly who deprives himself too much of the use of his own); one is reputed generous, one rapacious; one cruel, one compassionate; one faithless, another faithful; one effeminate and cowardly, another bold and brave; one affable, another haughty; one lascivious, another chaste; one sincere, another cunning; one hard, another easy; one grave, another frivolous; one religious, another unbelieving, and the like. And I know that every one will confess that it would be most praiseworthy in a prince to exhibit all the above qualities that are considered good; but because they can neither be entirely possessed nor observed, for human conditions do not permit it, it is necessary for him to be sufficiently prudent that he may know how to avoid the reproach of those vices which would lose him his state; and also to keep himself, if it be possible, from those which would not lose him it; but this not being possible, he may with less hesitation abandon himself to them. **And again, he need not make himself uneasy at incurring a reproach for those vices without which the state can only be saved with difficulty, for if everything is considered carefully, it will be found that something which looks like virtue, if followed, would be his ruin; whilst something else, which looks like vice, yet followed brings him security and prosperity.**

---

## Reflection and Discussion

1. Summarize Machiavelli's advice in one sentence.
2. How do you see vice and virtue at work within your organizational context?
3. In what ways do you think you are being politically-correct and being politically-astute?
4. In what ways do you agree or disagree with my assertions?
5. What other advice would you have given, besides reading Machiavelli?

* * * * * *

# Good Leaders Live in Reality
*Kelly O'Donnell*

## When is reality not reality?

I recently heard Dr. Robert Sternberg speak at Tufts University in Boston, USA. He is a psychologist and also Dean of the College of Arts and Sciences. He was also the President of the American Psychological Association. Dr. Sternberg spoke on "good leaders and bad leaders." His presentation was excellent, and it was both personally and professionally challenging for me.

All of us in leadership struggle at times with areas of weakness and even areas of wrongness. Sometimes though, people in positions of responsibility can consistently "go down the wrong road" and negatively impact the well-being of others. Sternberg would refer to such people as being "bad" leaders. Based on his research and experience, he emphasized that bad leaders ultimately deny/distort reality. This denial of reality is essentially what *dysfunction* is all about. He also made many other points. Some examples:

- They see themselves as being above accountability—"ethics" are for other people.
- They do not avail themselves of needed input from others to complement, balance, and correct themselves.
- They lapse into an unrealistic and often disguised sense of omnipotence, inerrancy, mega-importance, unrealistic optimism, and invulnerability.
- They become entrenched in their ways, even when it is obvious to others that these leaders are digging a bigger pit of mistakes into which they and others will fall.
- They may have high intelligence, but ultimately all the above makes them "foolish."

Ultimately, bad leaders distort and ignore reality.
They create their own reality.
Bad leaders also display a significantly diminished moral competency.

---

**Reflection and Discussion**

1. What would be five positive qualities of effective, ethical leadership?
2. How are these positive qualities developed?
3. What can lead to the development of dysfunctional leaders?

4. Consider these quotes below form Ayn Rand (*The Virtue of Selfishness,* 1964) and G.K. Chesterton (*Everlasting Man*, 1925/1993). Both adamantly assert in different ways that: "something always happens when we do nothing."

> It is not justice or equal treatment that you grant to men when you abstain equally from praising men's virtues and from condemning men's vices. When your impartial attitude declares, in effect, that neither the good nor the evil may expect anything from you—whom do you betray and whom do you encourage? (p. 82)

> If there is one fact we really can prove, from the history we really do know, it is that despotism can be a development, often a late development and very often indeed the end of societies that have been highly democratic. A despotism may almost be defined as a tired democracy. As fatigue falls on a community, the citizens are less inclined for that eternal vigilance which has truly been called the price of liberty; and they prefer to arm only one single sentinel to watch the city while they sleep (p. 58-59).

\* \* \* \* \* \*

# Leadership Listening and AV² Encounters:
## Helping Staff Deal with Difficult Experiences
*Kelly O'Donnell*

Death, discord, disillusionment, depression, danger. What helps our staff grow through such difficult experiences? How can people move from being "stuck in the mire of ministry life" towards having a greater sense of inner peace, healthy attitudes, and good relationships? To begin, everyone benefits from having a safe place and a safe person with whom to talk. Particularly helpful are special times that we have to talk with a trusted leader in our organization. We call such times "AV² encounters."

Mission/aid life can thrash even the most robust of us. Of particular note are the chronic exposure to misery and relationship struggles on field projects or in headquarter offices (e.g., the two main stressors in Carter's 1999 study: "seeing needs I am unable to meet" and "confronting others when necessary"). How do we help ourselves and others navigate such difficult experiences?

**Quality Leaders Listen.** Group and individual debriefings can really help of course, including support from external consultants or in-house resources like colleagues with counseling/debriefing training or counselors in an Employee Assistance Program. In addition, there is something reassuring about connecting with an organizational

145

leader, especially a "busy" albeit trusted person, who really takes the time to listen and understand. Talking with such leaders can be very valuable even if the leader does not always agree with the perspectives shared, or even if the leader can do little in response to the person's concerns. In my experience most staff usually appreciate sharing their difficult experiences with such a leader, provided that the leader is indeed "safe" (low risk)—that is, keeps complete confidence, is genuinely concerned, and does not use staff concerns against them. They have integrity/skill (Ps 78:72).

**Growing and Learning Together.** Most hurting staff, if we could really probe their yearnings, are wanting something like what I call "AV² Encounters" with leaders. AV² primarily refers to having one's thoughts/feelings Acknowledged and Validated (AV-1), possibly followed by both an Apology and Vindication (AV-2). It relates to things like relational discord, project struggles, and organizational grievances. This type of encounter is characterized by mutual respect and the freedom to express one's thoughts (concerns) and emotions (especially sadness and anger). It helps people and organizations put greater closure on unresolved issues and moves them further along the cycle of learning/growth.

**Acknowledge and Validate Staff.** One key for leaders is to pay careful attention to feelings of anger. Anger is a "relational" feeling, comprised of both thoughts and emotions. It is mediated by a sense of *helplessness* and a sense of *violation*. In order to feel more *empowered* (less helpless), people need to have their concerns Acknowledged: "Yes, I hear and understand what you are saying. This is really important to you and to me." And they also need their concerns to be Validated: "Yes, what you are feeling and saying makes sense." This is AV-1. It is very *affirming*, people feel more valued, and it helps create an inner shift so that one's feelings and focus are less negative.

**Apologize and Vindicate if Possible.** AV-2 deals with the desire for *justice* and the sense of having been unfairly treated (violation). People benefit from some type of authentic Apology. Even a small/vicarious, "I'm sorry" can help. People also benefit when some measure of Vindication is experienced. An affirmation of *rightness,* although not necessarily implying full absolution from being wrong/weak, is nonetheless significant. This also creates an inner shift that frees one's attention for more positive things.

**Summary.** AV-1 is basic. Active listening by leaders, or any respected person, helps facilitate it. People feel *empowered*. AV-2 though is trickier. In many situations involving relationship, project, and organizational issues—in spite of encounters with safe leaders—apologies and vindication do not happen. *Justice* may not be served to one's satisfaction. Divergent views and differing people cannot be reconciled. Dysfunctional aspects of systems and people can seemingly prevail. This challenges people to be realistic about what to expect; to consider their own possible distortions and weaknesses; and to use this difficult experience for personal growth—letting it bring out the best in them and not the worst. And for those in the Christian faith-based sector, it can encourage them and even goad them to "entrust themselves into the hands of a faithful Creator in doing what is right" (I Pet. 4:19).

## Leaders and AV² Encounters

**AV-1:** Acknowledgement and Validation
Helps to affirm our sense of truth
Helps us feel more empowered (less helpless)
Helps lighten the burden on our shoulders

**AV-2:** Apology and Vindication
Helps to affirm our sense of justice
Helps us feel more valuable (less violated)
Helps lighten the burden in our heart

AV-2 encounters affirm our sense of reality, ethics, and self-worth.
They reinforce who we are as a "person" created in God's image.
They are "protective factors" which further develop our resiliency.
People in leadership shepherd people with integrity/skill (Ps. 78:72).

Let's consider another type of encounter: AV-3.
These are the wrong kind of encounters.

**AV-3:** Attack and Vilify
Covers up truth and distorts reality
Discredits a person's character, competence, and contributions
Reinforces an organizational ethos of fear, impunity, and dysfunction

AV-3 encounters destroy.
People in leadership "stomp, smear, sneak" (Ps. 56, *The Message*)

---

### References
Carter, J. (1999). Missionary stressors and implications for care. *Journal of Psychology and Theology, 27(2)*, 171-180.

**Reflection and Discussion**

1. How do AV² Encounters reflect an organization's ethos of staff development?
2. To whom do leaders go for AV² Encounters?
3. What if the leader is part of the problem or may use disclosures against the person, or staff are too afraid to confront an errant leader or unhealthy practice/system?
4. When might it be better to talk to an ombudsman or an outside consultant rather than to a leader?
5. What happens if staff distort the facts, and/or correction rather than empathy is needed?
6. Conversely, what if leaders distort the facts, or only give empathy when action is what is needed?
7. List a few examples in your experience of AV3 Encounters (attack and vilify). What can be done to prevent such encounters?

\* \* \* \* \* \*

# Preventing Corruption in Humanitarian Assistance

Executive Summary, 2008 (for the full *Report*, see the link below)
Feinstein International Center, Humanitarian Practice Group,
Transparency International
*www.transparency.org/publications/publications/other/
humanitarian_assistance_report_2008*

Reprinted from *Preventing Corruption in Humanitarian Assistance:
Final Research Report.*
©2008 Used with permission. Transparency International: the global coalition against corruption. For more information, visit www.transparency.org

This report describes research on the problem of corruption in humanitarian assistance, carried out in 2007 and 2008 by the Feinstein International Center of Tufts University (FIC) in collaboration with the Humanitarian Policy Group (HPG) at the Overseas Development Institute in London (ODI) and the sponsoring organization, Transparency International (TI). Seven major international humanitarian NGOs volunteered to be part of the project and allowed researchers access to their headquarters staff and documentation along with similar access to field programs in seven crisis affected countries.

The research does not try to assess the degree of corruption in any one agency or country. Rather it seeks to document perceptions of corruption in humanitarian operations, including the context of humanitarian assistance, the risks and consequences of corruption, the policies and practices to mitigate or manage corruption risks, and remaining gaps in addressing corruption. This report provides some examples of prevalent corrupt practices and the range of measures the cooperating agencies are using to counter the temptation of corruption, guard operations against corruption and allow for its detection. It does not attempt to evaluate the effectiveness of these measures in reducing corruption. But more importantly, the research provides the basis for TI to develop a handbook of good practices in managing corruption risk and combating corrupt practices in humanitarian assistance, which will be issued in early 2009. This report is limited to the research findings.

The research was carried out on the strict understanding that both individuals and agencies would remain anonymous. For this reason, the data presented in this main report are in aggregate form only. More detailed information has been fed back to the individual agency headquarters and field programs respectively. This report is necessarily void of some of the contextual details that might have compromised the identity of either individuals or agencies, and is deliberately limited to generic descriptions. This is not because the study turned up any new cases of corruption—it did not, nor was it intended to—but rather to respect the confidentiality required to have an honest discussion with agency staff about corruption risks and their means of dealing with them.

This analysis suggests that, in recent years, humanitarian agencies have become more aware of the risks of corruption and have taken many steps to deal with these risks. However, there are remaining gaps that could be addressed both by better sharing of good practices within the humanitarian community, and by looking to good examples from outside of it. Also, many of the mechanisms agencies use to track and control normal financial and human resource procedures along with program quality mechanisms can be used to mitigate the risk of corruption and counter its effects. Agencies have put in place specific mechanisms to mitigate corruption risks, most notably "whistleblower" programs and strengthened internal audit functions. However, findings here suggest that the former are better known in headquarters than in field operations.

These findings also suggest that many humanitarian workers have a narrow view of what constitutes corruption, seeing it primarily as a financial issue, rather than abuse of power.

This report makes a series of recommendations as to how the humanitarian community might move forward to increase discussion of corruption issues, develop improved systems to mitigate risk and better ensure its detection.

Based on findings from this study, recommendations to humanitarian agencies include:

- Work to reduce or remove the "taboo" in discussing corruption in humanitarian assistance and promote greater transparency in reporting corrupt abuse of aid, by providing leadership, changing staff incentives and setting up safe and effective complaint mechanisms

- Communicate to staff that preventing corruption is an important part of the current focus on program quality and accountability, not purely a program-support issue, particularly through incorporating the issue of corruption in induction and training programs
- Communicate that corruption extends beyond fraudulent financial practices to "nonfinancial corruption" such as nepotism/cronyism, sexual exploitation and abuse, coercion and intimidation of humanitarian staff or aid recipients for personal, social or political gain, manipulation of assessments, targeting and registration to favour particular groups, and diversion of assistance to non-target groups
- Incorporate corruption risk analysis into emergency preparedness and disaster risk reduction strategies and strengthen surge capacity
- Ensure that agency policies and procedures that can directly or indirectly mitigate corruption (for example, whistleblower policies) are effectively disseminated and implemented at field level and that standard policies are adapted for emergency contexts
- Give greater attention to setting up good financial, administrative, procurement and human resources systems from the very beginning of an emergency response, including mechanisms to guard against "burn rate" pressures
- Improve the overall transparency of information (resource flows, assessments, program elements, targeting criteria, aid recipient lists, entitlements, etc.)
- Allocate greater resources to program monitoring, especially field monitoring
- Address corruption risks in the selection, monitoring and capacity-building of partners
- Strengthen downward accountability practices as a way of preventing and detecting corruption
- Deepen the scope of audits beyond "the paper trail" to include forensic objectives and practices
- Increase the use of independent external evaluation, including peer review mechanisms
- Encourage inter-agency coordination at national and international levels for information sharing and for joint action on corruption emanating from the external environment

**Reflection and Discussion**

1. What are some reasons why mission/aid workers may "have a narrow view of what constitutes corruption, seeing it primarily as a financial issue, rather than abuse of power?"
2. List three ways that the recommendations can apply to your organization/setting.
3. What can you do personally to help prevent financial fraud and "non-financial corruption"?
4. Comment on Christ's statements in Luke 12:15 and 16:11: Beware and be on your guard against every form of greed. If you have not been faithful in using unrighteous riches, then who will entrust you with true riches?

\* \* \* \* \* \*

# Healing the Body
*Kelly O'Donnell*

### Member Care and the Body of Christ: Part 2

*Agnus Dei qui tollis peccata mundi*
*miserere nobis.*

We are looking at "wounds" in the Body of Christ. We are relating specific paintings of Christ's "passion" from *El Prado* Museum in Madrid, to the mission/member care world. The level of health/dysfunction (wounds) in our own communities will be reproduced in the communities that we seek to strengthen and form. This goes for teams, churches, families, organizations, and movements.

The painting below, *The Descent from the Cross*, was done around 1435 by the Flemish artist Rogier van der Weyden. Who among us also, like Joseph of Arimathea and Nicodemus the Pharisee (John 19:38-39) has the moral courage to request and to hold and to care for the broken Body?

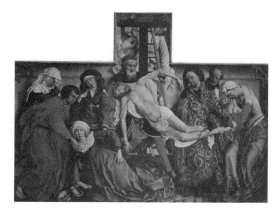

"He shall crush you on the head and you shall bruise him on the heel."
(Gen. 3:15)

---

**Reflection and Discussion**

1. Is there something within your sphere of influence that requires you to respond with moral courage?

2. In what ways have you requested, held, and cared for the broken Body?

3. Cover ups, at any level, ultimately work against those who try to hide wrongdoing. Comment on this statement in light of this verse: We will not prosper if we cover a transgression. But if we confess and forsake our transgressions, we will find mercy (Prov. 28:13).

# PART THREE
## Ethics and Human Rights in Member Care
## Developing Guidelines for Mission/Aid

*"All human beings are born free and equal in
dignity and rights. They are endowed with reason
and conscience and should act towards one another
in a spirit of brotherhood."*

UNIVERSAL DECLARATION OF HUMAN RIGHTS, 1948

Shining light on rights and wrongs. © 2008 Kelly O'Donnell

W E IN MEMBER CARE ARE QUITE A DIVERSE GROUP. We come from so many countries, training backgrounds, and organizations. Part Three discusses the need to further develop ethical care in light of our diversity. The two broad purposes are to provide a relevant framework for member care ethics and to discuss how an understanding of human rights is essential for good member care. Both the emphasis on a broad-based ethical framework and the relevance of human rights are new contributions to the development of the member care field.

By "ethical" I mean in accordance with recognized guidelines which promote responsible care and good practice. Such guidelines deal with areas like confidentiality, skill competencies, continuing growth, accountability, sensitivity to human diversity, and organizational responsibility for staff care.

## "Better a broken heart than a broken promise."
### FAMILY PROVERBS

Part Three of *Pearls and Perils* is an expanded and updated version of "Upgrading Member Care: Five Stones for Ethical Practice," originally published in *Evangelical Missions Quarterly* July 2006, pp. 344-355. Chapter 9 describes a rationale for ethics and gives several examples of ethical issues in member care. These foundational comments set the stage to consider five types of guidelines that are important for ethical practice. The first four guidelines are explored in Chapter 10: member care worker commitments, sending group principles, ethical rationalizations, and specific ethics codes. Chapter 11 delves deeply into human rights principles, addressing how this overlooked area is essential for good practice in member care. Throughout these chapters I have interspersed several "Ethics Sensitizers" which are short exercises to help you think through and apply the material. I finish, as in all three Parts of *Pearls and Perils,* with several materials to stimulate your personal and professional growth (Chapter 12).

> *"I will prescribe regimens for the good of my patients*
> *according to my ability and my judgment*
> *and never do harm to anyone."*
>
> HIPPOCRATIC OATH, 5TH CENTURY BC

Part Three can thus help us all to upgrade the ethical quality of the supportive care that we offer mission/aid staff. The material is meant for caregivers from different cultural backgrounds, including member care workers, leaders, staff, and sending organizations (agency/church).

Ethical care is not a code but rather a mentality, a practice, and a commitment. It is based on moral law and our duty to fellow humans.

# PEARLS
## ENHANCING AND ENRICHING GOOD PRACTICE

*The commitment to doing good and doing no harm are bedrocks of ethical practice.*

*An ethical mentality helps us to think and work through ethical issues.*

*Sacrifice and suffering are a normal part of mission/aid work.*

*Christ's relationship with us models the types of healthy relationships we have with others.*

*Regular consultation with others helps safeguard our ethical practice.*


# PERILS
## ENCUMBERING AND ENDANGERING GOOD PRACTICE

*Confusion about normative ethics due to limited experience and the diversity of member caregivers.*

*Standards in one country/discipline can dominate how we harmonize ethics internationally.*

*Only emphasizing common sense and personal morality for practicing ethical member care.*

*Sending groups and member care workers do not anticipate and discuss together possible ethical issues.*

*Not taking the time to reflect and ask questions about the ethical nature of our work.*

# CHAPTER 9

# Encountering Ethical Member Care

"I BELIEVE IN DISCRETION MORE THAN CONFIDENTIALITY WHEN
DEALING WITH SENSITIVE INFORMATION."

"OUR TEAM IS FAR TOO BUSY TO FOLLOW-UP THIS DIFFICULT MATTER—
SOMEONE ELSE WILL HAVE TO DO IT."

"THIS MISTAKE MUST NOT DISCREDIT OUR ORGANIZATION AND
REPUTATION BY COMING INTO PUBLIC VIEW."

"IF PEOPLE FOCUS ON RIGHTS THEN THEY WILL BECOME SELF-CENTERED
AND NEGLECT THEIR RESPONSIBILITIES."

———————

There are some tricky waters to navigate when we provide member care. What is confidential information? When are we working outside of our competencies? To what extent are senders responsible to safeguard the well-being of their workers? We need to think ethically and to act ethically, based on recognized standards, as we seek to support the mission/aid community with our services and resources.

Member care is a broad field with a wide range of people who provide it. As this field continues to grow, it is important to offer guidelines to further clarify and shape good practice. Any guidelines must carefully consider the fact of the field's international diversity, and blend together the best interests of both service receivers and service providers. They also need to be applicable to member care workers (MCWs) with different types of training and experience. No one set of standards from a particular country or a particular health-related discipline should dominate. This is a challenging task to undertake, and it is one that must be done in consultation with many others and on an ongoing basis. Trying to differentiate between codes, guidelines, frameworks, and suggestions is yet another important aspect of this challenging task.

## RATIONALE FOR AND REVIEW OF ETHICS

Let's begin with a bit of history and look at five premises that influence the ethical practice of member care (see Box 1). Underlying all of these premises are the core commitments of *beneficence and nonmaleficence*. These terms simply mean that we intentionally seek *to do good* and *to do no harm, respectively,* within our spheres of practice and influence. They are embedded in the *Hippocratic Oath* from the 5th century BC and explicitly mentioned or reflected in so many of the ethical codes in human health areas (e.g., American Psychological Association, *Ethical Principles of Psychologists and Code of Conduct,* 2002, p. 3). For more information on the applications of the *Hippocratic Oath* to member care, see the weblog entries from June through September 2009 at: www.COREmembercare.blogspot.com.

---

### Box 1. Five Premises for Ethical Member Care

First, staff are *humans with intrinsic worth* and not just *resources with strategic worth*. We appreciate for who they are as well as for what they do.

Second, ethical care is concerned with both the *well-being of every one* involved in mission in aid. This includes the well-being of the organization, its purposes, and its personnel.

Third, *sacrifice and suffering* are normal parts of mission/aid work. We acknowledge yet try to mitigate against the serious negative consequences that accompany work in risky places.

Fourth, we encourage balancing the demands of professional work with the desires for personal growth. Personnel need to find a good work-life balance so they can both *run well and rest well.*

Fifth, *how* we provide services to staff is as significant as the actual services themselves. We respect the dignity and rights of all people and thus provide quality care, *carefully.*

---

These five premises are both values and commitments that can be explicitly identified, discussed and further developed. These premises need to be understood for how they positively influence the ethical decisions necessary for good member care practice. They also can be understood as being *protective factors* to safeguard the purposes and personnel of sending groups. Consider the following three examples of some common ethical challenges in mission/aid (Box 2). As you will see, applying these premises is not always a straightforward process. How would you apply these five premises in light of the commitment to do good and to do no harm?

---

### Box 2. Common Ethical Challenges in Member Care

**Competence.** An experienced consultant makes recommendations to a humanitarian organization based in Asia. The consultant is addressing the care of their emergency staff working in a mass disaster area, rampant with cholera and malaria. The consultant is vaguely familiar with that cultural context and the organization itself. To what extent does the consultant need to inform the agency about limitations in his/her background? When is it OK to "stretch" beyond one's areas of training and experience? What if no one else is readily available to offer advice? So is the consultant acting competently?

**Confidentiality.** A compassionate leader informally exchanges a few emails with a man in their organization who has marital struggles. The man tells the leader that he and his wife have frequent fights that can be overheard by African neighbors. He is also drinking a local alcoholic beverage most nights. Later, the leader prays with his own wife about the other couple's struggles. Is it OK for one's spouse to know such things? Is the disclosure of "significant problems" protected information? Would asking the leader to not share be "secretive"? So what type of confidentiality is appropriate?

**Responsibility.** A reputable sending organization shortens a family's field preparation from three months to one month. The reason is so that the husband, a medical doctor, can cover a crucial and vacant position in a refugee clinic in the Middle East. To what extent does making such "adjustments" simply reflect the realities of mission/aid work? What if "lives," or a large funding grant, are at stake? So to what extent is the organization acting responsibly towards the family and towards the refugee patients?

---

Many other types of ethical issues get stirred up in mission/aid settings, not the least of which are managing multiple roles and different types of relationships with sending groups/workers (Barber and Hall, 1996). Just a few of the many examples are listed in Box 3. It is important for sending groups and MCWs to anticipate and discuss such issues together. We thus need to be very conversant with the values, ethical principles, and guidelines that shape our decisions It is also important to acknowledge that our personal morality and common sense are helpful but usually only go so far. We all want to do a good job at managing and supporting our mission/aid staff. The materials here and in the remaining chapters will help us move in this direction!

---

### Box 3. More Ethical Issues in Mission/Aid

- Assessing physical/mental disabilities during selection, including those of children (e.g., whether hiring, locating, or promoting staff is based on such disabilities)
- Determining who has access to personnel files (e.g., if team leaders have access to team members' personnel files, especially "negative" information)
- Working in stressful settings with limited supervision, contingency plans, and personal debriefing (e.g., whether senders can support staff adequately in isolated settings and/or with extreme stressors)
- Consulting with people with whom one has many types of social/work relationships (e.g., whether to do conflict mediation for an interagency group that includes folks from your agency)
- Confronting the unhealthy and harmful practices of leaders and other staff
- (e.g., how to protect staff that point out problems; whether certain lifestyle choices are private affairs)

---

## PERSPECTIVES ON GOOD PRACTICE

Good practice is a term and a concept that is widely used in the health care, mission, and many other fields. It refers to principles and standards for practice in a field which are derived from expert consensus and/or evidence-based research. Two examples are the Sphere Projects' *Humanitarian Charter and Minimum Standards in Disaster Response* (2004, available in over ten languages at www.sphereproject.org; revision in 2011) and the *Code of Conduct* of the International Red Cross (1994, www.ifrc.org/publicat/conduct/). From a Christian perspective, I see good practice in member care as being rooted in the example of the care offered by Christ, the "Good Practitioner." Consider the "continuum of care" in Box 4 below, which is adapted from chapter 1 in *Doing Member Care Well* (2002). It illustrates how Christ's relationship with us serves as a foundation for our interaction with others.

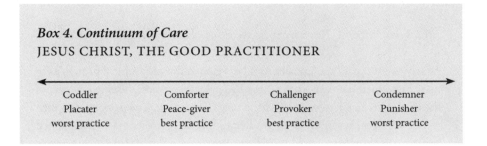

**Box 4. Continuum of Care**
JESUS CHRIST, THE GOOD PRACTITIONER

| Coddler | Comforter | Challenger | Condemner |
|---------|-----------|------------|-----------|
| Placater | Peace-giver | Provoker | Punisher |
| worst practice | best practice | best practice | worst practice |

The middle two dimensions of being *comforted/challenged* are normative for us, and reflect many of Christ's encounters with disciples in the New Testament. The extremes on the continuum represent "worst practice" and do not reflect His relationship with us. Likewise, they should not reflect our relationships with mission/aid personnel—that is, overly protecting them and not sufficiently challenging them (coddling), or blaming them for having needs/frailties (condemning). Christ is both tender and at times tough with us, in His relentless love for us to be conformed to His image—what is best for us. His example points the way for us as we provide and develop member care ethically.

Good practice in member care involves more than simply identifying the right general ethical guidelines and then trying to apply them in appropriate, situation-specific ways. Rather it is fundamentally a way of *thinking through* problems, our practices, and the possible consequences of our actions. It is a *mentality*. It is a mentality which in my experience is still lacking in much of the mainstream member care community. It is not a question of morality, but rather a reflection of the need to develop a pervasive mental mindset for ethics over time through training, experience, and reviewing various scenarios with others.

Let's take our encounter with ethics one step further. Ethical reflections must also be included in any of the collaborative work we do. So this means exploring the ethical dimension not just in how we help others but how we help others review how they help others. In other words, *the way* we set up and conduct things like peer consultation, supervision, and case discussions is clearly within the domain of ethical reflection as well. Good ethical thinking is needed in all of our work.

Here are three materials that I have found helpful to further strengthen my skills and thinking about ethics. I like these materials because they are filled with so many cases, real struggles, challenging issues, and seasoned principles related to ethical practice. The first two are books: *Culture and the Clinical Encounter* (1996), *Ethics in Plain English* (2005), and *Assessing and Managing Risk in Psychological Practice* (2006). The third item is the special issue on ethics in an outstanding publication, *Psychotherapy Networker* (03/2003, www.psychotherapynetworker.org). These materials are written mostly in a North American context yet you will likely find many commonalities and applications to other locations.

*Ethics Sensitizer 1. Reviewing Some Ethics History in Member Care*

Nearly twenty years ago my wife and I developed five core ethical principles to help guide member care work. These five principles were presented as part of the case study in Chapter 19 of *Missionary Care* (1992). The principles in turn were built upon seven previous guidelines that were presented and explained in some depth in Chapter 44 in *Helping Missionaries Grow* (1988). Let's have a look at these five principles again from 1992. They can give us a better sense of some of the ethical thinking in our field and what ethics entail.

**Organizational Responsibility**. Mission agencies acknowledge responsibility for the quality of care they provide staff. They seek to develop integrated, comprehensive member care services which are periodically reviewed to determine their effectiveness. They also make reasonable efforts to ensure the appropriate use of these services.

**Confidentiality**. Mission organizations and member care workers have clear policies based on the legal and organizational limits of confidentiality. Ownership and accessibility to counseling and personnel records must be clarified in advance with staff. In general, staff have the right to determine how information which they have disclosed in confidence can be shared. Confidentiality procedures must be clarified for in-house consultants and counselors who are responsible to protect the interests of the organization in addition to the individual.

**Counselor/Consultant Competence**. Member care workers are dedicated to high standards of competence in the interest of the individuals and mission agencies which they serve. They recognize the limits of their training, experience, and skills and work only in those areas where they are qualified. They also endeavor to maintain and develop their competencies.

**Use of Testing**. Only qualified individuals are to administer and interpret psychological, educational, and vocational tests. Those who provide testing services safeguard their tests and take precautions to prevent the inappropriate use of test results. Individuals have the right to receive feedback on their test results and to know the basis for arriving at any recommendations and decisions.

**Personal Values and Legal Standards**. Member care workers and mission leaders are aware of the values and standards held by the organization and the society in which they work. They are sensitive as to how these values, as well as their own, might impact the agency and its staff. Legal regulations regarding the provision of mental health services are understood and followed.

### Applications

1. How would you apply some of these principles to a member care situation in which you are currently involved?
2. Are there any additional core principles that guide your work and should be included in this list? If so, which ones?
3. Which ethical issues are you most likely to face in your settings?

## FINAL THOUGHTS

I want to conclude with a concrete example about having an ethical mentality that shapes our practice. Let's suppose that a mission worker sends us an email expressing her concerns about her five year old child who is constantly "misbehaving" at home. She is Swiss and lives and works in Uganda. We as member care providers are Brazilian and live and work in Singapore. Four countries in four continents are "represented" here.

Before we send an email response to the question about how to handle a child's misbehavior, we want to shift into ethics mode and to "think ethically." The same goes for any other issues such as consulting about: a depressed team member, an alcoholic relative back in a person's passport country, residual fears for local staff following a major earthquake, or a manager's conflict with an organizational policy. We thus pause and ask ourselves how ethics is involved in this matter:

- Are there any special jurisdiction issues and special laws regarding the countries involved?
- Who may be seeing our communications, now and in the future?
- Do the communication exchanges need to be encrypted?
- Do I respond informally as a colleague or officially on behalf of an organization or as an MCW?
- Do I have enough information to offer input and how accurate is the information that I do have?
- Should I consult with anyone about the situation?
- Which ethical guidelines are relevant?
- What may be the consequences of my response/advice?

Do the above questions sound familiar? Or do some seem a bit strange to you? Are there other questions that could be asked? The last question is especially important and is something to always consider after we have gone through our usual questions. *Remember, there is always an ethical context and mentality that accompany our member care work!*

# PEARLS
## ENHANCING AND ENRICHING GOOD PRACTICE

*Ethical practice requires recognized standards, quality services,
and ongoing development.*

*Member care workers are committed to provide the best services in the
best interests of others.*

*Character, competence, and compassion are core parts of member caregivers'
qualities and qualifications.*

*Sending groups regularly monitor how member care is being integrated into their
overall goals.*

*Get the core ethical guidelines that you need and don't be overwhelmed with the many
codes and guidelines available.*


# PERILS
## ENCUMBERING AND ENDANGERING GOOD PRACTICE

*There can be a mismatch between the diversity of member care workers
and the types of ethical guidelines that are available.*

*Many senders have minimal resources and limited experience for supporting
and managing their staff well.*

*The mission/aid settings with the greatest needs are often the riskiest
for mission/aid workers.*

*We are all hard-wired to rationalize the various mistakes and ethical
blunders that we make.*

*You will likely do yourself and others harm if you do not take advantage
of the consolidated wisdom found in relevant ethical guidelines
and experienced colleagues.*

# CHAPTER 10

# Pursuing Trans-Cultural Ethics

ETHICAL CARE AND ETHICAL GUIDELINES CAN MEAN DIFFERENT THINGS TO
DIFFERENT PEOPLE. HOW CAN WE HARMONIZE OUR DIFFERENT AND AT TIMES
DIVERGENT WAYS OF DOING ETHICAL MEMBER CARE? IS IT POSSIBLE TO EVEN DO SO?
LET'S HAVE A CLOSE LOOK AT FOUR BROAD AREAS (CALLED STONES) FOR
PRACTITIONERS AND SENDERS THAT INCLUDE RECOMMENDED GUIDELINES
AND APPLICATIONS. WE ARE ON A JOURNEY TO FIND AN ETHICAL FRAMEWORK AND
ETHICAL PRINCIPLES THAT ARE RELEVANT FOR THE DIVERSITY
OF PEOPLE IN MISSION/AID.

Many types of professional ethical codes exist that can relate to the practice of member care. For some practitioners, these codes are essential and are a good "fit." But one size does not fit all! For example, as a psychologist and as international affiliates of the American Psychological Association (APA), my wife and I abide by the APA's *Ethical Principles of Psychologists and Code of Conduct* (2002). But a skilled Nigerian pastor providing trauma training/care in Sudan may not find this code so helpful. Such ethical codes are primarily relevant for the disciplines and countries for which they were intended. Yet many member care workers (MCWs) enter the member care field via a combination of their life experiences and informal training, and are not part of a professional association with a written ethics code. So appealing to another country or discipline's ethical code can result in a rather cumbersome mismatch between the person and the code.

This "mismatch" is akin to the story of David being outfitted in Saul's armor as he prepared to fight Goliath. The armor was far too cumbersome for his smaller body size and hence it would likely be more of a liability than an asset in battle. He clearly needed his more familiar, custom-fitted arms that fit his frame and fighting strategy: namely, his staff and his sling along with five carefully-selected, smooth stones (I Sam. 17).

By analogy, like David we need to carefully identify *relevant ethical guidelines* that fit into our cultural and experiential "slings." In other words, MCWs and sending groups must choose stones which can further shape their ethical mentality and guide their member care practice. What might some of these stones and guidelines look like? In this chapter I will discuss four types of stones and in the next chapter a fifth stone (see Box 1). I will also recommend some core guidelines as part of each stone.

*Box 1. Five Stones for Ethical Member Care*

Stone 1: Good Practice Commitments for MCWs
Stone 2: Good Practice Principles for Senders
Stone 3: Sub-standards for Poor Practice
Stone 4: Specific Codes for Good Practice
Stone 5: Human Rights Principles (see Chapter 11)

Each of these five stones are under-girded by the commitment to do good and to do no harm (that is, of *beneficence and nonmaleficence* (as described in Chapter 9). They promote four indispensable emphases.

- *Quality services* by MCWs and senders
- *Ongoing development* for senders and MCWs
- *Recognized standards* for those who are using/providing MCW services
- *Protection* for service receivers via safeguards.

✶ ✶ ✶ ✶ ✶ ✶

# Stone One
## Good Practice Commitments for Member Care Workers[1]

Stone One reflects the need for a generic set of guidelines for all types MCWs. The specific example given offers ten basic *commitments*. It focuses on the personal characteristics, backgrounds, and relationships needed to practice member care ethically. The underlying principle is for MCWs to provide the best services possible in the best interests of the people whom they serve. Like all the stones, Stone One is intended to be referred to regularly, to be discussed with colleagues, and to be applied in light of the variations in our backgrounds. Further, it requires serious reflection and a serious consideration of the implications for one's life and work—these are not just "suggestions" but commitments. The "look before you leap" warning in Prov. 20:25 is instructive here: "It is a snare for a person to say rashly, 'It is holy!' and after the vows to make inquiry."

Stone One is also relevant for sending groups. Sending groups that solicit/receive MCW services for their staff are responsible to carefully choose MCWs, both in-house and outside MCWs. The ten commitments in this Stone One example, in combination with reviewing references and educational/experiential backgrounds, can thus also serve as a grid to help evaluate prospective service providers.

---

### Stone One. Recommended Guidelines
TEN COMMITMENTS FOR MEMBER CARE WORKERS

1. Ongoing training, personal growth, and self-care.
2. Ongoing accountability for my personal/work life, including consultation/ supervision.
3. Recognizing my strengths/limits and representing my skills/ background accurately.
4. Understanding/respecting felt needs, culture, and diversity of those with whom I work.
5. Working with other colleagues, and making referrals when needed.
6. Preventing problems and offering supportive/restorative and at times pro bono services.
7. Having high standards in my services and embracing specific ethical guidelines.
8. Acknowledging different disciplinary/regulatory norms for different MCWs.
9. Abiding by any legal requirements for offering member care where I reside/ practice.
10. Growing in my relationship to Christ, the Good Practitioner.

---

### Core Personal Qualities and Qualifications ($Q^2$ core)
Character, competence, and compassion are necessary for good practice in member care. These "three C's" are both qualities for MCWs to develop and qualifications for MCWs to demonstrate. The same goes for any person with member care responsibility or who is in a caregiver role. The centrality of one's character, competence, and compassion are embedded in the ten commitments identified in Stone One.

**Character**: This $Q^2$ core refers to moral virtue, emotional stability, and overall maturity. Basically, the qualifications for leaders in I Tim. 3 and Titus 1 reflect the types of character traits needed for MCWs (e.g., being: above reproach, temperate, prudent, respectable, hospitable, able to teach, managing one's household well, sensible, just, devout, self-controlled, etc.). Those in member care ministry have positions of trust and responsibility, and work with people who are often in a vulnerable place. Therefore they need to model godly characteristics as they minister responsibly—to protect/provide for those who receive their services.

**Applications**: MCWs like anyone else can experience serious problems, including emotional, family, or moral struggles. In such cases, the quality of MCWs' services can decrease, and MCWs will need help, accountability, and often a break for restoration. If MCWs cannot manage their own life well, how will they manage the mission/aid "household" (1 Tim. 3:4-5)? Member care receivers expect Christian MCWs to model a healthy, godly lifestyle, and to maintain a close relationship with the Lord.

*Commitments 1, 2,* and *10* are the most relevant for MCW character. These include personal growth, accountability, and relationship with Christ.

**Competence**: This $Q^2$ *core* refers to having the necessary skills to help well (via life experience and training). I have found that competence is not necessarily based on degrees or certification, although the systematic training that is required to get these "validations" is a very important consideration. Others without such institutional validation are also capable of doing member care well (usually via more supportive than specialized care), and indeed in many places they are the primary service providers (e.g., peers, team leaders). Note that MCWs, like others in the health care fields, can be "stretched" at times to work in ways that may go beyond their skill level. And many services can be in ambiguous, complex, and difficult settings, with the outcomes (positive or negative) not easy to predict. Note also that certification as a "professional" and skill sets useful in one country may not be relevant in other locations. Caution and consultation with others are needed in such cases.

**Applications**: Christian workers in South Asia are being trained to provide pastoral care for staff in their organizations. Most do not have backgrounds in the health sciences. But they are mature people who have been chosen by their leaders to receive special training twice a year, in areas like basic counseling, crisis care, running a personnel office, and team building. They also have access to the trainers for case consultation via email/telephone. These MCWs reflect a growing number of caregivers who are recognized within their organizations as being able to offer helpful services. Another example is the "peer debriefers" being trained in Africa as a first line of help when critical incidents occur.

*Commitments 1, 2, 3, 8,* and *9* are especially important for MCW competence. These include ongoing training, getting consultation/supervision, knowing strengths/limits, acknowledging different MCW norms, abiding by legal requirements.

**Compassion**: This $Q^2$ *core* refers to our core motivation for member care work. It is the love of Christ that compels us. We value people and we provide our services to people because of their inherent worth, and not just because of their "important" work. Likewise experiencing a sense a fulfillment in our member care work, although desirable and an honorable motive, is not the primary reason for why we do what we do. Our motives for providing member care are often refined by the many challenges that ripple through our lives and work—especially disappointments via such experiences as minimal recognition, minimal compensation, and/or minimal opportunities within one's "career trajectory."

**Applications**: MCWs often sacrificially give of themselves. They do so not to compensate for personal deficits but rather from a compassionate commitment to help others grow. Compassion has limits, and MCWs need to be aware of their boundaries and practice self-care. Nonetheless, there are times and even seasons when serving others is costly— and helping may be done out of a sense of duty and obedience; and it may temporarily "interrupt" our commitment to self-care (e.g., the tired disciples being asked to serve the crowds—Luke 9:10-17).

 *Commitments 1, 5,* and *10* are key for maintaining MCW compassion. These include self-care, respecting felt needs, and relationship with Christ.

---

*Stone One Ethics Sensitizer. Reflection and Discussion*
WHEN IS INFORMATION CONSIDERED "CONFIDENTIAL" ?

The basic consensus among professional codes of ethics is that any information shared during the course of professional services is considered to be "privileged" information. This means that only the "client" (the person asking for help/receiving services) can determine when and how this information can be shared by the helper/member care worker. There are a few important exceptions however when there is a danger to self/others . Confidentiality is a core part of the helping relationship, and a foundation for trust and good practice. It is not just a matter of MCWs simply being "discrete" —which can be interpreted in many different ways—and relying on one's own "good" judgment concerning disclosures. Rather the MCW abides by a strict standard that honors the client's rights. Here are two confidentiality examples.

**Example One: Member Care Associates**
**Confidentiality (from Service Agreement)**
We want you to know that what you share with us is confidential. The only exception, in compliance with most laws (e.g., American and European), is when: a) you or someone's life may be in danger (e.g., child/elder abuse, suicidal/homicidal threat, gravely disabled); or b) explicit written permission by you has been given to waive confidentiality. Other types of personal struggles can significantly interfere with one's work role and/or credibility of one/s organization (e.g., abusive leadership, addictions, major depression, moral failure, serious marital conflict.) In such cases we usually encourage you to inform a leader whom you trust within your organization(s). We see such struggles as being larger than the helping relationship, and thus usually best handled with the involvement and support of others. Note for group or debriefing services: The material shared by others during the group/debriefing sessions will be kept strictly confidential by the participants.

**Example Two: American Association for Marriage and Family Therapy (AAMFT)**
**Confidentiality (*Code of Ethics*, July 2001)**
*www.aamft.org/resources/lrm_plan/Ethics/ethicscode2001.asp*
Marriage and family counselors/therapists often work with more than one person in a family. It is important to guard each client's confidence but it can be challenging at times. The AAMFT has developed six points relating to confidentiality. The main ideas in each point are listed below. Be sure to see the full code at the AAMFT site listed above.

1.  Discuss the nature of confidentiality to clients and any others involved in the case.
2.  Do not disclose information without written authorization or unless disclosure is required by law.
3.  Confidentiality is protected when using examples for teaching, writing, research, etc.
4.  Clarity about how to safeguard and destroy records of clients
5.  Clarity about how to deal with client records when closing a practice, moving, or dying.
6.  When/how to disclose information if one consults with colleagues about a case.

**Applications**

1. In what ways are the above standards relevant to member care workers who provide more "informal" services, or who do not have a "professional" certification, or who are not therapists, or who come from different countries?

2. How thorough and how specific should such standards be, for different settings, including counseling, team meetings, or internet communications?

3. Confidentiality sometimes leads to misunderstandings. For example, it can be seen as being secretive and withholding important information from an organization about its staff. How can this be minimized?

\* \* \* \* \* \*

## Stone Two
### Good Practice Principles for Sending Organizations

Stone Two focuses on the crucial role of sending groups to responsibly support and manage their staff well, including their international staff, local/national staff, home office staff, and family members of their staff. It also considers the big picture of member care from recruitment through retirement and the commitment to nurture both organizational and staff health. The international model of member care in Chapter 1 of *Doing Member Care Well* (2002) refers to sending groups as the "sustainers" of member care. "They demonstrate (their) commitment by the way they invest themselves and their resources, including finances, into staff care. Sending groups aspire to have a comprehensive, culturally relevant, and sustainable approach to member care, including a commitment to organizational development." (p. 18). Sending groups do well to offer quality services for staff and to expect quality services from staff.

The specific example for Stone Two is from the *Code of Good Practice in the Management and Support of Aid Personnel*[2] (2003) developed by People In Aid in the United Kingdom. It includes seven principles and several key indicators (specific criteria to demonstrate how the principles are practiced). Sending groups can use it to help them monitor how their member care (human resources) policies are integrated into their overall goals. These principles are effective when they are understood and embraced at all levels of the sending group, and implemented by skilled managers with integrity. For more information see the complete Code and related documents at: www.peopleinaid.org.

*Stone Two. Recommended Guidelines*
SEVEN PRINCIPLES FOR SENDERS

*(Code of Good Practice from People In Aid, 2003)*

**Principle 1: Human Resources Strategy.**
*Human resources are an integral part of our strategic and operational plans.*
    The organization allocates sufficient human and financial resources to achieve the objectives of the human resources strategy.

**Principle 2: Staff Policies and Practices.**
*Our human resources policies aim to be effective, fair and transparent.*
    Polices and practices that relate to staff employment are in writing, monitored, and reviewed. Staff are familiarized with policies and practices that affect them.

**Principle 3: Managing People.**
*Good support, management and leadership of our staff is key to our effectiveness.*
    Staff have clear work objectives and performance standards, know whom they report to and what management support they will receive. All staff are aware of grievance and disciplinary procedures.

**Principle 4: Consultation and Communication.**
*Dialogue with staff on matters likely to affect their employment enhances the quality and effectiveness of our policies and practices.*
    Staff are informed and adequately consulted when we develop or review human resources policies or practices that affect them.

**Principle 5: Recruitment and Selection.**
*Our policies and practices aim to attract and select a diverse workforce with the skills and capabilities to fulfil our requirements.*
    Written policies and procedures outline how staff are recruited and selected to positions in our organization. Our selection process is fair, transparent, and consistent.

**Principle 6: Learning, Training and Development.**
*Learning, training and staff development are promoted throughout the organization.*

Adequate induction, and briefing specific to each role, is given to all staff. Written policies outline the training, development, and learning opportunities staff can expect from the organization.

**Principle 7: Health, Safety and Security.**
*The security, good health, and safety of our staff are a prime responsibility of our organization.*

Written policies are available to staff on security, individual health, care and support, health and safety. Program plans include written assessment of security, travel and health risks specific to the country or region, reviewed at appropriate intervals.

Before an international assignment, all staff receive health clearance. In addition, they and accompanying dependents receive verbal and written briefing on all risks relevant to the role to be undertaken, and the measures in place to mitigate those risks, including insurance… Briefings are updated when new equipment, procedures, or risks are identified. All staff have a debriefing or exit interview at the end of any contract or assignment. Health checks, personal counseling, and careers advice are available. Managers are trained to ensure these services are provided.

## *Where There Are No (Well-Resourced) Senders*

There are a couple important counterpoints for the guidelines suggested in Stone Two. First, not all mission/aid workers actually have "senders." At least many may not have an ongoing long-term sender as they may work from contract to contract and from agency to agency. Others workers do things much more on their own without a sending group per se. Their charitable work and Christian witness are done as part of their lifestyle in a host culture. Many mission/aid workers surely wish that a sender would be able to support and manage them in ways that are recommended in Stone Two!

Second, for some sending groups themselves, these guidelines may seem overly idealistic at best and inappropriately constrictive at worst. Senders coming from philosophically different, or less-experienced, or financially-limited settings may not be on the same page about what is "needed" to do mission/aid and member care well. For instance some senders may default to the practice of sending out "naked" mission workers who have no apparent resources other than to follow the biblical injunction Christ gave his disciples to go without an extra coat, staff, or money. These folks embody that commitment, without an expectation of returning to their home country for furlough or retirement. This may seem extreme, but it does reflect the other end point of the sender's continuum for providing "comprehensive" member care. On a related note, in her concluding chapter in *Sharing the Front Line and Back Hills* (2002), Danieli describes how some potential contributors to her edited work dismissed her effort as "preposterous or obscene." The reason was that she was focusing on aid workers themselves—the protectors and providers—rather than on what was perceived to be the far more needy victims who needed help (p. 388).

**Applications**: A sending church in Europe helps support ten mission/aid workers. The workers are part of separate agencies and they work on four different continents. Their biggest issue is maintaining communication with these workers, and feeling connected with each other. Most of the responsibilities for "managing and supporting staff" are assumed to lie with the sending agency rather than the church. During the past year one of these workers was severely injured in a car crash and needs months of intensive physiotherapy, while another suffers from recurrent malaria. What to do?

**Good Practice**: Each worker is assigned a volunteer advocate from church who stays in monthly contact with the worker. The mission coordinator reviews these seven good practice principles with the church pastors and elders. They agree to adopt these principles, and send copies of the *Code of Good Practice* to the volunteer advocates, the workers, and the sending agencies. Over the next two months the mission coordinator talks with each personnel director from the sending agencies. They review how best to support the respective workers, taking special note of *Principles 4, 6,* and *7* (communication with staff, learning opportunities, health/safety issues.)

**Poor Practice**: The sending church agrees to help send three more mission workers. The addition of three more photos looks pretty good on their world map in the entrance to the church. The mission coordinator gets a copy of the *Code of Good Practice*, reads it with appreciation, and dutifully files it...until a new crisis hits one of their thirteen mission/aid workers.

*Stone Two Ethics Sensitizer. Reflection and Discussion*
WHEN IS IT ETHICAL FOR WORKERS TO BE SENT TO AND
KEPT IN RISKY AREAS?

Workers who serve in cross-cultural settings are often subject to a variety of extreme stressors. Natural disasters, wars, sudden relocation, imprisonment, sickness, and protracted relationship conflicts are but a few of the examples. The general consensus seems to be that sending groups that deploy their people into potentially adverse situations have an ethical responsibility to do all they can to prepare and support them. This thinking is in line with Principle 7 from the People In Aid *Code of Good Practice* (2003) which states, "The security, good health and safety of our staff are a prime responsibility of our organization."

There are so many locations where the social/political situation is very unstable, where there is the possibility of death or serious physical/emotional injury in the course of helping others, and/or more isolated places where there are few supportive member care resources available. The very places that are the neediest are also often the riskiest for mission/aid workers.

**Applications**

1. Risk can also be understood as being part of one's job description, and continuous with the reality that there are always risks in life regardless of one's location or job. But to what extent should mission/aid workers take risks? Does one help victims of car accidents without having protective barriers that can prevent the transmission of HIV through the victims' blood? Does one obey an organizational requirement to evacuate from a war zone knowing that there may be far more dire consequences to the nationals/locals that remain without the protective presence of international peacekeepers and providers? How much information about risk does one need to know in advance of an assignment?

2. How does your theology (or understanding) of sacrifice and suffering fit into the type of risks to which mission/aid workers are exposed? Here are two perspectives/quotes to consider.

   Effective pre-mission training must begin with instilling awareness of the need for security and psychosocial support in the culture of organizations. Patched together, ad hoc, or solely programmatic ef forts will have only minimal impact. Security and support must be integrated, both structurally and functionally, into the mainstream of pre-field mission operations: mission planning, staffing, and budgeting. Yael Danieli (Editor), *Sharing the Front Line and the Back Hills* (2002), p. 383

We have had to ensure that our philosophy of member care, along with our crisis and contingency management approach, respect what God asks of our workers, even though they sometimes go against the prevailing attitude of "safety, security, and reduction of stress levels at all costs," that is characteristic of many Western cultures. Although no worker morbidly desires others to go through pain or suffering, we have come to realize that such experiences, according to scripture and history, normally accompany the spread of God's kingdom. Steve and Kitty Holloway, Responsible Logistics for Hostile Places, *Doing Member Care Well* (2002), p. 447

\* \* \* \* \* \*

## Stone Three
### Sub-Standards for Poor Practice

Stone Three addresses our propensity for rationalizations about our mistakes and errors in making ethical decisions. These rationalizations can be seen as sub-standards that we can unfortunately all-too-easily tolerate or even adopt. The prefix *sub* here refers to standards that are both inferior and wrong.

The recommended guidelines for Stone Three consist of ten common rationalizations for our *faux pas* as practitioners. They are cover-ups. And cover ups, of course, can be just as bad or even worse than the ethical mistakes themselves. Sending organizations and MCWs would benefit by adding to these ten items in light of one's own "preferred" rationalizations. But beware: we can rationalize our rationalizations with "meta-rationalizations." One of the prime examples of a meta-rationalization is the self-serving belief that we do not in fact rationalize. Or a corollary meta-rationalization is to believe that even if we do rationalize, we do so for a very ethical or even noble reason.

I have drawn upon the work of Ken Pope and Melba Vasquez (1999) by adding to and adapting some of the rationalizations that they have identified in the practice of psychology. In the words of these psychologists:

Faced with the complex demands, human costs, constant risks, and often limited resources from our work, we may be tempted to simplify life by changing or overlooking our ethical responsibilities. Not wanting to view ourselves or have others view us as being unethical, we use common fallacies and rationalizations to justify our unethical behaviors and quiet a noisy conscience. These attempts to disguise our unethical behaviors might be called *ethical sub-standards*, although they are not really ethical (p. 1).

Dealing with rationalizations, like dealing with ethical situations, is a skill that we can develop. It is not an all or nothing proposition, but more like a continuum of competence that we develop. It ranges, to borrow from Bennett *et al's* (2006) "taxonomy of risk management," from: "knowledge, comprehension, application (lower levels) to analysis, synthesis, evaluation" (higher levels) (p. 9).

*Stone Three. Recommended Guidelines*
TEN RATIONALIZATIONS TO MONITOR

1. It is ethical as long as you don't know a Bible verse, law, or ethical principle that prohibits it.
2. It is ethical as long as your colleagues or service receivers do not complain about it; or as long as no one else knows or wants to know; or as long as you can convince others that it is OK.
3. It is ethical as long as you or your telecommunications technology were having a "bad day," thus affecting your usual quality of work; or as long as the circumstances and decision were difficult; or as long as you are busy, rushed, or multi-tasking.
4. It is ethical as long as you follow the majority of your ethical guidelines; or as long as you only intend to do it one time.
5. It is ethical as long as there is no intent to do harm, you are being sincere, "your heart is in the right place," and you are trying to do the best that you can.
6. It is ethical as long as you are a moral person; or a nice, competent, or respected person; or as long as you provide *free* services.
7. It is ethical as long as you "take responsibility" for your decision/behavior; or as long as you were acting with "integrity" ; or as long as it does not seem to negatively impact your behavior/emotions.
8. It is ethical as long as the matter is not completely black and white; or as long as someone else is also "wrong or more wrong" than you are; or as long as others do it; or as long as someone in authority over you reassures you or pressures you and asks you to do it.

9. It is ethical as long as you believe/feel it is not unethical or as long as you think God is on your side.

10. It is ethical as long as you are an important person or the most powerful person.

## Trusting and Distorting

Stone Three is part of a larger process and commitment for both sending groups and MCWs to regularly look in the mirror of our hearts. We do this individually and with others in order to scrutinize both our motives and the ethical quality of our member care work. Our own capacity for self-deception and self-justifying revisions of our personal and work-related history give cause for much concern. In addition to reviewing the copious amount of Scriptures that expose our prevarication-prone human nature (e.g., Jer. 17:9), see the compelling work of Tavris and Aronson (2007) on how we distort reality: *Mistakes Were Made (But Not by Me): Why We Justify Foolish Beliefs, Bad Decisions, and Hurtful Acts*). So we have to trust ourselves surely, yet we also must have a healthy respect for the possibility of our own distortions.

**Applications**: At an international member care conference, a group of mission leaders and MCWs discuss member care issues during a special interest group. The facilitator uses the above 10 items as a springboard to discuss how quality services can be compromised. Many tricky examples are voiced: "I needed to do what I thought was best as there was not opportunity to consult a book or colleague;" "I do prayer ministry for depressed people and so professional ethics are not relevant;" and "I am a good person and my good intentions significantly guide how I run the personnel department." The participants then break into small groups to relate these 10 rationalizations with sayings from the book of Proverbs. They also identify a couple safeguards from Stone One (Ten MCW Commitments) to help prevent them from lapsing into ethical sub-standards.

## *Stone Three Ethics Sensitizer. Reflection and Discussion*
### THE CASE OF PHILLIP FAITHFUL[3]

The following fictitious account includes at least twenty-five poor or potentially poor (unethical) practices. Read this study and identify several problems. What is the central problem? How would you help? For some answers check out the analysis of the related case in Chapter 19 of *Missionary Care* (1992) available online at: www.sites.google.com/site/membercaravan/test/mc-counting-the-cost-book.

### The Faithful Family
Phillip, Anne (parents), Fatima, Jerome (children)

Phillip Faithful is a 28-year-old staff member of a large church in Southeast Asia. On the average he works nine to ten hour days and is almost always available to help out when there is a need in the office. He is the type of person who doesn't say no to those over him, sometimes at the expense of his own needs. He often uses part of his vacation time for helping others.

Phillip was raised in Singapore and went to a university in England for two years where he met his wife, Anne. He married at age 24 and has two healthy children, Fatima (age 3) and Jerome (age six months). Currently he and his family live in Jakarta and are involved in work locally and throughout the Asia.

During the last three months Phillip, who is usually very friendly, has become increasingly irritable with his colleagues and somewhat withdrawn with his family. His supervisor noticed these changes and talked to Phillip's wife about what he viewed as "pride and independence" in Phillip. She confided in him that they both feel apathetic and that she has little energy to take care of her home and work responsibilities. The supervisor shares some scripture with her. He then encourages her to talk to Phillip about taking time off to "get back into work shape" and that he talk to someone about his problems. She follows his advice.

Phillip was too busy to take time off but he did agree to contact the Director of Training, Ms. Bartell, for counseling. She is a North American woman who has taken some counseling courses at a Christian University and is recognized for her ability to listen and offer appropriate advice. She also provides counseling to Christians from some of the local churches to supplement her income.

Ms. Bartell works on a fundraising committee in the church with Phillip and three others which meets once a month. Phillip approaches her after a meeting and schedules a time with her to talk and pray about his problems. She also begins to pray regularly for Phillip with the Pastoral Care Committee.

Ms. Bartell obtained Phillips personnel files from the temporary secretary in the Personnel Department to better acquaint herself with his background. Phillip had taken two personality tests as part of the screening process to be accepted on staff. He scored high on the "depression" scale, so she wondered if he had tendencies towards a serious emotional disorder.

Ms. Bartell also decided to speak to Phillip's wife and supervisor to better understand his struggles. The supervisor recommended that Ms. Bartell borrow a "temperament analysis" test and administer it to Phillip in order to further explore his personality. She administered the test and then spoke with the supervisor, suggesting that Phillip be put in a department with less paperwork and more people contact.

Phillip and Ms. Bartell meet for four counseling sessions. They spend most of their time talking about the challenges of raising his two children, his past relationship with his father, and his apprehension to openly talk about his work frustrations with leaders. Ms. Bartell spends time listening for what might be the "root" of his problems, and subsequently advises him to work fewer hours, spend more time with his family, and be more assertive with colleagues.

After the fourth session, Ms. Bartell tells Phillip that she would like to recommend his seeing a visiting leader from a Christian charity from Europe. She feels this person can encourage him and possibly give him more insights into his current situation. Phillip gives her a small honorarium for her services, and a few days later approaches the visiting leader. The leader has never heard anything about Phillip.

\* \* \* \* \* \*

# Stone Four
## Specific Codes for Good Practice

Stone Four involves the need for *specific* guidelines. These guidelines are identified and/or developed for specific MCWs and sending organizations so as to fit with their background and context.

**MCWs.** Some MCWs are specialists and have advanced degrees/certification in their respective disciplines. So in addition to making use of the previous three stones, they possess a fourth stone, which is their respective disciplinary/professional association's code of ethics.[4] For example, for those whose main emphasis and professional identity is human resource management, the code of the Society for Human Resources Management (SHRM, the largest international human resources association) could be a good fit and hence one's forth stone. SHRM's code includes six core principles. The fuller version includes a description of the intentions and guidelines for each principle (www.shrm.org).

*Stone Four. Recommended Guidelines*
SIX PRINCIPLES FOR HUMAN RESOURCE PERSONNEL

*SHRM Code of Ethical and Professional Standards in Human Resource Management*

**Professional Responsibility**
Core Principle: As HR professionals, we are responsible for adding value to the organizations we serve and contributing to the ethical success of those organizations. We accept professional responsibility for our individual decisions and actions. We are also advocates for the profession by engaging in activities that enhance its credibility and value.

**Professional Development**
Core Principle: As professionals we must strive to meet the highest standards of competence and commit to strengthen our competencies on a continuous basis.

**Ethical Leadership**
Core Principle: HR professionals are expected to exhibit individual leadership as a role model for maintaining the highest standards of ethical conduct.

**Fairness and Justice**
Core Principle: As human resource professionals, we are ethically responsible for promoting and fostering fairness and justice for all employees and their organizations.

**Conflicts of Interest**

Core Principle: As HR professionals, we must maintain a high level of trust with our stakeholders. We must protect the interests of our stakeholders as well as our professional integrity and should not engage in activities that create actual, apparent, or potential conflicts of interest.

**Use of Information**

Core Principle: HR professionals consider and protect the rights of individuals, especially in the acquisition and dissemination of information while ensuring truthful communications and facilitating informed decision-making.

Other MCWs have less formal or less systematic training routes (e.g., workshops, life experience.) Currently there is no generic accreditation or professional association for MCWs in this category. The first three *stones* will be very helpful for them. In addition, and in view of *Commitment 7* in Stone One they are strongly encouraged to practice member care in light of specific code of ethics that "fits" for them (Commitment 7: Having high standards in my services and embracing specific ethical guidelines). It could be a code developed by a national or international organization/discipline, such as codes for Christian counselors, coaches, spiritual directors, or ombudsmen. They are also encouraged to have a written endorsement from their organization that attests to their competence and accountability. Note also that many field leaders and team leaders regularly function in member care roles—it is part of their job description in many cases. These leaders may not need a specific code per se—Stone Four—but at the very least they need to be thoroughly informed by ethical guidelines such as those described in this article.

**Sending Groups**. Many sending groups are either too small or perhaps too inexperienced to maintain a professional personnel department. However, this does not excuse them (as per some of the rationalizations in Stone Three) from the need to understand and adopt good practice principles. All sending groups, regardless of their size and experience, are encouraged to develop, endorse, or adapt a *code of good practice* for managing and supporting their staff that fits their context (e.g., Stone Two).

Two additional codes are especially relevant for senders in the Christian mission/aid community. The first is the *Code of Best Practice in Member Care* (2001) by the Evangelical Fellowship of Canada. This Code includes principles and key indicators that are categorized into six sections: Organizational Policy and Practice; Selection, Training and Career Care; Community Life; Family and Missionary Children; Relationships with

Churches; and Crisis/Contingency Care. This is available at http://files.efc-canada.net/out/ BestPractice_MemberCare.pdf and is also included in *Doing Member Care* (2002).

A second code has been developed in the United Kingdom: *Guidelines for Good Practice for Mission Member Care* (2009*)*. It is one of the most detailed member care codes to date (www.globalconnections.co.uk/resources/standardsinmissionpractice/ membercareguidelines).

As is true of the Canadian code, senders from different nations and organizations could adjust and build upon it to fit their own context. These guidelines relate to those who are expecting to be overseas for more than two years. For shorter periods of service, see the *UK Code of Best Practice in Short-Term Mission* (Chapter 26 in *Doing Member Care Well*, 2002 and also available on the Global Connections Web site) and the *Standards of Excellence in Short-term Mission* (www.stmstandards.org/standards). The UK *Guidelines* include two broad areas: *core values* which every mission organization or sending church that adopts this code should aim to meet, and *detailed guidelines* for those who want further information about how the values can be put into practice.

### How Do We Mainstream Codes?
Here's an imaginary but not unlikely scenario for senders. It can help to better understand what is involved in choosing and implementing a sender code.

**Applications**: An international Christian mission focuses on orphanage work in Africa. Many children are helped and receive a good education and vocational training. But people both at the home office and field personnel in Africa average only two years of service. They have a personnel department with three full-time staff, but the leaders as well as the personnel staff are only vaguely familiar with good practice codes for senders and have not formally adopted such a code. What to do?

**Good Practice**: Appoint a group to review the management and support of staff. Get three good practice codes for senders. Talk to three other organizations about their staff-related practices and experiences. Get information from current and former staff. Leaders discuss staff input in light of the good practice principles and the mission's goals. They apologize as needed, sincerely. They talk about the agency "culture" of work and care, policies, and the leadership styles that might contribute to staff growth or turnover. They ask hard questions about: their own spiritual life and that of staff; maintaining work-life balance; structures to help staff support each other (email access, small groups, retreats, briefing and debriefing); funds to further train staff; a referral list for specialist services; and the agency's connections with mission and member care networks. And they pray!

**Poor Practice:** The leaders actually do not meet, nor talk openly, probably because they feel too threatened. And they are too busy. They also don't get the perspectives of staff. Nor do they have records, surveys, or exit interviews that can provide objective data. They talk about issues one-on-one usually. It's a bit cathartic. But no one does anything. There is no review process in place regarding work-life balance, staff effectiveness, staff development, organizational practices, and staff morale. Someone else is always to blame. Good practice codes are seen to embody either common sense principles that everyone knows already or else are seen as restrictive principles that are not in the Bible and which can instill false expectations in staff. They do not want to hinder their sacrificial focus on the needs of others. OK. Rest in peace and rest in pieces.

---

*Stone Four Ethics Sensitizer. Reflection and Discussion*
HOW DO WE NAVIGATE THE MANY ETHICAL CODES AND
PRINCIPLES AND THEIR ADAPTATIONS?

By now you may be feeling just a bit overwhelmed. Perhaps the giants (challenges) in your member care practice also include the challenge of identifying, adjusting, and mainstreaming appropriate ethical guidelines into your work or sending group. What ideas do you have for doing this? Here are a few items to also consider. See also *A Guide to Developing Your organization's Code of Ethics* (2001) by the Society for Human Resource Management http://www.shrm.org/ethics/organization-coe.pdf.

1. Get input. Ask for examples from other MCWs and sending groups about what they are using. How have they integrated such codes into their member care practice and organizational ethos? Don't assume you know a lot or a little. Use this article as a foundation for exploration and interaction too.

2. Go with the core. Get what you need, and focus on the basics. Don't try to put on "armor" that does not fit you or your discipline, culture, or organization. Less is probably better, especially at first.

3. Be realistic and maintain perspective. Consider these principles from *Assessing and Managing Risk in Psychological Practice* (2006): "Strive for excellence, not perfection....You will make mistakes. You cannot help everyone. You will not know everything. You cannot go it alone. It is helpful to have a proper mix of confidence and humility." (p.5).

4.  Review your guidelines openly and regularly. Get input from current and former staff about the way staff are managed and supported. Be sure to establish "key indicators" to help you determine the extent to which you are putting into practice your core ethical principles.

5.  Think organizational *ethos* and practitioner *mentality*. Developing good ethical practice is a process which involves inner shifts and not just behavioral shifts. We think ethically and we act ethically, and each one influences the other.

## FINAL THOUGHTS

I like to think of these ethical stones as representing *ideals* and the guidelines themselves as representing the *particulars*. The ideals of these stones move us in the direction of a trans-cultural *framework*. The particulars in the guidelines help move us in the direction of trans-cultural *applications*.

The proposed framework includes developing ethical principles for MCWs and senders (stones, 1, 2, 4); developing a process for monitoring sub-standards (stone 3); and developing our understanding of human rights principles (stone 5, to be discussed in Chapter 11). The recommended guidelines include principles that are malleable and can be carefully shaped to fit one's culture, discipline, and organization.

The main goal in Part Three of *Pearls and Perils* is not developing something trans-cultural per se. That is quite a job and hard to measure of course! The main and realistic goal is to develop and offer guidelines that are as *relevant* as possible for as many people as possible. So this means people with member care responsibility from all kinds of backgrounds who are able to adjust and apply them as necessary. Perhaps a more accurate term to consider would be *trans-relevant ethics*.

Finally, let us remember that our quest for ethical member care has a destination. It ultimately leads us to the doorsteps of the world in need. Our quality, ethical care bolsters the many diverse segments of the mission/aid community. It supports those who in turn reach out in so many noble ways to help fellow humans in this struggling world.

# PEARLS
## ENHANCING AND ENRICHING GOOD PRACTICE

*Human rights are foundational for good practice and ethical member care.*

*United humanity, in all of our diversity, identified and agreed upon basic human rights via the Universal Declaration of Human Rights (1948).*

*Many people are willing to risk their own rights and well-being for the sake of others.*

*Both rights and responsibilities are emphasized as workers and senders relate together.*

*Human rights and human morality make sense because they have a "Prescriber" —God.*


# PERILS
## ENCUMBERING AND ENDANGERING GOOD PRACTICE

*It is risky to provide member care to vulnerable populations in places where human rights violations are normative.*

*Training in international human rights instruments is neglected in the mission/aid community.*

*Serious forms of poor practice do in fact exist and even flourish in some mission/aid settings.*

*People with intact human rights can ignore blatant human rights violations for others in order not to jeopardize their own assets or lifestyles.*

*Social and economic human rights are elusive dreams for a large majority of people who simply struggle to survive in the face of vast inequalities.*

# CHAPTER 11

# Extending the Foundations of Good Practice

STONE FIVE APPROXIMATES A UNIVERSAL SET OF PRINCIPLES TO HELP SHAPE OUR ETHICAL PRACTICE. IT IS THE CORNERSTONE UPON WHICH THE OTHER STONES ARE SET. THIS STONE INVOLVES OUR DUTY TO SACRIFICIALLY HELP OTHERS AND OUR COMMITMENT TO RESPECT THE RIGHTS AND DIGNITY OF ALL PEOPLE. UNDERSTANDING HUMAN RIGHTS BASED ON MORAL LAW IS FUNDAMENTAL FOR LIVING ETHICAL LIVES AND FOR DOING MEMBER CARE WELL. IT IS A CRUCIAL AREA FOR THE MISSION/AID COMMUNITY TO EMBRACE.

---

This chapter explores what I believe is the foundational stone in our search for trans-culturally relevant ethics. Stone Five is fascinating! It based on doing what we "know" is morally right to do. It shines light on our inner sense of *duty*. I believe that it must especially take into account *human rights* in a way which hitherto has received minimal consideration in the member care field. This includes understanding and protecting the rights of mission/aid staff and the people with whom they work, as described for example in international human rights documents (discussed below).

However, the primary focus of this stone is not just mission/aid staff. It is also on the ethical responsibility—ethical imperative—for personal and group duty (often sacrificial duty) on behalf of humanity. *It is about the duty and choice to risk one's own rights and well-being in order to extend member care, broadly speaking, to vulnerable populations.* More specifically, it is a principled commitment to improve the quality of life and seek justice for those whose human rights, including religious liberties and freedom of conscience as well as physical safety and economic livelihood, are habitually threatened through neglect, disasters, poverty, discrimination, fear, and persecution.

\* \* \* \* \* \*

# Stone Five
## Human Rights Principles

I like to refer to Stone Five as the "known" stone—our moral knowledge and moral duty—that impels us to help others even if it inconveniences us or leads to difficult consequences. It is not just knowledge-based however, but also affect-based (e.g., involving "moral emotions," Leffel, *et al*, 2008). It makes us "groan" with pain and compassion, even as all creation groans in futility and brokenness (Rom. 8:22). I thus also refer to this stone as the "groan stone." As an example, consider how the following account can stir up your own "known-groan stone" and sense of duty to do good.

> I just returned from Sulawesi yesterday where I met with leaders who oversee about 2000 church-planters, pastors, and evangelists in the Maluku islands, Indonesia. They have lost about 100 workers in the last several months. Some were burnt alive and others cut to pieces. One evangelist had his head cut off and placed in a public place…One pastor lost his children and grand children. Another pastor was forcibly circumcised along with his children, including his five-year year old girl. I am just so overwhelmed with pain in my heart. As I sat with them I couldn't bear to listen. But even more painful, is what one pastor asked me: "Why doesn't anyone care for us?" (Report from Beram Kumar, Member Care Network-Malaysia; February, 2001; quoted in "Human Rights Advocacy in Missions" by Wilfred Wong, *Doing Member Care Well*, 2002)

### Human Rights (HR) and Member Care (MC): From Sulawesi to Starbucks
It is difficult to follow the despicable account above with the next personal anecdote. It is hard because this anecdote took place in the serenity and security of a lovely setting where human rights are the accepted norm. Life is filled with such strange juxtapositions though, and often tinged with the dissonant recollection of others suffering while we ourselves relax in comfort. It is such dissonance however, as I describe below, that can rally us to consider our personal and ethical responsibilities.

I was recently facilitating a one-week consultation on developing member care. The day before the event began, I participated in a "self-consultation" at the local Starbucks, sipping an iced coffee over a two hour period. I spent my entire time scrutinizing the *United Nation's Universal Declaration of Human Rights* (UDHR, 1948) including the *Preamble* and its *30 Articles* (principles). I had become engrossed in serious reflection on just how much human rights seemed to be foundational for good member care. It was amazing! But was this merely a transient caffeine-induced "revelation"? Or had I, along with a myriad of other competent member care practitioners, missed this central and possibly self-evident truth over the last two decades? I wondered.

****

*I had become engrossed in serious reflection on just how much human rights seemed to be foundational for good member care.*

****

I also timidly wondered to what extent I would be willing to further look into my own heart, as Stone Four (ethical sub-standards) instructs us to do. Had I rationalized away some of my duty to help others in dire need, such as the one hundred martyred Christian workers in the Sulawesi account above, or the estimated one billion slum-dwellers on our planet whose lack of economic and social opportunities/rights are nothing short of horrific? How much did I really understand human rights (see Box 1) and to what extent were human rights integrated into my personal and professional life? Again, I wondered...and stared in astonishment as the experiential contours of both the known stone and the groan stone started to emerge out of my own inner fog of humanity-related ethics. My understanding of human rights, ethics, and member care would never be the same again.

---

### Box 1. What Are Human Rights?

United Nations Office of the High Commission for Human Rights
(www.ohchr.org)

- Human rights are rights inherent to all human beings, whatever our nationality, place of residence, sex, national or ethnic origin, colour, religion, language, or any other status. We are all equally entitled to our human rights without discrimination. These rights are all interrelated, interdependent and indivisible.
- Universal human rights are often expressed and guaranteed by law, in the forms of treaties, customary international law, general principles and other sources of international law. International human rights law lays down obligations of Governments to act in certain ways or to refrain from certain acts, in order to promote and protect human rights and fundamental freedoms of individuals or groups.

- The principle of universality of human rights is the cornerstone of international human rights law. This principle, as first emphasized in the *Universal Declaration of Human Rights* in 1948, has been reiterated in numerous international human rights conventions, declarations, and resolutions. The 1993 Vienna World Conference on Human Rights, for example, noted that it is the duty of States to promote and protect all human rights and fundamental freedoms, regardless of their political, economic and cultural systems.
- Human rights are inalienable. They should not be taken away, except in specific situations and according to due process. For example, the right to liberty may be restricted if a person is found guilty of a crime by a court of law.
- All human rights are indivisible, whether they are civil and political rights, such as the right to life, equality before the law and freedom of expression; economic, social and cultural rights, such as the rights to work, social security and education; or collective rights, such as the rights to development and self-determination The improvement of one right facilitates advancement of the others. Likewise, the deprivation of one right adversely affects the others.

www.ohchr.org/EN/Issues/Pages/WhatareHumanRights.aspx

For me, the more I explore the *MC-HR* relationship, the stronger my convictions grow of the central, ubiquitous role of HR for the member care field. I have continued to build upon my Starbucks experience with the *UDHR* document and other subsequent human rights documents, relating MC in HR terms and how HR principles could inform MC practice. My ideas roughly fit into two broad areas of inquiry regarding the MC-HR connection.

1. How does HR provide a foundation for our responsibility to manage and support our mission/aid staff?
2. How does HR provide a foundation for our responsibility in mission/aid work to help vulnerable populations including those who have experienced human rights abuses?

A good starting point for answering these two core questions is found in the opening statements of the *UNDHR Preamble*. The foundational assertion is found in the first line, in that we recognize "the inherent dignity and equal and inalienable rights of all members of the human family." This assertion applies to all people, and for our purposes it applies to both mission/aid staff and the people with whom staff work. It is no wonder, as Paul

Kennedy says in his brilliant treatment of the history of the United Nations, that this international document was quickly referred to as the "Magna Carta of mankind," and translated into almost every language (*The Parliament of Man*, 2006, p.180).

Take some time to read the *Preamble* in Box 2. Be sure to note the powerful contrasts that are used (bold/italics added) that reflect humanity's very inconsistent understanding and application of human rights throughout history: e.g., recognition and disregard, progress/development and oppression, promote/protect and contempt, reaffirm and outrage, freedom and tyranny, peace and fear. We humans have a cyclical history of wounding ourselves, then bandaging ourselves, then wounding ourselves again, then bandaging ourselves again. Helping to break this cycle is one of the purposes of human rights instruments (plus "the rule of *just* laws"), which fits well with the goals of many mission/aid groups.

---

### Box 2. When is it ethical for workers to be sent to and kept in risky areas?

*United Nations 1948 (www.un.org/en/documents/udhr/index.shtml)*

Whereas **recognition** of the inherent dignity and of the equal and inalienable rights of all members of the human family is the foundation of freedom, justice and **peace** in the world,

Whereas **disregard** and **contempt** for human rights have resulted in barbarous acts which have **outraged** the conscience of mankind, and the advent of a world in which human beings shall enjoy **freedom** of speech and belief and freedom from **fear** and want has been proclaimed as the highest aspiration of the common people,

Whereas it is essential, if man is not to be compelled to have recourse, as a last resort, to rebellion against **tyranny** and **oppression**, that human rights should be **protected** by the rule of law,

Whereas it is essential to **promote** the **development** of friendly relations between nations,

Whereas the peoples of the United Nations have in the Charter **reaffirmed** their faith in fundamental human rights, in the dignity and worth of the human person and in the equal rights of men and women and have determined to **promote** social **progress** and better standards of life in larger freedom,

Whereas Member States have pledged themselves to achieve, in co-operation with the United Nations, the **promotion** of universal respect for and observance of human rights and fundamental freedoms,

---

Whereas a common understanding of these rights and freedoms is of the greatest importance for the full realization of this pledge,

Now, therefore the General Assembly proclaims this *Universal Declaration of Human Rights* as a common standard of achievement for all peoples and all nations, to the end that every individual and every organ of society, keeping this Declaration constantly in mind, shall strive by teaching and education to promote respect for these rights and freedoms and by progressive measures, national and international, to secure their universal and effective recognition and observance, both among the peoples of Member States themselves and among the peoples of territories under their jurisdiction.

I want to make five key applications of the *Preamble* to the mission/aid community. These applications are core principles that form my main recommendations for Stone Five. Note that both rights and responsibilities are emphasized, and that moral duty underlies these principles.

### Stone Five. Recommended Guidelines
FIVE PRINCIPLES FOR HUMAN RIGHTS AND MEMBER CARE

1. We recognize the dignity and equality of our staff and of the people that are the focus of our services. The pursuit of freedom, justice, and peace are responsibilities that are reflected in our core values and goals.
2. We promote friendly relations, social progress, and better standards of life within our organizations and within the people that are the focus of our services.
3. We are gravely concerned ("outraged" in the *Preamble*) when basic rights are disregarded within our organizations and within the people that are the focus of our services. We seek to protect people's rights and we oppose ("rebellion" in the *Preamble*) those entities that stifle freedoms of speech and beliefs and the freedom from fear.
4. We reaffirm our ongoing commitment to basic human rights in both our organizations and in the people who are the focus of our services.
5. We are willing to prudently make sacrifices in order to safeguard and promote the rights and well-being of vulnerable people, including mission/aid personnel and the people whom they serve.

## More Perspectives on Human Rights and Member Care

Up until now HR has not been in any discussion that I am aware of within the member care field (i.e. regarding the support and management of staff). Rather, principles from Christian scripture (e.g., see Glen Taylor's article, "A Theological Perspective on Missionary Care" in *Enhancing Missionary Vitality,* 2002) and professional ethics/good practice codes (as discussed at length in this article) have been the main influences and standards. What I am advocating for is: a) to foster a greater understanding of human rights *and* their affirmation via application, which will produce healthier organizations and staff, and b) to include HR along with Christian scripture and good practice/ethical codes in our foundational understanding of member care.

One practical outworking would be the inclusion of HR in our mission/aid and member care-related training programs. Specifically, I suggest studying the human rights instruments that make up the *International Bill of Human Rights.* These instruments are the *UDHR* (1948), and the *International Covenants on Human Rights* (including the *International Covenant on Social, Economic, and Political Rights* (1966) and the *International Covenant of Civil and Political Rights* (1966) at www.ohchr.org/Documents/Publications. For more discussion on the historical and philosophical development of human rights see chapters one through four in Michal Haas' book, *International Human Rights: A Comprehensive Approach* (2008). Also see these books: *25+ Human Rights Documents* (2005) by Martin; *Introduction to the Human Rights Regime* (2003) by Nowack; and *Human Rights: Between Idealism and Realism* (2003) by Tamushut.

Box 3 for example, lists specific economic rights primarily related to work, which need to be understood by the mission/aid community both for itself as well as for the people with whom they work. Keep in mind though that these rights are still dreams for a large majority of people whose life experience consists of unemployment, poverty, poor health, and vast social inequalities. One can only wonder what seismic shifts have to occur politically, environmentally, spiritually, and in our own lifestyles in order to see such basic human rights realized in our world (see Collier, 2007, *The Bottom Billion*; and Pantuliano, 2009, *Uncharted Territory*).

---

### Box 3. International Bill of Human Rights (excerpts)
UNITED NATIONS OFFICE OF THE HIGH COMMISSIONER FOR HUMAN RIGHTS

*(www2.ohchr.org/english)*

\*\*\*\*\*

*Excerpts—Universal Declaration of Human Rights (1948)*

Article 22

Everyone, as a member of society, has the right to social security and is entitled to realization, through national effort and international co-operation and in accordance with the organization and resources of each State, of the economic, social and cultural rights indispensable for his dignity and the free development of his personality.

Article 23

(1) Everyone has the right to work, to free choice of employment, to just and favourable conditions of work and to protection against unemployment.

(2) Everyone, without any discrimination, has the right to equal pay for equal work.

(3) Everyone who works has the right to just and favourable remuneration ensuring for himself and his family an existence worthy of human dignity, and supplemented, if necessary, by other means of social protection.

(4) Everyone has the right to form and to join trade unions for the protection of his interests.

Article 24

Everyone has the right to rest and leisure, including reasonable limitation of working hours and periodic holidays with pay.

Article 25

(1) Everyone has the right to a standard of living adequate for the health and well-being of himself and of his family, including food, clothing, housing and medical care and necessary social services, and the right to security in the event of unemployment, sickness, disability, widowhood, old age or other lack of livelihood in circumstances beyond his control.

(2) Motherhood and childhood are entitled to special care and assistance. All children, whether born in or out of wedlock, shall enjoy the same social protection.

*****

*Excerpts— International Covenant on Economic, Social and Cultural Rights* (1966)

Article 7
The States Parties to the present Covenant recognize the right of everyone to the enjoyment of just and favourable conditions of work which ensure, in particular:
>    (a) Remuneration which provides all workers, as a minimum, with:
>>    (i) Fair wages and equal remuneration for work of equal value without distinction of any kind, in particular women being guaranteed conditions of work not inferior to those enjoyed by men, with equal pay for equal work;
>>    (ii) A decent living for themselves and their families in accordance with the provisions of the present Covenant;
>    (b) Safe and healthy working conditions;
>    (c) Equal opportunity for everyone to be promoted in his employment to an appropriate higher level, subject to no considerations other than those of seniority and competence;
>    (d) Rest, leisure and reasonable limitation of working hours and periodic holidays with pay, as well as remuneration for public holidays.

## Problems: Recognizing, Regarding, and Promoting HR

People and organizations violate human rights all the time. Violations happen through ignorance and through intention, or a combination of both. Christian workers and sending groups are definitely not immune from the failure to recognize, regard, and promote the rights of others. Here are some examples.

**Problem one.** There are problems when we do not *recognize* the reality that humans have dignity and rights. Certain people or groups (especially those we don't like, for whatever reason) can be viewed as being less human and thus merit human wrongs rather than human rights (remember Zimbardo's Stanford Prison Experiment in 1971 where "normal" university students quickly became abusive, a reflection of the countless other examples of abuse in our human history). Freedom of speech, conscience, and religion, at the state level for example, are often the first universal rights to be repressed. At the family, group, or organizational levels, repressing human rights via the maladaptive trio of "don't talk, don't feel, don't trust" can become pervasive dysfunctions. The upshot of not recognizing human rights is that it becomes easier and more acceptable to ignore, neglect, or hurt people, to not be "aware" of any wrongdoing, and to even excuse it. We redefine human rights to our own advantage. Reality gets distorted at the expense of humans.

**Problem two.** Not recognizing HR overlaps with a second problem: a lack of *regard* for the dignity and rights of humans. This further distortion can lead to controlling and exploiting others. For mission/aid personnel including leaders, not regarding human rights is often done to stay safe, not disturb the status quo, not to be shamed, and not jeopardize ones position and livelihood. Fear can be a major influence, leading to blind loyalty, self-protection, poor practice, low morale, group stagnation, and above all, injustice. In all the above examples, we can end up succumbing, as Christopher Hitchens says in his commentary on George Orwell's *Animal Farm* and *1984*, to a "mentality of servility" and to "the lethal temptation to exchange freedom for security: a bargain that invariably ends up with the surrender of both." (2003, *Introduction to Animal Farm and 1984*)

**Problem three.** There are also problems when we do not *promote* dignity and rights and instead oppress people. We think more of our own interests than the interests of others. Rebellion may eventually result. In its healthiest form such rebellion is a sincere and virtuous attempt to create change that will protect people from abuses and promote their well-being. The *UDHR Preamble* refers to this as fostering "social progress and better standards of life in larger freedom."

✳✳✳✳✳

*Seeking to promote and/or protect human rights, especially on behalf of those who are oppressed, and in ways which are seen to challenge the status quo and to be politically incorrect, does not always have a happy ending.*

✳✳✳✳✳

One example of "virtuous rebellion" is in I Sam. 11, in which Saul responds to the threat of serious human rights violations from an invading army (the intentional failure to regard and recognize the rights of others). The invading army had surrounded the town of Jabesh-Gilead and threatened to gouge out the right eye of all of its citizens. Saul is informed about this menace, becomes outraged, puts his livelihood on the line by slaughtering his oxen and then risks his life in order to rally his compatriots to action, fight, and protect others. The result is that the invading army is routed, the citizens are protected, the national identity/unity is strengthened, and justice is done.

A second example with a far less positive outcome is in I Kings 22. Here, Micaiah the prophet takes unknown risks in order to speak publicly to two kings and their entourage about what God tells him to say: "As the Lord lives, what the Lord says to me, that I will speak" (v. 14). He prophesies disaster, is struck in the face, then thrown in prison, and never heard of again in the pages of scripture. Seeking to promote and/ or protect human rights, especially on behalf of those who are oppressed, and in ways which are seen to challenge the status quo and to be politically incorrect, does not always have a happy ending.

### Applications: States and Senders.

The sending group's responsibility for the good practice of member care is analogous to the nation-state's responsibility for the good practice of human rights. Sending groups can learn from the experience of nation-states! Consider these thoughts from David Little in the Foreword of *For All People and All Nations: Christian Churches and Human Rights* (2005).

> ...the Human Rights Commission (1945) went on to bring into being the Universal Declaration (1948) and thereby to make way for and inspire a whole array of subsequent human rights documents on civil, political, economic, social, cultural, racial, gender, minority, environmental, and other issues, that today set international standards for what is expected of nation-states, both within and outside their borders. Although these standards are not universally enforced around the world, they are more and more taken to comprise the basic international requirements of political legitimacy. It is simply the case now that states found systematically and grossly to these violate standards are regarded as pariahs (x).

When senders/states consistently do not recognize or when they even deny the basic rights of their staff/citizens, then their very legitimacy in the eyes of their respective communities—the mission/aid community and the international community respectively—will be seriously questioned. In the worst cases, senders and states would be viewed as "illegitimate or failed entities" and "poor-practice pariahs." Unfortunately, this last point though extreme, does occur in both nation-states and the mission/aid community. Further, for the mission/aid community, more moderate albeit serious forms of poor practice do in fact exist and even flourish in some settings. Human rights are violated and human beings are injured, sometimes irreparably. We all must courageously acknowledge such poor practice! "Christians are called to fearlessly seek and name the truth of what has happened. Deformed ways of remembering the past (and present) include denial, social amnesia, a spirit of unforgiveness, and uncritical affirmation of one's own group and it's history" (Reconciliation Network, 2005, p. 7). We protect staff/ citizens from such practices/violations when we recognize, regard, and promote both human rights and the truth.

### Moral Law: The Foundation for Human Rights and Member Care

Article 29 of the *UDHR* says that "Everyone has duties to the community..." It is this sense of duty that makes us want to *recognize, regard,* and *promote* the rights and well being of others. This duty is synonymous with our sense of "moral obligation" in Stone Five. It is what Immanuel Kant referred to as the "categorical imperative": an absolute, unconditional requirement to do the right thing, applicable to any person in similar circumstances. "Act only according to that maxim whereby you can at the same time will that it should become a universal law" (*Grounding for the Metaphysics of Morals* (1785/1993). Underlying the notion of human rights then, is the notion of intrinsic, universal moral law.

Human rights as conceptualized by the authors of the *UDHR*, are understood to be universal, yet not based on any partisan or creedal belief. They are simply a given and something which humankind acknowledges. David Little explains this in his Foreword to John Nurser's book, *For All Peoples and All Nations: Christian Churches and Human Rights* (2005).

> Human beings are held to possess human rights, and to be accountable and to live up to them simply because they are human, not because they are Muslim, or Christian, or Buddhist, or Jewish, or Hindu, or a member of any particular religious or philosophical tradition. The whole point of human rights is that they are taken to be binding and available, regardless of identity or worldview. This does not mean, of course, that people are not free to harbor their own personal reasons—religious or otherwise—for believing in human rights. It only means that such views may not be taken as "official" or in any way binding on others who do not share them (xi).

The framers of the *UDHR* did well to find a neutral, common point to which people from most if not all backgrounds could agree (Note there are some exceptions/adjustments as seen in the 1990 *Cairo Declaration on Human Rights in Islam*, 1990). I approach the universality and "given-ness" of HR though as something which cannot stand on its own merit. In other words, human rights are not simply substantiated by "personal reasons" or simply because they are "human" as per the perspective cited above. The human focus of HR is indeed a reasonable rallying point, but philosophically it is very weak.

I see HR as being based on something more substantial and transcendental—moral law. And the corollary of course is that moral law comes from a Moral Law-giver. "In other words, there is a "prescription" to do good, that has been given to all humanity," to quote Geisler and Turek's (2004) argument for the existence of a moral law "Prescriber" in *I Don't Have Enough Faith to be an Atheist* (p.170). God is understood to have infused moral law in the human beings that He has created. Hence our sense of morality, our yearning for justice, and our "universal" human rights are based on God. Human rights make sense because God makes sense.

These thoughts are also reflected in the "Guiding Principles" recorded in an obscure but definitely not obsolete document, "A Message from the National Study Conference on the Churches and a Just and Durable Peace" which convened in the USA in 1942 under the auspices of the National Council of Churches.

> We believe that moral law, no less than physical law, undergirds our world. There is a moral order which is fundamental and eternal, and which is relevant to the corporate life of [humans] and the ordering of human society. If [humankind] is to escape chaos and recurrent war, social and political institutions must be brought into conformity with this moral order....We believe that the Eternal God revealed in Christ…is the source of moral law and the power to make it effective (Section II, Guiding Principles, pp. 10-14).

✳✳✳✳✳

*Rights and responsibilities are a two-way street, affecting both organizations and staff alike.*

✳✳✳✳✳

An important corollary to the HR and moral law relationship is to say that human rights violations are in fact infringements on moral law. From a Christian perspective, it is a consequence of the moral fragmentation in humanity that began with broken relationship with God, as related in the Genesis narrative. Humans became beset with the intractable flaws of self-centeredness (a core part of narcissism) and deception (a core part of sociopathy). One way to look at it is that in spite of our moral goodness and beauty—having been made in God's image—we are all guilty of "crimes against ourselves and crimes against others." The pernicious combination of human and devilish wrongs leads to the demise of humanity's well-being: we end up maiming human rights and moaning for human rights. We yearn for our *rightful* ontological and experiential place as children of God (Rom. 8:18-25). We are back to the affective component of Stone Five, the notion of the "groan stone."

### Rights and Responsibilities in Perspective

Rights and responsibilities are a two-way street, affecting both organizations and staff alike. Mission/aid sending groups have a responsibility to manage and support their staff well, as discussed in Stone Two (principles for senders), for instance. Mission/aid staff have the right to expect/receive good supportive/managerial services from their sending groups. In addition, staff also have a responsibility to provide quality services to/through their sending groups and support the purposes of their sending groups. Sending groups also have a right to make sure that their staff are providing quality services. Think of the rights and responsibilities of senders and workers as a 2 X 2 matrix (Box 4). This matrix could be used as a grid to discuss and clarify mutual obligations and expectations.

199

## Box 4. Responsibilities and Rights for Senders and Staff

|  | Responsibilities | Rights |
|---|---|---|
| Senders | Provide quality support and management to staff | Require accountability for staff and quality services from staff |
| Staff | Provide quality services and embrace organizational goals | Receive quality support and management from the organization |

When there is a breakdown in the recognition of these mutual rights and responsibilities, by either senders and staff, the result is low morale, poor performance, conflicts, and attrition. For some related thoughts and issues see also Chapter 16, Employee Rights and Discipline, in Mathis and Jackson, *Human Resource Management* (2003, 10th ed., pp. 508-540).

Theologically, human rights must also be understood in the light of Divine "rights." God has the "right" as our Creator, to ask us to obey Him, trust Him, and serve Him. He always does this based on His character of love—His immutable attributes of moral goodness—even though we may not fully understand His ways. One prime example in scripture is the extra measure of hardship experienced by Baruch, the scribe of Jeremiah, due to his obedience to God and his subsequent challenge to be content with simply being alive (surviving the destruction of the Babylonian invasion and his subsequent voluntary exile to Egypt, Jer. 45:1-5). One of life's greatest challenges can be to embrace how Divine sovereignty outweighs human preferences.

### Applications: Member Care for Persecuted Humans

Recently I was part of a team of psychologists providing member care services to workers in a Central Asian country. These workers were a mixture of locals and internationals who were living in a country where religious and other civil liberties were routinely violated. In addition to teaching on parenting skills, marriage, stress management, and grief/loss, there was also teaching on understanding human rights and surviving difficult experiences. Difficult experiences included both *external stressors* like persecution, harassment, and relationship conflict, and *internal struggles* like depression, fear, and frustration.

Most of the local workers knew well first-hand about how to survive some fairly harsh circumstances (e.g., economic hardship, government surveillance). Yet almost all of them had limited knowledge of national laws and international instruments (such as the *UDHR*) that pertained to their rights. The same was true for the international workers present. For many of the local workers, it seemed that generations of "learned helplessness" had left them with little sense that something could be done to change human rights abuses. Many of these rights and laws were said to be arbitrarily interpreted by government officials, not surprisingly, in terms of the "national interests" or at least in terms of the interests of the people with the most power. Confronting human rights violations could lead to serious negative consequences to one's well-being and that of their family and colleagues.

We listened a lot and discussed survival strategies and human rights in light of scripture. We reviewed, in the national language, Articles 18, 19, 20 of the *UDHR* (Box 5). Lights seemed to go on as people understood much better the "universal, indivisible, and inalienable rights" that the signatory State's of the *UDHR* have been "recognizing, regarding, and promoting" for nearly sixty years. It was not just the value that scripture and God put on human rights. It was also the value that united *humanity,* in all of its diversity, was putting on human rights.

---

**Box 5. Universal Declaration of Human Rights, Articles 18-19**

18. Everyone has the right to freedom of thought, conscience and religion; this right includes freedom to change his religion or belief, and freedom, either alone or in community with others and in public or private, to manifest his religion or belief in teaching, practice, worship and observance.

19. Everyone has the right to freedom of opinion and expression; this right includes freedom to hold opinions without interference and to seek, receive and impart information and ideas through any media and regardless of frontiers.

20. (1) Everyone has the right to freedom of peaceful assembly and association.

(2) No one may be compelled to belong to an association.

---

Persecution can be viewed along a continuum going from disinformation and discrimination, to physical harassment and detention, to torture and death. It involves things like imprisonment without a fair or any trial, sectarian violence, extra-judicial execution, psychiatric detention, and laws restricting religious freedom. Those who have their religious liberties violated, as outlined in Articles 18, 19, 20 of the *UNDHR* and subsequent international instruments/laws, often need human rights advocacy (e.g., *Declaration on the Elimination of All Forms of Intolerance and of Discrimination Based on Religion or Belief by the United Nations* in 1981). Wilfred Wong (2002) with Jubilee Campaign based in the United Kingdom writes:

To engage in human rights advocacy is basically to raise concerns about human rights violations and to call on the responsible government to rectify this injustice. It also involves getting Parliamentarians, governments and members of the public in other countries to put pressure on the responsible government to end the human rights violations. Human rights advocacy can be done at different levels, ranging from very public and strong pressure to quiet negotiations to persuade a government to stop the human rights abuses. Some examples of human rights advocacy organizations are Jubilee Campaign, Christian Solidarity Worldwide, and Amnesty International.

....As Christians, I believe we must show solidarity with other believers who are facing persecution. Failing to do what we can to try and help them in their time of need is akin to failure to help the wounded stranger on the road.... Human rights advocacy is not just about human rights but is also a key form of mission support. It involves speaking out against injustices and trying to have such situations rectified. We believe in a God of Justice (Isa. 30:18) whose prophets, like Amos, uncompromisingly called for justice (Amos 5:24). It thus amazes me when Christians think that closing one's eyes to injustice is somehow the more "spiritual" thing to do. Human rights advocacy is not about seeking political power, it is about seeking justice. It should not be considered as any more political than the prophetic utterances of Amos, Elijah, Isaiah, or any of the other prophets of the Bible (2002, pp. 477-479).

Wong also identifies seven guidelines about how to prepare for and respond to human rights-related crises on the mission/aid field (see the Stone Five Ethics Sensitizer). Our duty to help—Stone Five—must lead to prudence rather than temerity. It requires accurate information, connections, solidarity with others, and as necessary, risk. Justice does not happen unless one actively pursues it. It takes patience, prayer, and professionalism. For a good overview of religious advocacy issues, approaches, and case examples, see Knox, *et al's International Religious Freedom Advocacy: A Guide to Organizations, Law, and NGOs* (2009).

People though may be unwilling to help: to inconvenience themselves, to threaten their livelihood, to be ostracized by others, and above all to "change one's way of life." This is true of individuals, organizations, communities, and countries. Fortunately, there are some people however who cannot simply look the other way and ignore gross injustice. These people are resolutely committed to pursue truth and justice, and will not take "no" for an answer. They are willing to face extreme negative consequences, including defamation and sometimes even death, in order to act with integrity and help others. This is Stone Five at its core, and humans at our best.

## Stone Five Ethics Sensitizer. *Reflection and Discussion*
### HOW DO WE PRACTICALLY HELP PEOPLE WHOSE RELIGIOUS LIBERTIES ARE VIOLATED?

*Based on Wilfred Wong (2002), Human Rights Advocacy in Missions*

One reason why there is persecution in so many different countries today is because the church is expanding its frontiers throughout the world. More than at any other time in the history of Christianity we can truly regard the church as a global community. It is because the church is growing in places traditionally hostile to the Gospel that in many of these locations the backlash of persecution occurs. Governments or religious extremists feel threatened by the spread of Christianity and try all sorts of methods to stop its growth, ranging from murder and genocide to more subtle measures such as the introduction of restrictive laws on church registration, which is common in a number of countries.

### Overview of the Seven Guidelines
1. Pray for God's guidance. If possible, get others to pray and fast about the situation and for you while you take action.
2. Identify possible sources of information. Verify the information by getting independent corroboration of the facts. When a problem is starting to arise, one should start to gather the relevant facts in case advocacy needs to be used and for the purposes of informing others so they can pray.
3. Discuss the issue of authorization for advocacy or whatever course of action needs to be taken, with the appropriate person. The best people to give authorization are first the person/victim, then the closest immediate family of the person, and then the leader of the church/fellowship group to which the person belongs.
4. Communicate the information and request for prayer and action (if authorization has been given) to the relevant contacts in as speedy and secure a manner as possible. Follow this up with further updates as more information is obtained and as the situation develops
5. Consider contacting a lawyer if a person is being detained; someone who may be already known to the person, sympathetic to the case, and able to help.
6. Consider approaching any locally based people (such as sympathetic diplomats in the foreign embassies or local human rights groups) for assistance. But be sure that these people are trustworthy and bear in mind the implications this may have for your own security.

7. Consider whether the person has any dependants who may need assistance as a result of the crisis; e.g., the person may be in prison and unable to provide for the families needs. It is usually better for funds to be channeled through the local church/fellowship, via the approval of the leader, unless there are exceptional circumstances.

**Applications**

1. Who in your immediate sphere of contacts is the most vulnerable to serious human rights violations? What are you able and willing to do to help these people?
2. A follower of Christ is imprisoned for his faith and held without any contact with outsiders. His wife wants human rights advocacy on his behalf but his local church leader is opposed to it because he's very frightened of any actions that may potentially cause problems for his church. Whose view should have priority in deciding whether to authorize human rights advocacy?
3. Imagine you are working in a country where Article 18 of the Universal Declaration of Human Rights is not honored (freedom of religion/conscience and freedom to change one's religion). Anti-Christian persecution by certain people in the government has not yet started but with the growing number of citizens freely choosing to become Christians, it's likely to happen in the near future. What sort of preparations for persecution can you, other colleagues, and the local Christians make now, in advance?
4. In what ways can human rights violations happen within sending organizations?
5. Comment on these assertions:
   - There are consequences for defending human rights—including our own and those of others.
   - There are consequences for providing member care to workers whose human rights have been violated through harassment, discrimination, forced exile, and imprisonment.
   - There are consequences for not defending human rights or not helping those whose rights are violated.

# FINAL THOUGHTS

## *When Stone Guidelines Become Human Guidelines*

We in member care are committed to acknowledge and respect our diversity. We also want to be committed to acknowledge and respect our similarity as people who affirm basic human rights and basic human responsibilities. We want to grow together in the mission/aid community as we upgrade how we think about and how we practice ethical member care.

Taken together, the five stones discussed in chapters ten and eleven provide a relevant framework for doing member care ethically. I also believe they help move us more towards a trans-cultural framework for ethical member care. I have found it very helpful to review these stones regularly, discuss them with colleagues, and above all use them!

For most of us, I believe these five stones can fit well into our "cultural and experiential" slings. For others though, these stones may still feel cumbersome and "foreign," just like Saul's armor was for David. In such cases I encourage colleagues to see them as aspirational points of departure, seriously consider them, and to apply them in view of their cultural and organizational contexts and ongoing experience.

Where do we go from here? I believe it would be very helpful to form an international working group along with an ongoing internet-based forum where the area of member care ethics, along with these five stones in particular, could be further discussed and refined. It would also be helpful to convene an international consultation or to include as the main theme within an existing member care conference, the topic of international member care ethics. One of the priorities, similar to the approach of Part Three in *Pearls and Perils*, could be to consider a framework that would include ethical guidelines relevant for the diversity of member care practitioners and sending organizations.

Ethical member care is founded upon the imperative to help workers in mission/aid through good management and support. We esteem their dignity and equality. It also involves integrating Christ's universal declaration for agape love (John 13:24, 25) with the United Nations' universal declaration for human rights—on behalf of both mission/aid workers and the people they serve. Ethical member care does not simply promote good *practice*. It is a mindset, a set of behaviors, and part of a lifestyle that promotes *humans*. And as humans are promoted via good ethical practice, these stone guidelines for member care incarnate: they become alive. They become living guidelines for living as human beings.

Living guidelines for living as human beings, Red Cross Museum, Geneva, Switzerland.
© 2008 Kelly O'Donnell

# RESOURCES

CHAPTER 12

# Resources for Good Practice

BUT THE WORLD IS NOT SO HAPPY A PLACE...
CAN WE REALLY OFFER JUSTICE AND FREEDOM FROM WANT
TO A MID-TWENTY-FIRST-CENTURY EARTH OF PERHAPS NINE BILLION PEOPLE,
ONE-THIRD OF WHOM MAY LIVE IN SQUALOR AND DESPERATION?
PAUL KENNEDY, *THE PARLIAMENT OF MAN*, 2006, P. 289

This chapter provides materials to encourage your personal and professional growth. As good practitioners we want to continue to develop our character (virtues and resiliency) and competence (skills and knowledge). We grow together with others. We have clear and strong ethical commitments to do good and to provide quality services. We go broadly and grow deeply as we follow the Good Practitioner and the Heart of Member Care, Jesus Christ.

Materials in this Chapter:

- A Call for Christian Risk
- Universal Declaration of Human Rights
- Fragile States and Neglected Emergencies
- Marley's Ghost
- Psychological Dynamics of Intractable Ethnonational Conflicts
- Moral Courage and Courageous Action
- Healing the Body: Part Three

\* \* \* \* \* \*

# A Call for Christian Risk
*John Piper, Desiring God Ministries, May 29, 2002*

www.desiringgod.org/ResourceLibrary/TasteAndSee/
ByDate/2002/1203_A_Call_for_Christian_Risk

*By removing eternal risk, Christ calls his people to continual temporal risk.*

For the followers of Jesus the final risk is gone. "There is now no condemnation for those who are in Christ Jesus" (Rom. 8:1). "Neither death nor life…will be able to separate us from the love of God in Christ Jesus our Lord" (Rom. 3:38-39). "Some of you they will put to death…But not a hair of your head will perish" (Luke 21:16, 18). "Whoever believes in me, though he die, yet shall he live" (John 11:25).

When the threat of death becomes a door to paradise the final barrier to temporal risk is broken. When a Christian says from the heart, "To live is Christ and to die is gain," he is free to love no matter what. Some forms of radical Islam may entice martyr-murderers with similar dreams, but Christian hope is the power to love, not kill. Christian hope produces life-givers, not life-takers. The crucified Christ calls his people to live and die for their enemies, as he did. The only risks permitted by Christ are the perils of love. "Love your enemies, do good to those who hate you, bless those who curse you, pray for those who abuse you" (Luke 6:27-28).

With staggering promises of everlasting joy, Jesus unleashed a movement of radical, loving risk-takers. "You will be delivered up even by parents…and some of you they will put to death" (Luke 21:16). Only some, which means it might be you and it might not. That's what risk means. It is not risky to shoot yourself in the head. The outcome is certain. It is risky to serve Christ in a war zone. You might get shot. You might not.

Christ calls us to take risks for kingdom purposes. Almost every message of American consumerism says the opposite: Maximize comfort and security—now, not in heaven. Christ does not join that chorus. To every timid saint, wavering on the edge of some dangerous gospel venture, he says, "Fear not, you can only be killed" (Luke 12:4). Yes, by all means maximize your joy! How? For the sake of love, risk being reviled and persecuted and lied about, "for your reward is great in heaven" (Matt. 5:11-12).

There is a great biblical legacy of loving risk-takers. Joab, facing the Syrians on one side and the Ammonites on the other, said to his brother Abishai, "Let us be courageous for our people…and may the LORD do what seems good to him" (2 Sam. 10:12). Esther broke the royal law to save her people and said, "If I perish, I perish" (Esther 4:16). Shadrach and his comrades refused to bow down to the king's idol and said, "Our God whom we serve is able to deliver us…But if not, be it known to you, O king, that we will not serve your gods" (Dan. 3:16-18). And when the Holy Spirit told Paul that in every city imprisonment and afflictions await him, he said, "I do not account my life of any value nor as precious to myself, if only I may finish my course" (Acts 20:24). "Every Christian," said Stephen Neil about the early church, "knew that sooner or later he might have to testify to his faith at the cost of his life" (*A History of Christian Missions*, Penguin, 1964, p. 43). This was normal. To become a Christian was to risk your life. Tens of thousands did it. Why? Because to do it was to gain Christ, and not to was to lose your soul. "Whoever would save his life will lose it, but whoever loses his life for my sake will find it" (Matt 16:25).

The price of being a real Christian is rising around the world. Things are getting back to normal in "this present evil age." Increasingly 2 Tim. 3:12 will make sense: "All who desire to live a godly life in Christ Jesus will be persecuted." Those who've made gospel-risk a voluntary life-style will be most ready when we have no choice. Therefore I urge you, in the words of the early church, "Let us go to him outside the camp and bear the reproach he endured. For here we have no lasting city, but we seek the city that is to come" (Heb. 13:13-14). When God removed all risk above/He loosed a thousand risks of love.

* * * * * *

# Universal Declaration of Human Rights
http://www.un.org/en/documents/udhr/index.shtml

The General Assembly of the United Nations adopted the Universal Declaration of Human Rights on December 10, 1948. The Assembly called upon all member countries to publicize the text of the Declaration and "to cause it to be disseminated, displayed, read and expounded principally in schools and other educational institutions, without distinction based on the political status of countries or territories." To access the Declaration in over 360 languages/translations, go to: http://www.ohchr.org/EN/UDHR/Pages/Introduction.aspx

## *Preamble*
Whereas recognition of the inherent dignity and of the equal and inalienable rights of all members of the human family is the foundation of freedom, justice and peace in the world,

Whereas disregard and contempt for human rights have resulted in barbarous acts which have outraged the conscience of mankind, and the advent of a world in which human beings shall enjoy freedom of speech and belief and freedom from fear and want has been proclaimed as the highest aspiration of the common people,

Whereas it is essential, if man is not to be compelled to have recourse, as a last resort, to rebellion against tyranny and oppression, that human rights should be protected by the rule of law,

Whereas it is essential to promote the development of friendly relations between nations,

Whereas the peoples of the United Nations have in the Charter reaffirmed their faith in fundamental human rights, in the dignity and worth of the human person and in the equal rights of men and women and have determined to promote social progress and better standards of life in larger freedom,

Whereas Member States have pledged themselves to achieve, in co-operation with the United Nations, the promotion of universal respect for and observance of human rights and fundamental freedoms,

Whereas a common understanding of these rights and freedoms is of the greatest importance for the full realization of this pledge,

Now, Therefore THE GENERAL ASSEMBLY proclaims THIS UNIVERSAL DECLARATION OF HUMAN RIGHTS as a common standard of achievement for all peoples and all nations, to the end that every individual and every organ of society, keeping this Declaration constantly in mind, shall strive by teaching and education to promote respect for these rights and freedoms and by progressive measures, national and international, to secure their universal and effective recognition and observance, both among the peoples of Member States themselves and among the peoples of territories under their jurisdiction.

Article 1. All human beings are born free and equal in dignity and rights. They are endowed with reason and conscience and should act towards one another in a spirit of brotherhood.

Article 2. Everyone is entitled to all the rights and freedoms set forth in this Declaration, without distinction of any kind, such as race, colour, sex, language, religion, political or other opinion, national or social origin, property, birth or other status. Furthermore, no distinction shall be made on the basis of the political, jurisdictional or international status of the country or territory to which a person belongs, whether it be independent, trust, non-self-governing or under any other limitation of sovereignty.

Article 3. Everyone has the right to life, liberty and security of person.

Article 4. No one shall be held in slavery or servitude; slavery and the slave trade shall be prohibited in all their forms.

Article 5. No one shall be subjected to torture or to cruel, inhuman or degrading treatment or punishment.

Article 6. Everyone has the right to recognition everywhere as a person before the law.

Article 7. All are equal before the law and are entitled without any discrimination to equal protection of the law. All are entitled to equal protection against any discrimination in violation of this Declaration and against any incitement to such discrimination.

Article 8. Everyone has the right to an effective remedy by the competent national tribunals for acts violating the fundamental rights granted him by the constitution or by law.

Article 9. No one shall be subjected to arbitrary arrest, detention or exile.

Article 10. Everyone is entitled in full equality to a fair and public hearing by an independent and impartial tribunal, in the determination of his rights and obligations and of any criminal charge against him.

Article 11. (1) Everyone charged with a penal offence has the right to be presumed innocent until proved guilty according to law in a public trial at which he has had all the guarantees necessary for his defense. (2) No one shall be held guilty of any penal offence on account of any act or omission which did not constitute a penal offence, under national or international law, at the time when it was committed. Nor shall a heavier penalty be imposed than the one that was applicable at the time the penal offence was committed.

Article 12. No one shall be subjected to arbitrary interference with his privacy, family, home or correspondence, nor to attacks upon his honour and reputation. Everyone has the right to the protection of the law against such interference or attacks.

Article 13. (1) Everyone has the right to freedom of movement and residence within the borders of each state. (2) Everyone has the right to leave any country, including his own, and to return to his country.

Article 14. (1) Everyone has the right to seek and to enjoy in other countries asylum from persecution. (2) This right may not be invoked in the case of prosecutions genuinely arising from non-political crimes or from acts contrary to the purposes and principles of the United Nations.

Article 15. (1) Everyone has the right to a nationality. (2) No one shall be arbitrarily deprived of his nationality nor denied the right to change his nationality.

Article 16. (1) Men and women of full age, without any limitation due to race, nationality or religion, have the right to marry and to found a family. They are entitled to equal rights as to marriage, during marriage and at its dissolution. (2) Marriage shall be entered into only with the free and full consent of the intending spouses. (3) The family is the natural and fundamental group unit of society and is entitled to protection by society and the State.

Article 17. (1) Everyone has the right to own property alone as well as in association with others. (2) No one shall be arbitrarily deprived of his property.

Article 18. Everyone has the right to freedom of thought, conscience and religion; this right includes freedom to change his religion or belief, and freedom, either alone or in community with others and in public or private, to manifest his religion or belief in teaching, practice, worship and observance.

Article 19. Everyone has the right to freedom of opinion and expression; this right includes freedom to hold opinions without interference and to seek, receive and impart information and ideas through any media and regardless of frontiers.

Article 20. (1) Everyone has the right to freedom of peaceful assembly and association. (2) No one may be compelled to belong to an association.

Article 21. (1) Everyone has the right to take part in the government of his country, directly or through freely chosen representatives. (2) Everyone has the right of equal access to public service in his country. (3) The will of the people shall be the basis of the authority of government; this will shall be expressed in periodic and genuine elections which shall be by universal and equal suffrage and shall be held by secret vote or by equivalent free voting procedures.

Article 22. Everyone, as a member of society, has the right to social security and is entitled to realization, through national effort and international co-operation and in accordance with the organization and resources of each State, of the economic, social and cultural rights indispensable for his dignity and the free development of his personality.

Article 23. (1) Everyone has the right to work, to free choice of employment, to just and favourable conditions of work and to protection against unemployment. (2) Everyone, without any discrimination, has the right to equal pay for equal work. (3) Everyone who works has the right to just and favourable remuneration ensuring for himself and his family an existence worthy of human dignity, and supplemented, if necessary, by other means of social protection. (4) Everyone has the right to form and to join trade unions for the protection of his interests.

Article 24. Everyone has the right to rest and leisure, including reasonable limitation of working hours and periodic holidays with pay.

Article 25. (1) Everyone has the right to a standard of living adequate for the health and well-being of himself and of his family, including food, clothing, housing and medical care and necessary social services, and the right to security in the event of unemployment, sickness, disability, widowhood, old age or other lack of livelihood in circumstances beyond his control. (2) Motherhood and childhood are entitled to special care and assistance. All children, whether born in or out of wedlock, shall enjoy the same social protection.

Article 26. (1) Everyone has the right to education. Education shall be free, at least in the elementary and fundamental stages. Elementary education shall be compulsory. Technical and professional education shall be made generally available and higher education shall be equally accessible to all on the basis of merit. (2) Education shall be directed to the full development of the human personality and to the strengthening of respect for human rights and fundamental freedoms. It shall promote understanding, tolerance and friendship among all nations, racial or religious groups, and shall further the activities of the United Nations for the maintenance of peace. (3) Parents have a prior right to choose the kind of education that shall be given to their children.

Article 27. (1) Everyone has the right freely to participate in the cultural life of the community, to enjoy the arts and to share in scientific advancement and its benefits. (2) Everyone has the right to the protection of the moral and material interests resulting from any scientific, literary or artistic production of which he is the author.

Article 28. Everyone is entitled to a social and international order in which the rights and freedoms set forth in this Declaration can be fully realized.

Article 29. (1) Everyone has duties to the community in which alone the free and full development of his personality is possible. (2) In the exercise of his rights and freedoms, everyone shall be subject only to such limitations as are determined by law solely for the purpose of securing due recognition and respect for the rights and freedoms of others and of meeting the just requirements of morality, public order and the general welfare in a democratic society. (3) These rights and freedoms may in no case be exercised contrary to the purposes and principles of the United Nations.

Article 30. Nothing in this Declaration may be interpreted as implying for any State, group or person any right to engage in any activity or to perform any act aimed at the destruction of any of the rights and freedoms set forth herein.

✶ ✶ ✶ ✶ ✶ ✶

# Fragile States and Neglected Emergencies
*Global Future, Ian Gray[1] (2008, Number 2, pp. 22-23)*
www.globalfutureonline.org

*What are the operational and funding restrictions that hamper the effectiveness of non-governmental organizations in neglected emergencies? The key contributor to whether an emergency becomes chronic and neglected is the fragility of the state.*

In order to reduce poverty, a state needs to be able to deliver the safety and security of its citizens, functioning public institutions and services, and sound economic management. State fragility not only exacerbates suffering in times of acute humanitarian need, but also increases the likelihood of emergencies becoming neglected because they are awkward or complex to deal with, especially if their root causes are chronic and pervasive. In order to address this, donors need to summon up the political will to address the underlying causes of fragility, whilst providing more sustainable solutions to addressing the symptoms.

Fragile states have become a major focus for donors and others in the humanitarian and development community over the past five years. In many poor countries, the tax base is insufficient and the state's capabilities weak, so there is a heavy reliance on aid to support core functions. How does donor policy affect the ability of *nongovernmental organisations* (NGOs), the main deliverer of basic services or the poor in *fragile states affected by conflict* (FSACs), to ensure that emergencies do not sink into neglect?

A number of donors, including the UK's Department for International Development (DFID), identified this problem of aid dependency and switched their development funding to a mechanism called Direct Budgetary Support. This approach has been in place for around five years for many countries whose Poverty Reduction Strategies DFID assists.

But what if a state is unwilling or unable to carry out its core functions? The traditional donor approach has been to by-pass the state altogether and fund the United Nations and NGOs to deliver basic services using humanitarian budget lines.

Fragile state policy, particularly that coming through the OECD [Organization for Economic and Co-operative Development] Fragile States Group,[2] has focused on how to best support states emerging from conflict. This has mainly been in the form of Multi-Donor Trust Funds and Transitional Results Matrices,[3] aimed at relieving the burden of donor engagement for the state, whilst providing a "coherent" aid package. The overall design of such funding mechanisms should mirror existing or developing state policies for service sectors (such as health) and the method of implementation the state would use if it had the capacity to do so.

These positive steps have resulted in a broader, more coherent approach. However, there is still a lack of donor understanding of the role of civil society as the primary delivery mechanism, and funding timeframes remain woefully short (for example, the last Basic Services Fund[4] round in Sudan was for 18 months).

## Impact of donor funding

Generally finance comes in the form of grants for less than one year and are based on humanitarian need. Donors such as the European Commission Humanitarian Aid (ECHO), for instance, have supported basic services in countries such as Somalia for more than ten years using six- to twelve-month funding cycles. Volatility of funding for services in fragile states afflicts the planning and implementation of service deliverers (usually NGOs) with short-termism, hampering effective management of their supply chain and retention of key staff. It ultimately weakens relationships with the communities, as delivery of services can be patchy, and since funding is often for particular sectors, communities' development needs are rarely assessed holistically, and the services are frequently delivered in a myopic fashion, diluting their ultimate impact.

Emergencies that do not appear to have "straightforward" solutions are less attractive to many international media and donors. States are most prone to fall back into conflict in the first five years following hostilities, and often take at least another 10 years to function effectively.[5]

Donors also struggle with disparity of information between those delivering services on the ground and those making funding decisions in the humanitarian capitals. Clearly, a bigger-picture approach is needed to emergencies that risk slipping into protracted neglect and human insecurity

## *Can't private funds be raised?*

Private donations are the other major source of funding. However, gaining funds for such contexts is exceptionally difficult, primarily due to the psychology behind private individual charitable giving.

Research has shown that most private donors are driven in their philanthropic decision-making by what cognitive psychologists call "system one" thinking, which is a highly intuitive and emotional approach. Motivation for such giving usually comes from an unconscious bias towards seemingly solvable, personally identifiable problems. Empathy for man-made, conflict-related chronic emergencies is not so common. Fewer people base their philanthropic decisions on "system two" thinking, which is conscious and rational. Therefore, it is extremely difficult to raise money for vastly complex, seemingly intractable problems faced by people living in FSACs.[6]

## *So what is the solution?*

There are no "quick win" solutions. However, if the donor community funded the long-term integrated programming of NGOs—which seek to balance service delivery with building the capacity of states, societies and markets to be pro-poor and pro-vulnerable—we could see substantial changes for the poor in FSACs and help prevent some emergencies from descending into a cycle of neglect.

World Vision has decided to "practise what it preaches" by trialling this approach in three fragile contexts to date, carrying out holistic in-depth assessments that have led to multi-year programming, which has attracted significant funding commitments. Unfortunately some of this funding is still short-term. However, this experience does highlight the value of good quality assessment data from fragile contexts where donors traditionally have had difficulties.

## Note of caution

For NGOs working in FSACs, advocating for more development oriented funding mechanisms comes with a health warning: the issue of "humanitarian space." The very concept of humanitarian space is being heavily contested in some quarters, and is most strained at the juncture of programming in fragile contexts.

If NGOs decide to translate fragile states policy into programme design, they are essentially buying into the "state building" project. What does this mean for the impartiality and independence of the NGO? This is of particular consequence for neglected emergencies in fragile states, where the levels of vulnerability and hazard mean that NGOs often need to carry out emergency relief alongside their longer-term developmental work. This conundrum needs to be addressed in both NGO and donor thinking on fragile states policy and in the current "coherency" and "whole of government" approach.

Note from the book author—some more materials on fragile states and the poor:

- *Development, Security and Transition in Fragile States* (2010, Overseas Development Institute, www.odi.org.uk/resources) by Samir Elhawary, Marta Foresti, and Sara Pantuliano
- *The Bottom Billion: Why the Poorest Countries Are Failing and What Can Be Done About It*, (2007, Oxford: Oxford University Press) by Paul Collier
- *Social Justice Handbook: Small Steps for a Better World* (2009, Downers Grove, IL USA: Intervarsity Press) by May Elise Cannon
- *When Helping Hurts: How to Alleviate Poverty Without Hurting the Poor and Yourself* (2009, Chicago, IL USA: Moody Publishers) by Steve Corbett and Brian Fikkert.

\* \* \* \* \* \*

# Marley's Ghost
### *A Christmas Carol, Charles Dickens (1843)*

http://dickens.thefreelibrary.com/Christmas-Carol

When it had said these words, the spectre took its wrapper from the table, and bound it round its head, as before. Scrooge knew this, by the smart sound its teeth made, when the jaws were brought together by the bandage. He ventured to raise his eyes again, and found his supernatural visitor confronting him in an erect attitude, with its chain wound over and about its arm.

"It is required of every man," the Ghost returned, "that the spirit within him should walk abroad among his fellow-men, and travel far and wide; and if that spirit goes not forth in life, it is condemned to do so after death. It is doomed to wander through the world—oh, woe is me!—and witness what it cannot share, but might have shared on earth, and turned to happiness!"

Original illustration 1843, John Leech

"Oh! captive, bound, and double-ironed," cried the phantom, "not to know, that ages of incessant labour by immortal creatures, for this earth must pass into eternity before the good of which it is susceptible is all developed. Not to know that any Christian spirit working kindly in its little sphere, whatever it may be, will find its mortal life too short for its vast means of usefulness. Not to know that no space of regret can make amends for one life's opportunities misused! Yet such was I! Oh! such was I!"

The apparition walked backward from him; and at every step it took, the window raised itself a little, so that when the spectre reached it, it was wide open.

It beckoned Scrooge to approach, which he did. When they were within two paces of each other, Marley's Ghost held up its hand, warning him to come no nearer. Scrooge stopped.

Not so much in obedience, as in surprise and fear: for on the raising of the hand, he became sensible of confused noises in the air; incoherent sounds of lamentation and regret; wailings inexpressibly sorrowful and self-accusatory. The spectre, after listening for a moment, joined in the mournful dirge; and floated out upon the bleak, dark night.

Scrooge followed to the window: desperate in his curiosity. He looked out.

The air was filled with phantoms, wandering hither and thither in restless haste, and moaning as they went. Every one of them wore chains like Marley's Ghost; some few (they might be guilty governments) were linked together; none were free. Many had been personally known to Scrooge in their lives. He had been quite familiar with one old ghost, in a white waistcoat, with a monstrous iron safe attached to its ankle, who cried piteously at being unable to assist a wretched woman with an infant, whom it saw below, upon a door-step. The misery with them all was, clearly, that they sought to interfere, for good, in human matters, and had lost the power for ever.

Whether these creatures faded into mist, or mist enshrouded them, he could not tell. But they and their spirit voices faded together; and the night became as it had been when he walked home.

---

### Reflection and Discussion

Dicken's fantastical description of roaming, anguishing ghosts poignantly describes our responsibility and accountability to do good—now. How did the story affect you? List a few ways that it applies to you now?

\* \* \* \* \* \*

## Psychological Dynamics of Intractable Ethnonational Conflicts
*Nadim N. Rouhana and Daniel Bar-Tal*
*(American Psychologist, 53, 1998, pp. 761-770)*

Conflicts between and among states that dominated the international scene for decades are gradually being replaced by conflicts between ethnic, religious, linguistic, and national groups within the states often termed *ethnonational conflicts* (Connor, 1994). The conflicts between Catholics and Protestants in Northern Ireland, Tamils and Hindus in Sri Lanka, Muslims and Serbs in Bosnia, and Tutsi and Hutu in Rwanda are only a few examples of ethnonational conflicts raging around the world. Dealing with these conflicts introduces new challenges to the international system because of the ostensible intractability of the conflicts; the underestimation of the psychological dynamics that can contribute to their escalation, stalemate, and perpetuation (Rubin, Pruitt, & Kim, 1994); and the difficulty of applying traditional efforts to their resolution (Rouhana. 1998). These conflicts, also termed *deep-rooted* (Burton, 1987), *enduring rivalry* (Goertz & Diehl, 1993), or *protracted social conflicts* (Azar, 1990), are often transformed into intractable social conflicts (Kriesberg, 1993) that defy traditional negotiation and mediation efforts (Azar, 1990; Burton. 1990).

Although psychological factors contribute to the perpetuation of these conflicts, it should be made clear at the outset that they are neither a psychological epiphenomenon nor conflicts generated mainly by psychological factors. These are conflicts over vital tangible resources in which basic human needs such as identity and security become central to the conflicts and their resolution (Burton, 1990). These conflicts can be resolved only when both the tangible disputed resources are adequately negotiated and the unaddressed human needs that fuel the conflicts are satisfactorily addressed. Yet, because they have psychological bases too, social psychology can and should be able to offer insights into their intractable dynamics and contribute to designing approaches to their resolution.

## Characteristics of Intractable Conflicts That Increase Their Resistance to Resolution

Our analysis in this article is limited to ethnonational conflicts, such as those in Northern Ireland and Sri Lanka, that are less amenable to peaceful conflict-resolution efforts. We refer to such conflicts as *intractable ethnonational conflicts*. They share characteristics that differentiate them from tractable conflicts, which are more amenable to peaceful negotiation (Bar-Tal, 1998; Kriesberg, 1993). The most important characteristics are described below.

**Totality**. Intractable ethnonational conflicts often concern existential and basic needs such as recognition and security, the fulfillment of which is essential for existence and survival. Often. Therefore, they are multifaceted, touching on wider aspects of political and cultural life. The conflicts penetrate the societal fabric of both parties and force themselves on individuals and institutions. Leaders, publics, and institutions-such as educational and cultural systems-become involved in the conflicts. At some stages of the conflicts, even intellectual life and scholarly inquiry become politicized as interest in the other society originates in the motivation to "know your enemy" and inquiries become guided by security needs and considerations.

**Protractedness**. Intractable ethnonational conflicts last at least a generation, often many generations. Their duration means that both parties have deep-rooted animosity and prejudice, that their collective memories are affected by conflict-related events, and that the individuals and societies adapt their lives to the conflicts.

**Centrality**. The centrality of intractable ethnonational conflicts is reflected in the group members' preoccupation with the conflicts. Thoughts related to the conflicts are highly accessible and are relevant to various discussions within each society (Bar-Tal, Raviv, & Freund, 1994). The centrality of such conflicts is further reflected in their saliency on the public agenda. The media and the political and intellectual elites are greatly preoccupied with the conflicts and their developments.

**Violence**. Intractable ethnonational conflicts usually involve violent events, including full-scale wars, limited military engagements, or terrorist attacks. The continual cycle of violence afflicts civilian and military casualties and causes property destruction and, often, population displacement. The violence and its vividness and saliency in each society are another reason for the conflicts' centrality in public life; they also generate intense animosity that becomes integrated into the socialization processes in each society and through which conflict-related emotions and cognitions are transmitted to new generations. Virtually every civilian can be the potential target of a random attack, and mundane daily decisions are affected by the conflicts.

**Perception of Irreconcilability.** Societies embroiled in intractable ethnonational conflicts often see them as zero-sum and view their differences as irreconcilable. Each side perceives its own goals as essential for its own survival and, therefore, does not see a place for the concessions regarded by the other side as essential for conflict resolution. The minimum requirements for one party to reach an agreement are not provided by the other. Societies fail to develop integrative solutions and present them for public discourse.

See also the article, "Peace Psychology for a Peaceful World", including the extensive reference section, by Daniel Christie, Barbara Tint, Richard Wagner, and Deborah DuNann Winter (*American Psychologist*, September, 2008, pp. 540-552).

* * * * * *

## Moral Courage and Courageous Action
### Matthew 10, *The Message*

**Stay alert**. This is hazardous work I'm assigning you. You're going to be like sheep running through a wolf pack, so don't call attention to yourselves. Be as cunning as a snake, inoffensive as a dove.

**Don't be naive**. Some people will impugn your motives; others will smear your reputation—just because you believe in me. Don't be upset when they haul you before the civil authorities. Without knowing it, they've done you—and me—a favor, given you a platform for preaching the kingdom news! And don't worry about what you'll say or how you'll say it. The right words will be there; the Spirit of your Father will supply the words.

When people realize it is the living God you are presenting and not some idol that makes them feel good, they are going to turn on you, even people in your own family. There is a great irony here: proclaiming so much love, experiencing so much hate! **But don't quit. Don't cave in**. It is all well worth it in the end. It is not success you are after in such times but survival. Be survivors! Before you've run out of options, the Son of Man will have arrived

A student doesn't get a better desk than her teacher. A laborer doesn't make more money than his boss. **Be content**—pleased, even—when you, my students, my harvest hands, get the same treatment I get. If they call me, the Master, "Dungface," what can the workers expect?

**Don't be intimidated**. Eventually everything is going to be out in the open, and everyone will know how things really are. So don't hesitate to go public now.

**Don't be bluffed into silence** by the threats of bullies. There's nothing they can do to your soul, your core being. Save your fear for God, who holds your entire life—body and soul—in his hands. What's the price of a pet canary? Some loose change, right? And God cares what happens to it even more than you do. He pays even greater attention to you, down to the last detail—even numbering the hairs on your head! **So don't be intimidated** by all this bully talk. You're worth more than a million canaries.

Stand up for me against world opinion and I'll stand up for you before my Father in heaven. If you turn tail and run, do you think I'll cover for you?

If you don't **go all the way with me**, through thick and thin, you don't deserve me. If your first concern is to look after yourself, you'll never find yourself. But if you **forget about yourself and look to me**, you'll find both yourself and me.

---

### Reflection and Discussion

1. Which of these imperatives are the most relevant for you right now?
2. What other imperatives by Christ, besides the words in bold above, do you find in the text?
3. Who do you know that has modeled putting these imperatives into practice?
4. How is acting with moral courage in difficult places related to one's relationship with Christ?
5. Any other applications for your life and work?

✶ ✶ ✶ ✶ ✶ ✶

# Healing the Body
*Kelly O'Donnell*

### Member Care and the Body of Christ: Part 3

This painting is undoubtedly my favorite work of art in El Prado museum. It was done by Antonello da Messina circa 1476, oil on panel. The most striking aspect for me is the beautiful, anguished face of the angel, grieving over the broken, beloved Christ.

*Tu nobis vicor Rex, miserere.*

I too grieve. I grieve for the broken, beloved member care body of Christ. I grieve when we inflict it with injury, either by ignorance or by intentionality. This can change. We can grow together, loving truth, peace, and people, in the mission/aid community and beyond.

*Steep yourself in God-reality, God-initiative, God-provisions.*
*You'll find all your everyday human concerns will be met.*
*Don't be afraid of missing out. You're my dearest friends!*
*The Father wants to give you the very kingdom itself.*
Luke 12:31-32, *The Message*

---

## Reflection and Discussion

1. How can the mission/aid community develop the additional capacity it needs in order to protect and promote the health of the Body?

2. Sometimes people acknowledge how they have participated in the wounding of the Body, through ignorance and/or intentionality. They apologize and they offer restitution. They are genuinely contrite and they change their ways. Give a few examples.

3. Our core motivation, goal, and approach for bringing healing is described by Paul: "The authority the Master gave me is for putting people together, not taking them apart" (2 Cor. 13:10, *The Message*). Who are some people and what are some situations right now that you could help "put together"?

# Afterword

What lies ahead for the member care field, and indeed for our world at large? What are our future challenges and opportunities for member care in mission/aid and beyond?

Our developing field needs "good learners-practitioners" who are growing in their character (virtues), competency (skills), and compassion (love). We need to be willing to "cross domains" (e.g., international health and humanitarian sectors), "cross disciplines" (e.g., human resources, personnel management), and "cross deserts" (e.g., internal journeys of faith and external settings of difficulty) in order to work effectively. We must grow together through the hard times. As earthen vessels we must develop the personal resiliency and mature faith that can sustain us as we take risks and resolutely confront evil in its many forms.

As a diverse, resilient, international community of member care workers, we will need to have clear ethical commitments in order to provide/develop quality services to mission/aid workers in many cultural settings, often in unstable locations permeated with conflict, calamity, and corruption.

The material in this book and the historical flow of our field are intentionally heading us towards an ultimate destination. Our destination is also the foundation and motivation for our field: resilient love. Sacrificial and celebratory love. Agape.

*Amo neniam pereas.*
Love never fails.

# References

## PART ONE: EXPLORING MEMBER CARE IN MISSION/AID

A boy plants a flower after taking a swim in pools formed by rain waters
in the Mathare slums, Kenya.
©2008 Julius Mwelu/IRIN www.irinnews.org

Addicott, E. *Body Matters: A Guide to Partnership in Christian Mission*. Edmonds, WA: Interdev
Partnership Associates, 2005.

Adeney, M. *Kingdom Without Borders: The Untold Story of Global Christianity*. Downers Grove,
IL: Intervarsity Press, 2009.

Andrews, L. (Ed.). *The Family in Mission: Understanding and Caring for Those Who Serve*. Palmer
Lake, CO: Mission Training International, 2009.

APA Office of International Affairs, International Snapshots, *Psychology International* 9 (3),
(1998): 10.

Butler, P. *Well Connected: Releasing Power, Restoring Hope Through Kingdom Partnerships*.
Waynesboro, GA: Authentic Media, 2006.

Carter, J. Missionary Stressors and Implications for Care. *Journal of Psychology/Theology 27
(1999)*: 171-180.

Collins, M. *Who Cares About the Missionary?* Chicago, IL: Moody, 1974.

Companjen, A. *Hidden Sorrow, Lasting Joy: The Forgotten Women of the Persecuted Church*.
Wheaton, IL: Tyndale, 2000.

Corwin, G. Understanding the Global South(s). *Evangelical Missions Quarterly* 46 (2010): 134-
135.

Danieli, Y. (Ed.). *Sharing the Frontlines and the Back Hills: Peacekeepers, Humanitarian Aid Workers,
and the Media in the Midst of Crises*. New York: Baywood Press, 2001.

De Berens, B. Stress Issues and Humanitarian Activities. (Research presented at *Traumatic Stress
in Emergency Services, Peacekeeping Operations, and Humanitarian Aid Organisations*,

17-20 March, 2006, University of Sheffield, UK. (Organized by Trent RHA and European Society for Traumatic Stress Studies), 1996.

Eriksson, C., Bjorck, J., & Abernethy, A. Occupational Stress, Trauma and Adjustment in Expatriate Humanitarian Aid Workers. In J. Fawcett (Ed.). *Stress and Trauma Handbook: Strategies for Flourishing in Demanding Environments* (pp. 68-100). Monrovia, CA: World Vision, 2003.

Eriksson, C., Foy, D., & Fawcett, J. Humanitarian Aid Worker: Exposure to Chronic and Traumatic Stress. Presentation Given at the *Managing Stress of the Humanitarian Aid Worker* organized by Centers for Disease Control and Antares Foundation, Amsterdam, The Netherlands 6-8 September 2001.

Fawcett, J. (Ed.). *Stress and Trauma Handbook: Strategies for Flourishing in Demanding Environments.* Monrovia, CA: World Vision, 2003.

Foyle, M. *Honourably Wounded: Stress Among Christian Workers.* London, UK: Monarch, 2001 (rev.).

———. *Can It Be Me?* London, UK: Christian Medical Fellowship, 2006.

Friedman, T. *The World is Flat: A Brief History of the Twenty-First Century.* New York: Picador, 2007.

Gardner, L. Missionary Care and Counseling: A Brief History and Challenge. In J. Powell & J. Bowers (Eds.). *Enhancing Missionary Vitality: Mental Health Professions Serving Global Mission* (pp. 41-48). Palmer Lake, CO: Mission Training International, 2002.

Gish, D. Sources of Missionary Stress. *Journal of Psychology and Theology* 11 (1983): 238-242.

Global Connections. *Guidelines for Good Practice for Mission Member Care.* www.global connections.co.uk, 2009.

Hattaway, P. (Ed.). *Back to Jerusalem: Called to Complete the Great Commission.* Waynesboro, GA, Authentic and Carlisle, UK: Piquant Editions, 2003.

Hay, R., Lim, V., Blocher, D., Ketelaar, J., & Hay, S. *Worth Keeping: Global Perspectives on Best Practice in Missionary Retention.* Pasadena, CA: William Carey Library, 2007.

Hess, M., & Linderman, P. *The Expert Expat: Your Guide to Successful Relocation Abroad.* Boston, MA: Nicholas Brealey, 2007.

Hill, M., Hill, H., Bagge, R., & Miersma, P. *Healing the Wounds of Trauma: How the Church Can Help.* Nairobi, Kenya: Paulines Publications, publications@paulines africa.org, 2007.

Holtz, H., Salama, P., Cardozo, B., & Gotway, C. Mental Health Status of Human Rights Workers, Kosovo, June 2002. *Journal of Traumatic Studies* 15 (2000): 389-395.

International Federation of the Red Cross and Red Crescent Societies. Psychological Support Programme for Delegates. In *Psychological Support: Best Practices from Red Cross and Red Crescent Programmes* (pp. 18-21). Geneva, Switzerland; Author. (Available online for free from the World Health Organization, in the Mental Health section at: http://www.helid.desastres.net), 2001.

———. *Managing Stress in the Field.* Geneva, Switzerland: Author, 2001.

Johnson, T., Barrett, D., & Crossing, P. Christianity 2010: A View from the New *Atlas of Global Christianity. International Bulletin of Missionary Research* 34 (2010): 29-36.

Keckler, W., Moriarty, G., & Blagen, M. A Qualitative Study on Comprehensive Missionary Wellness. *Journal of Psychology and Christianity* 27 (2008): 205-214.

Lewis, T., & Lewis, B. Coaching missionary teams. In K. O'Donnell ). (Ed.), *Missionary Care: Counting the Cost for World Evangelization* (pp. 163-170). Pasadena, CA: William Carey Library, 1992.

Love, F., & Eckheart, J. (Eds.). *Ministry to Muslim Women: Longing to Call Them Sisters.* Pasadena, CA: William Carey Library, 2000.

MacArthur, B. *Surviving the Sword: Prisoners of the Japanese 1942-45.* London, UK: Abacus, 2005.

McKaughan, P. Challenges for a Constantly Changing Mission Context. *Evangelical Missions Quarterly* 46 (2010): 226-229.

Miller, R. Staying Sane and Healthy in an Insane Job: How One Relief Worker Kept Her Wits. *Together Magazine* (World Vision), (July/September 1998): 16-21.

O'Donnell, K. (Ed.). *Missionary Care: Counting the Cost for World Evangelization.* Pasadena, CA: William Carey Library, 1992.

———. An Agenda for Member Care in Frontier Missions. *International Journal of Frontier Missions* 9 (1992): 95-100.

———. From Rhetoric to Reality: Assessing the Needs and Coping Strategies of Frontier Mission Personnel. *International Journal of Frontier Missions* 12 (1995): 201-208.

———. (Ed.). *Doing Member Care Well: Perspectives and Practices from Around the World.* Pasadena, CA: William Carey Library, 2002.

———. Member Care in Missions: Global Perspectives and Future Directions. *Journal of Psychology and Theology* 25 (1997): 143-154.

———. Upgrading Member Care: Five Stones for Ethical Practice. *Evangelical Missions Quarterly* 42 (2006): 344-355.

———. Running Well and Resting Well: Twelve Tools for Missionary Life. In K. O'Donnell (Ed.). *Doing Member Care Well: Perspectives and Practices from Around the World* (pp. 309-322). Pasadena, CA: William Carey Library, 2002.

O'Donnell, K., & O'Donnell, M. (Eds.). *Helping Missionaries Grow: Readings in Mental Health and Missions.* Pasadena, CA: William Carey Library, 1998.

———. The Increasing Scope of Member Care. *Evangelical Missions Quarterly* 26 (1998): 418-428.

———. Understanding and Managing Stress. In K. O'Donnell (Ed.), *Missionary Care: Counting the Cost for World Evangelization* (pp. 110-122). Pasadena, CA: William Carey Library, 1992.

Parks, E. Challenges and Opportunities for Mental Health Providers. *Evangelical Missions Quarterly* 46 (2010): 174-178.

Parshall, P. How Spiritual are Missionaries? *Evangelical Missions Quarterly, 23,* 75-82, 1987.

Pascoe, R. *Raising Global Nomads: Parenting Abroad in an On-Demand World.* Vancouver, BC: Canada: Expatriate Press. 2006.

Pawlik, K. & d'Ydewalle, G. Psychology and the Global Commons: Perspectives of International Psychology. *American Psychologist* 51 (1996): 488-495.

People In Aid. *Code of Good Practice in the Management/Support of Aid Personnel.* London, UK: Author, 2003.

Philippine Missionary Care Congress. Member Care Declaration. *Global Member Care Briefing,* www.membercare.org, 2006.

Pirolo, N. *Serving as Senders: How to Care for Your Missionaries.* San Diego, CA: Emmaus Road, 1991.

Pollock, D., & van Reken, R. *The TCK Experience: Growing Up Among Worlds.* Boston: Intercultural Press, 1999.

———. *Third Culture Kids: Growing Up Among Worlds.* Boston, MA USA: Nicholas Brealey Publishing, 2009, 2nd ed.

Porter, B., & Emmens, B. *Approaches to Staff Care in International NGOs.* London: People in Aid www.peopleinaid.org, 2009.

Powell, J., & Bowers, J. (Eds.). *Enhancing Missionary Vitality: Mental Health Professions Serving Global Mission.* Palmer Lake, CO: Mission Training International, 2002.

Powell, J., and Wickstrom, D. The Annual Conference on Mental Health and Missions: A Brief History. In J. Powell and J. Bowers (Eds.). *Enhancing Missionary Vitality: Mental Health Professions Serving Global Mission* (pp. 3-11). Palmer Lake, CO: Mission Training International, 2002.

Quick, T. *The Global Nomad's Guide to University Transition.* Stamford, Lincolnshire UK: Summertime Publishing, 2010.

Quiroga, H. *Cuentos de la Selva.* Buenos Aires, Argentina: Editorial Losada, 1954.

Rajendran, K. Care for Christian Workers in India: Dark Obstacles and Divine Opportunities. In K. O'Donnell (Ed.), *Doing Member Care Well: Perspectives and Practices from Around the World* (pp. 77-86). Pasadena, CA: William Carey Library, 2002.

Rathnakumar, JJ. Care for the Builders of God's Kingdom. *Unpublished paper.* Author, 2004.

Ripkin, N. Servants in the Crucible. Findings from a Global Study on Persecution and the Implications for Sending Agencies and Sending Churches. (unpublished manuscript—soon to be in press), 2005.

Stewart, J. *To the River Kwai.* London: Bloomsbury, 1988.

Stringham, J. Likely Causes of Emotional Difficulties Among Missionaries. *Evangelical Missions Quarterly* 6 (1970): 193-203.

———. The Missionary's Mental Health. *Evangelical Missions Quarterly* 7 (1970): 1-9.

Strom, K., & Rickett, M. *Forgotten Girls: Stories of Courage and Hope.* Downers Grove, IL USA: Intervarsity Press, 2009.

Summerfield, D. The Social Experience of War and Some Issues for the Humanitarian Field. In P. Bracken & C. Petty (Eds.), (pp 9-37). *Rethinking the Trauma of War.* London, UK: Free Association, 1998.

Taylor, G. A Theological Perspective on Missionary Care. In J. Powell & J. Bowers (Eds.). *Enhancing Missionary Vitality: Mental Health Professions Serving Global Mission* (pp.55-62). Palmer Lake, CO USA: Mission Training International, 2002.

Taylor, W. (Ed). *Too Valuable to Lose: Exploring the Causes and Cures of Missionary Attrition* (85-104). Pasadena, CA USA: William Carey Library, 1997.

Tucker, R., & Andrews, L. Historical Notes on Missionary Care. In K. O'Donnell (Ed.). *Missionary Care: Counting the Cost for World Evangelization* (pp. 24-36). Pasadena, CA: William Carey Library, 1992.

United Nations High Commissioner for Refugees. *UNHCR Handbook for the Protection of Women and Girls*. Geneva, Switzerland: Author. http://www.unhcr.org/protect/PROTECTION/47cfae612.html, 2008.

Wan, E., & Pocock, M. (Eds). *Missions from the Majority World: Progress, Challenges, and Case Studies*. Pasadena, CA USA: William Carey Library, 2009.

Webb, K. Coaching Mission/Aid Workers for On-Field Development. *Ethne-Member Care Update*, 3-4 http://ethne.net/membercare/updates, November, 2006.

Wilcox, D. Development of Regional Networks. In J. Bowers (Ed.). *Raising Resilient MKs: Resources for Caregivers, Parents, and Teachers* (pp. 456-464). Colorado Springs, CO: ACSI, 1998.

Wong, W. Human Rights Advocacy in Missions. In K. O'Donnell (Ed.), *Doing Member Care Well: Perspectives and Practices from Around the World* (pp. 477-488). Pasadena, CA: William Carey Library, 2002.

Woodberry, D. (Ed.). *From Seed to Fruit: Global Trends, Fruitful Practices, and Emerging Issues Among Muslims*. Pasadena, CA: William Carey Library, 2008.

# PART TWO: PROMOTING HEALTH IN MISSION/AID

The eagle represents the Gospel of John's profound and soaring description of Christ.
The serpent is also shown to be crushed under the pierced foot of Christ, the Pierced-One.
(Gen. 3:15, Rom. 16:20).
*Book of Kells*, Ireland, circa 8th century

Adie, K. *The Kindness of Strangers: An Autobiography*. London, UK: Headline, 2002.

American Psychiatric Association. *Diagnostic and Statistics Manual of Mental Disorders; Fourth edition*. Washington DC: Author, 1994.

Anello, E. *Ethical Infrastructure for Good Governance in the Public Pharmaceutical Sector*. Geneva: World Health Organization (www.who.int.org), 2006.

Arterburn, S., & Felton, J. *Toxic Faith: Experiencing Healing from Painful Spiritual Abuse*. Colorado Springs, CO: Shaw Books, 2001.

Babiak, P., & Hare, R. *Snakes in Suits: When Psychopaths Go to Work*. New York: HarperCollins, 2006.

Baker, K. What Do You Do When Sin Seems Ignored? *Evangelical Missions Quarterly* 41 (2005): 338-344.

Barrett, D., Johnson, T., & Crossing, P. Missiometrics 2008: Reality Checks for Christian World Communions. *International Bulletin of Missionary Research* 32 (2008): 27-30.

Behnke, S. Cited in Tori DeAngelis, An Elephant in the Office. *Monitor on Psychology* 39 (2008): 33-34.

Bennis, W., Goleman, D., & O'Toole, J. *Transparency: How Leaders Create a Culture of Candor*. San Francisco, CA: Jossey-Bass, 2008.

Bliss, W., & Thornton, G. *Employee Termination Source Book: A Collection of Practical Examples*. Alexandria, VA: Society for Human Resource Management, 2006.

Brinkman, R., & Kirschner, R. *Dealing with Difficult People: 24 Lessons for Bringing Out the Best in Everyone*. New York: McGraw-Hill, 2006.

Buckingham, M., & Coffman, C. *First Break All the Rules: What the World's Greatest Managers do Differently*. New York: Simon & Schuster, 1999.

Carozza, D. Interview with Dr. Hare and Dr. Babiak; These Men Know "'Snakes in Suits'. *Fraud Magazine* 22 (4) (July/August, 2008): 36-43.

Carozza, D. An interview with Cynthia Cooper, CFE, CISA: Extraordinary Circumstances. *Fraud Magazine* 22 (2) (March/April, 2008): 36-43.

Carter, J. Missionary Stressors and Implications for Care. *Journal of Psychology and Theology* 27 (1999): 171-180.

Chesterton, G. *The Everlasting Man*. San Francisco, CA: Ignatius Press, 1925/1993.

Cloud, H., & Townsend, J. *Safe People*. Grand Rapids, MI: Zondervan, 1995.

Cooper, C. A Dark Cloud Descending. *Fraud Magazine* 22 (2) (March/April, 2008): 36-43.

Drucker, P. *The Essential Drucker*. New York: Harper Collins, 2001.

Evangelical Council for Financial Accountability. *Policy on Suspected Misconduct, Dishonesty, Fraud, and Whistle-Blower Protection*. Author. (www.ecfa.org), nd.

Fawcett, J. *Stress and Trauma Handbook: Strategies for Flourishing in Demanding Environments*. Monrovia, CA: World Vision, 2003.

Fisher, K., & Fisher, M. *The Distance Manager. A Hands-on Guide to Managing Off-site Employees and Virtual Teams*. New York: McGraw-Hill, 2001.

Gish, D. Sources of Missionary Stress. *Journal of Psychology and Theology* 11 (1983): 238-242.

Handy, C. *Understanding Voluntary Organizations: How to Make Them Function Effectively*. NY: Penguin, 1988.

Harriman, D. Trust *Me! Trust Me! Building Trust in Development*. Unpublished manuscript, 2006.

Hay, R. (Ed.). *Worth Keeping: Global Perspectives on Best Practice in Missionary Retention*. Pasadena, CA: William Carey Library, 2007.

Hay, R. The Toxic Mission Organisation: Fiction or Fact. *Encounters Mission E-zine, 2,* 1-8. (www. generatingchange.co.uk), 2004.

Henry, J. *Enhancing Quality in HR Management in the Humanitarian Sector.* London, UK: People In Aid, 2004.

Henry, J. *Understanding HR in the Humanitarian Sector.* London, UK: People In Aid, 2004.

Hotchkiss, S. *Why is it Always About You? Saving Yourself from Narcissists in Your Life.* New York: Free, 2002.

Johnson, L. (Ed.). *HR Magazine Guide to Managing People: 47 Tools to Help Managers.* Alexandria, VA: Society for Human Resource Management, 2006.

Johnson, T., Barrett, D., & Crossing, P. Christianity 2010: A View from the New *Atlas of Global Christianity. International Bulletin of Missionary Research* 34 (2010): 29-36.

Karabell, Z. The Myth of Transparency, *Newsweek* 47 (July 7/14, 2008).

Lencioni, P. *Five Dysfunctions of a Team: A Leadership Fable.* San Francisco, CA: Jossey-Bass, 2002.

Lewicki, R., Barry, B., & Saunders, D. (4th ed.). *Essentials of Negotiation.* Boston, MA: USA: McGraw Hill, 2007.

Lewis. B. *Making Friends with the Women on Your Team.* (unpublished manuscript), nd.

Machiavelli, N. *The Prince.* New York: Bantam Books, 1513/1996.

Management Sciences for Health. *Human Resource Management Assessment Instrument for NGOs and Public Sector Health Organizations.* Boston, USA: Author. www.msh.org, 2005.

———. Strengthening HRM to Improve Health Outcomes. *eManager.* www.msh.org/Documents/ emanager/upload/eManager_2009 No1_HRM_English.pdf, 2009.

Markopolos, H. *No One Would Listen: A True Financial Thriller.* Hoboken, NJ, USA: John Wiley & Sons, 2010.

McIntosh, G., & Rima, S. *Understanding the Dark Side of Leadership: The Paradox of Personal Dysfunction.* Grand Rapids, MI: Baker Books, 1997.

McLemore, C. *Toxic Relationships and How to Change Them: Health and Holiness in Everyday Life.* San Francisco, CA: Jossey-Bass, 2003.

Memon, K. Employee Fraud in Humanitarian Organizations: Taking from the Givers. *Fraud Magazine* 22 (2) (March/April 2008): 20-23.

O'Donnell, K. (Ed.). *Missionary Care: Counting the Cost for World Evangelization.* Pasadena, CA: William Carey Library, 1992.

Obama, B. *Audacity of Hope.* Edinburgh, UK. Canongate, 2008.

Peacemakers International. *Peacemakers Pledge.* www.peacemaker.org, nd.

People In Aid. *Code of Good Practice in Managing and Supporting Aid Personnel.* London, UK: Author, 2003.

Pruitt, D., & Kim, S. (3rd ed.). *Social Conflict: Escalation, Stalemate, and Settlement.* Boston, MA, USA: McGraw Hill, 2004.

Puder-York, M. *The Office Survival Guide: Surefire Techniques for Dealing with Challenging People and Situations.* New York: McGraw-Hill, 2006.

Rand, A. *The Virtue of Selfishness.* New York: Signet, 1964.

Reconciliation Network. *Reconciliation as the Mission of God: Christian Witness in a World of Destructive Conflicts.* www.reconciliationnetwork.com, 2005.

Reddix, V. *Millie and the Mudhole.* New York, NY: Lothrop, Lee, & Shepherd Books, 1992.

Roembke, L. *Building Credible Multicultural Teams.* Pasadena, CA USA: William Carey Library, 2000.

Schaef, A., & Fassel, D. *The Addictive Organization.* San Francisco, CA: Harper & Row, 1988.

Schreiter, R. Reconciliation as a New Paradigm of Mission. *Conference on World Mission and Evangelism,* May 9-16, 2005, Athens Greece. World Council of Churches, 2005. http://www.oikoumene.org/uploads/media/PLEN_14_doc_1_Robert_Schreiter.doc Note: An adjusted version of this presentation is in Reconciliation as a new paradigm in mission. In J. Matthey (Ed.). *Come Holy Spirit, Heal and Reconcile* (213-219). Geneva, Switzerland: WCC Publications, 2008.

Schubert, E. Current Issues in Screening and Selection. In K. O'Donnell (Ed.), *Missionary Care: Counting the Cost for World Evangelization* (pp. 74-88). Pasadena, CA: William Carey Library, 1992.

Scott, G. *A Survival Guide for Working with Humans: Dealing with Whiners, Back-Stabbers, Know-it-Alls, and Other Difficult People.* New York: American Management Association, 2004.

Stahlke, L., & Loughlin, J. *Governance Matters: Balancing Client and Staff Fulfilment in Faith-Based Not-for-Profit Organizations.* www.Governance Matters.com, 2003.

Tavris, C., & Aronson, E. *Mistakes Were Made (but not by me): Why We Justify Foolish Beliefs, Bad Decisions, and Hurtful Acts.* Orlando, FL: Harcourt, 2007.

Tolkien, J. *The Fellowship of the Ring.* London, UK: HarperCollins Publishers, 1999.

Transparency International, Humanitarian Policy Group, & Feinstein International Center Preventing *Corruption in Humanitarian Assistance: Final Research Report.* www.transparency.org, 2008.

Ugolino, B. *The Little Flowers of Saint Francis,* Christian Classics Ethereal Library. http://www.ccel.org/ccel/ugolino/flowers.pdf, 1330/1997.

Vian, T., Savedoff, W., & Mathieson, H. (Eds.). *Anticorruption in the Health Sector: Strategies for Transparency and Accountability.* Herndon, VA USA: Kumarian Press/Stylus Publishing, 2010.

White, F. The Dynamics of Healthy Missions. In K. O'Donnell (Ed). *Missionary Care* (pp. 235-246). Pasadena, CA: William Carey Library, 1992.

White, J., & Blue, K. *Healing the Wounded: The Costly Love of Church Discipline.* Downers Grove, IL: InterVarsity Press, 1985.

Williams, K. *Sharpening Your Interpersonal Skills.* www.ITPartners.org, 2002.

Williams, M. *Fit In! The Unofficial Guide to Corporate Culture.* Sterling, VA: Capital Books, 2007.

Wilson, E. et. al. *Restoring the Fallen: A Team Approach to Caring, Confronting, and Reconciling.* Downers Grove, IL: InterVarsity Press, 1997.

Zimbardo, P. *The Lucifer Effect: Understanding How Good People Turn Evil.* New York; Random House, 2007.

# PART THREE: DEVELOPING GUIDELINES IN MISSION/AID

Shining light, unmasking darkness, safeguarding people.
Red Cross Museum, Geneva, Switzerland
©2008 Kelly O'Donnell

American Association of Marriage and Family Therapists. *Code of Ethics*. July, 2001. Alexandria, VA: Author http://www.aamft.org/resources/lrm_plan/Ethics/ ethic-scode2001.asp.

American Psychological Association. *Ethical Principles for Psychologists and Code of Conduct*. Washington, DC: Author. http://www.apa.org/ethics/code2002.html, 2002.

Bennett, B., Bricklin, P., Harris, E., Knapp, S., VandeCreek, L., Younggren, J. *Assessing and Managing Risk in Psychological Practice: An Individual Approach*. Rockville, MD: The Trust, 2006.

Bowers, J. (Eds.). *Enhancing Missionary Vitality: Mental Health Professions Serving Global Mission* (pp. 435-444). Palmer Lake, CO: Mission Training International.

*Cairo Declaration on Human Rights in Islam*. 1990. http://www.religlaw.org/interdocs/docs/ cairohrislam1990.htm, 2002.

Cannon, M. *Social Justice Handbook: Small Steps for a Better World*. Downers Grove, IL USA: Intervarsity Press, 2009.

Christie, D., Tint, B., Wagner, R., & Winter, D. Peace Psychology for a Peaceful World. *American Psychologist* 63 (2008): 540-552.

Collier, P. *The Bottom Billion: Why the Poorest Countries are Failing and What Can be Done About It*. Oxford, UK: Oxford University Press, 2007.

Corbett, S., & Fikkert, B. *When Helping Hurts: How to Alleviate Poverty Without Hurting the Poor and Yourself*. Chicago, IL USA: Moody Publishers, 2009.

Danieli, Y. (Ed). *Sharing the Front Line and the Back Hills: Peacekeepers, Humanitarian Aid Workers and the Media in the Midst of Crisis*. Amityvillle, NY: Baywood, 2002.

Dickens, C. *A Christmas Carol*. http://dickens.thefreelibrary.com/Christmas-Carol, 1843.

Elhawary, S., Foresti, M., & and Pantuliano, S. *Development, Security and Transition in Fragile States.* London, UK: Overseas Development Institute. www.odi.org.uk/ resources, 2010.

Evangelical Fellowship of Canada. Code of Best Practice in Member Care. In K. O'Donnell (Ed.). *Doing Member Care Well: Perspectives and Practices from Around the World* (pp, 272-276). Pasadena, CA: William Carey. http://files.efc-canada.net/out /BestPractice_MemberCare.pdf, 2002.

Gardner, R., & Gardner, L. Training and Using Member Care Workers. In K. O'Donnell (Ed.) Missionary *care: Counting the Cost for World Evangelization* (pp. 315-331). Pasadena, CA: William Carey Library, 2002.

Geisler, N., Turek, F. *I Don't Have Enough Faith to be an Atheist.* Wheaton, IL: Crossway, 2004.

Global Connections. *Guidelines for Good Practice for Mission Member Care.* www.globalconnections.co.uk, 2009.

Global Connections. UK Code of Best Practice in Short-Term Mission. In K. O'Donnell (Ed.). *Doing Member Care Well: Perspectives and Practices from Around the World* (pp, 269-272). Pasadena, CA: William Carey Library. www.globalconnections.co.uk.

Gray, I. (2008). Fragile States and Neglected Emergencies. *Global Future* (World Vision International), 2 (2002): 22-23.

Gropper, R. *Culture and Clinical Encounter: An Intercultural Sensitizer for the Health Professions.* Yarmouth, Maine USA: Intercultural Press, 1996.

Haas, M. *International Human Rights: A Comprehensive Approach (2008).* Abingdon, UK: Routledge, 2008.

Hall, M., & Barber, B. The Therapist in a Missions Context; Avoiding Dual Role Conflicts. *Journal of Psychology and Theology* 24 (1996): 212-219.

Hitchens, C. Introduction. In G. Orwell *Animal Farm and 1984.* Orlando, FL: Harcourt, 2003.

Holloway, S, & Holloway, K. The Perils of Pioneering: Responsible Logistics for Hostile Places. In K. O'Donnell (Ed.). *Doing Member Care Well: Perspectives and Practices from Around the World* (pp, 445-456). Pasadena, CA: William Carey Library.

International Federation of Red Cross and Red Crescent Societies *The Code of Conduct for the International Red Cross and Red Crescent Movement and NGOs in Disaster Relief.* Geneva, Switzerland: Author, 1994.

Kant, I. (3rd ed). In J. Ellington (retranslation). *Grounding for the Metaphysics of Morals.* Indianapolis, IN: Hackett, 1785, 1993.

Kennedy, P. *The Parliament of Man: The Past, Present, and Future of the United Nations.* New York: Vintage Books, 2006.

Knox, T., Seiple, C., & Rowe, A. *International Religious Freedom Advocacy: A Guide to Organizations, Law, and NGOs.* Waco, TX USA: Baylor University Press, 2009.

Leffel, G., Fritz, M., & Stephens, M. Who Cares? Generativity and the Moral Emotions, part 3. *Journal of Psychology and Theology* 36 (2008): 202-221.

Little, D. Foreword. In J. Nurser, *For All People and All Nations: Christian Churches and human Rights* (pp.ix-xii ). Geneva, Switzerland: WCC publications, 2005.

Martin, J. *25+ Human Rights Documents.* New York, USA: Columbia University, 2005.

Mattis, R., & Johnson, J. *Human Resource Management* (10th edition). Mason, Ohio USA: Thomson, 2003.

Nagy, T. (2nd ed.). *Ethics in Plain English: An Illustrative Casebook for Psychologists.* Washington D.C.: USA American Psychological Association, 2005.

National Council of Churches, Presbyterian Historical Society (1942). A Message from the National Study Conference on the Churches and a Just and Durable Peace (section II, guiding principles, pp. 10-14, 1942; National Council of Churches of Christ in the USA Records, Federal Council of Churches Records, Record Group 18, box 28, folder 9. Presbyterian Historical Society, Philadelphia, PA USA. In J. Nurser, *For all people and all nations: Christian Churches and Human Rights* (pp. 186-188). Geneva, Switzerland: WCC publications, 2005.

Nowack. M. *Introduction to the Human Rights Regime.* Lund, Sweden: Wallenberg Institute/ University of Lund,/Swedenartinus Nijhoff, 2003.

O' Donnell, K., & O'Donnell, M. Ethical Concerns in Providing Member Care Services. In K. O'Donnell (Ed.). *Missionary Care: Counting the Cost for World Evangelization* (pp. 260-269). Pasadena, CA: William Carey Library, 1992.

———. Some Suggested Ethical Guidelines for the Delivery of Mental Health Services in Mission Settings. In K. O'Donnell & M. O'Donnell (Eds.). *Helping Missionaries Grow: Readings in Mental Health and Missions.* (pp. 466-479). Pasadena, CA: William Carey Library, 1988.

———. Going Global: A Member Care Model for Best Practice. In K. O'Donnell (Ed.). *Doing Member Care Well: Perspectives and Practices from Around the World* pp, 13-22). Pasadena, CA: William Carey Library, 2002.

———. Upgrading Member Care: Five Stones for Ethical Practice. *Evangelical Missions Quarterly* 41 (2006): 344-355.

———. Guidelines for Member Care Workers: 15 commitments. *Connections: The Journal of the WEA Mission Commission* (June 2004): 95-97.

Pantuliano, S. ( Ed.). *Uncharted Territory: Land, Conflict and Humanitarian Action.* Bourton on Dunsmore, UK: Practical Action, 2009.

People In Aid. *Code of Good Practice in the Management and Support of Aid Personnel.* London: Author. www.peopleinaid.org, 2003.

Piper, J. A Call for Christian Risk. *Desiring God Ministries.* www.desiringgod.org, May 29, 2002.

Pope, K., & Vasquez, M. On Violating the Ethical Standards. *California Board of Psychology Update,* 1-2, May, 1999. (Excerpted from *Ethics in Psychotherapy and Counseling: A Practical Guide* 2nd ed. San Francisco, Jossey-Bass Publishers, 1998).

*Psychotherapy Networker.* Special Issue on Ethics. www.psychotherapy networker.org, March 2003.

Richardson, J. Ethical Principles for Mental Health Work with Missionaries. In J. Powell & J. Bowers, J. (Eds.). *Enhancing Missionary Vitality: Mental Health Professions Serving Global Mission* (pp. 435-444). Palmer Lake, CO: Mission Training International, 2002.

Rosik, C., & Brown, R. Professional Use of the Internet: Legal and Ethical Issues in a Member Care Environment. In J. Powell & J. Bowers, J. (Eds.). *Enhancing Missionary Vitality: Mental*

*Health Professions Serving Global Mission* (pp. 463-471). Palmer Lake, CO: Mission Training International, 2002.

Rouhana, N., & Bar-Tal, D. Psychological Dynamics of Intractable Ethnonational Conflicts. *American Psychologist* 53 (1998): 761-770.

Society for Human Resource Management. *A Guide to Developing Your Organization's Code of Ethics.* Author. http://www.shrm.org/ethics/organization-coe.pdf, 2001.

———. *Code of Ethical and Professional Standards in Human Resource management.* Author http://www.shrm.org/ethics/ code-of-ethics.asp, 2006.

Sphere Project. *Humanitarian Charter and Minimum Standards in Disaster Response.* Geneva, Switzerland: Author. www.sphereproject.org, 2004.

Tavris, C., & Aronson, E. *Mistakes were Made (but not by me): Why We Justify Foolish Beliefs, Bad Decisions, and Hurtful Acts.* Orlando, FL: Harcourt, 2007.

Tomushut, C. *Human Rights: Between Idealism and Realism.* Oxford, UK: Oxford University Press, 2003.

United Nations Office of the High Commission for Human Rights. *What are Human Rights? Author.* http://www.ohchr.org/EN/Issues/Pages/WhatareHumanRights.aspx, nd.

United Nations. *Universal Declaration of Human Rights.* Author, 1948. http://www.un.org/en/documents/udhr/index.shtml

———. *International Covenants on Human Rights (International Covenant on Social, Economic, and Political Rights; International Covenant of Civil and Political Rights).* Author. www.ohchr.org/Documents/Publications, 1966.

———. Declaration on the Elimination of All Forms of Intolerance and of Discrimination Based on Religion or Belief. General Assembly Resolution 36/55, http://www2.ohchr.org/english/law/religion.htm, 1981.

Wong, W. Human Rights Advocacy in Missions. In K. O'Donnell (Ed.). *Doing Member Care Well: Perspectives and Practices from Around the World* (pp, 477-488). Pasadena, CA: William Carey Library, 2002.

## Reference Notes

Preface. Quotation: Tolkien, J.R.R., *The Fellowship of the Ring.* London, HarperCollins Publishers (p. 457). Reprinted by permission of HarperCollins Publishers Ltd, ©1966 George Allen & Unwin, 1999.

Preface. Quotation: Sirach 2:1-6, *New Jerusalem Bible,* Reprinted with permission of Catholic Online www.catholic.org

Chapters 4, 8, 12 (Resources for Good Practice). These chapters include a painting of Christ the "Pantocrator," one of the most respected representations of Christ in the Eastern churches. The word *Pantocrator* (from the Greek Παντοκράτωρ) means "The Almighty." It is one of several titles used to describe God in the Scriptures. In the Septuagint the word Pantocrator was used as the Greek translation of the Hebrew *El Shaddai* (שדי לא), meaning God Almighty. Pantoctrator is used nine times in the book of Revelation in reference to Christ/God.

Chapter 7. Some of the scriptures from "New Testament Warnings" (Box 4) are taken from *THE MESSAGE*. Copyright © by Eugene H. Peterson, 1993, 1994, 1995, 1996. Used by Permission of NavPress Publishing Group.

Chapter 12. All of the Scriptures from "Moral Courage and Courageous Action" are taken from *THE MESSAGE*. Copyright © by Eugene H. Peterson, 1993, 1994, 1995, 1996. Used by Permission of NavPress Publishing Group.

For additional updates on the *Global Member Care* series, including new links and resources, visit www.membercareassociates.org.

# Endnotes

## Chapter 2

1 These leaders are from the "A4" regions, referring to Africa, Asia, Arabic-Turkic, and America-Latina regions. A4 overlaps with the terms "Newer Sending Countries" and "Global South(s)". See also the many accounts and stories in books such as *Kingdom Without Borders: The Untold Story of Global Christianity* by Miriam Adeney (2009, Downers Grove, IL USA: Intervarsity Press); *Missions from the Majority World: Progress, Challenges, and Case Studies* by Enoch Wan and Michael Pocock (2009, Pasadena, CA USA: William Carey Library); and *Forgotten Girls: Stories of Courage and Hope* by Kay Marshall Strom and Michele Rickett (2009, Downers Grove, IL USA: Intervarsity Press).

2 To receive Africa Member Care Updates contact mcsa@xsinet.co.za.

3 Adapted from *MemCa Global Briefing* 2/02 and Chapter 10 in *Doing Member Care Well, 2002.*

4 Excerpts from Chapter 27 *Doing Member Care Well, 2002.*

5 To receive Asia Member Care Updates contact member-care-asia@yahoogroups.com.

6 Missionary Upholders Trust, *Care and Serve Bulletin*, March 2004; excerpts p.3.

7 Excerpts from Care for the Builders of God's Kingdom by J. J. Rathnakumar (unpublished paper, October 2004); jjratnakumar@gmail.com.

8 To receive India Member Care Updates contact ima@imaindia.org.

9 Chinese-Asian Member Care Project (CHAMP) 2005; www.chinamembercare.com.

10 *Back to Jerusalem*, 2003, pp. 57, 58.

11 To receive Latin America Member Care Updates (Spanish) contact cuidadointegral@gruposyahoo.com. ar or www.cuidadointegralcomibam.blogspot.com.

12 Excerpts from Chapter 17, *Doing Member Care Well, 2002.*

13 Excerpts from Chapter 16, *Doing Member Care Well, 2002.*

14 *Servants in the Crucible. Findings from a Global Study on Persecution and the Implications for Sending Agencies and Sending Churches.* January 2005 by Nik Ripken. See also this author's article on persecution and suffering in *From Seed to Fruit*, 2009.

15 This section is adapted from the material by the author in "To the Ends of the Earth, To the End of The Age," in *Doing Member Care Well*, 2002, and in "Caring for Caregivers" in *Come Holy Spirit, Heal and Reconcile*, 2008.

16 Adapted from two sources: The results presented/discussed in *Worth Keeping*, 2007; and Detlef Blöcher, "ReMAP 2 Survey on Missionary Retention: Member Care Builds Up Mission Personnel," *MemCa Global Briefing*, 06/04, pp. 6-8; http://membercare.org/images/globalbriefings/june2004.pdf used by permission of Detlef Blöcher.

## Chapter 3

1 This material reflects some of the initial thinking of the Member Care working group from March 2006, which I have expanded and updated periodically. I am grateful for the contributions from the other facilitators of our working group as well as the insights of the participants. An early version, "Future Directions: 12 Treasures for Member Care" was originally published in *Encounters*, May/June 2006, pp.49-52. See www.momentum-mag.org.

## Chapter 10

1   I developed the initial guidelines with significant input from colleagues in Global Member Care Resources (MemCa). The initial guidelines were published in *Connections*, June, 2004 (pp. 95-97).

2   *People In Aid* is an international network of development and humanitarian agencies. It helps organizations to better manage and support their staff. The full version of their *Good Practice Code* is at www.peopleinaid.org.

3   This case study is adapted from Ethical Concerns in Providing Member Care (Chapter 19) in *Missionary Care* (1992). Refer to this article for commentary on the poor practices and ethical issues in this case.

4   See Chapter 23 in *Missionary Care*, 1992, Training and Using Member Care Workers; Chapter 52 in *Enhancing Missionary Vitality*, 2002, Excerpts from Professional Codes of Ethics; and the ethical guidelines from Chapter 44 in *Helping Missionaries Grow*, 1988.

## Chapter 12

1   Ian Gray is head of Humanitarian and Emergency Affairs for World Vision United Kingdom.

2   See www.oecd.org/dac/fragilestates.

3   For operational guidelines on Transitional Results Matrices, see
http://siteresources.worldbank.org/INTLICUS/Resources/TRM.pdf .

4   The Basic Services Fund for Southern Sudan was launched by DfID in January 2006 to assist the government of southern Sudan in providing basic services, via non-government actors, to the most under-served populations. See http://www.dfid.gov.uk/News/files/sudancrisis/sudan-health.asp.

5   See P. Collier, *Post-Conflict Recovery: How Should Policies Be Distinctive?*, Centre for the Study of African Economies, Department of Economics, Oxford University, 2007,
http://users.ox.ac.uk/~econpco/research/pdfs/PostConflict-Recovery.pdf, and P. Collier, A. Hoeffler & M. Soderbom in collaboration with the United Nations Department of Peace Keeping Operations and the World Bank, *Post-Conflict Risks*, Centre for the Study of African Economies, Department of Economics, Oxford University, 2006, http://users.ox.ac.uk/~econpco/research/pdfs/Post-Conflict-Risks.pdf.

6   For a more in-depth look at funding for chronic problems, see K. Epstein, "Fundraising and Markets," *Stanford Social Innovation Review*, Spring 2006, Leland Stanford Jr. University, pp. 48–57.

# Index

## K

Kant, Immanuel, 198

key indicators, 59, 106, 171, 182, 185

known stone, 188-89

      known-groan stone, 188

## L

language, 7, 24, 30, 32, 43-45, 54, 58-59, 62, 67-68, 84, 108, 114, 123, 130, 143, 160, 189, 191, 201, 209-10

LeaderLink, 55

leaders, 10, 17, 19, 24-26, 41, 43, 47, 52-53, 55, 58, 73-74, 86, 91, 94, 106, 124-25, 139, 142, 144-48, 155, 159-60, 167-68, 170, 180, 182-84, 188, 196, 203-04, 219

      anointed, 12

      bad, 144

      caring, 40

      church, 58, 204

      good, 137, 144

      member care, 15, 23

      mission, 12, 28, 55, 162, 178

leadership, 43, 55, 59, 69, 107, 125-26, 142, 144, 147, 150, 172, 181, 183

      abuse. *See* abuse.

      bad/poor, 90

      church, 32

      development, 59

      ethical. *See* ethical.

      lack of, 49

      listening, 137, 145

      style, 44, 106

learned helplessness, 201

learning, 18, 24, 59, 62, 65-66, 69-70, 90, 146, 173-74

      language, 30, 43, 67

legal

      advice, 133

      limit, 162

      protection, 121-22

      regulations, 162

      requirements, 167-68

      standards, 162

legalism, 90

less-reached people groups, 19

library, 65, 75

life coach training, 60

functional trust, 100, 103
    rifts, 104
    shifts, 103-04
    recreating, 106
*truthseekers, safeguarders,* and *peacemakers,* 120
tyranny, 191, 210

U
unforgiveness, 197
United Nations, 54, 80, 191, 201, 205, 209-11, 213-14
    United Nations Global Compact, 131
    United Nations High Commissioner for Human Rights, 56-57, 79, 189, 193
*Universal Declaration of Human Rights,* 57, 153, 186, 188, 190, 192-93, 201, 204, 207, 209-10
unreached people groups (UPGs), 11-12, 53-55, 58, 62
U.S. Center for World Mission (USCWM), 11
use of information, 182

V
validation, 147, 168
values, 18, 45, 96-97, 125-26, 129, 142, 158-59, 162, 183, 192
van der Weyden, Rogier, 151
variation, 104, 133, 166
vicarious trauma, 50
vice, 8, 134, 142-43, 145
victims, 14, 19, 56, 97, 174-75
Vienna World Conference on Human Rights, 190
vilify, 147-48
vindication, 146-47
virtrios, 97
virtual teams, 73, 128
virtue, 8, 10, 65, 85, 97, 99, 108-09, 132, 137, 142-43, 145, 167, 207, 223
virtuous rebellion, 196
voice over internet technologies (VOIP), 60
volunteer groups, 139
vulnerable, 40, 61, 71, 86, 97, 112, 119, 134, 204
    colleagues, 94
    people, 19, 192
    place, 167
    populations, 186-87, 190